The Lotus Boat

Studies in Oriental Culture, Number 18
Columbia University

The Lotus Boat

The Origins of Chinese *Tz'u* Poetry
in T'ang Popular Culture

MARSHA L. WAGNER

COLUMBIA UNIVERSITY PRESS
New York
1984

The Andrew W. Mellon Foundation, through a special grant,
has assisted the Press in publishing this volume.

Library of Congress Cataloging in Publication Data

Wagner, Marsha L.
The lotus boat.

(Studies in Oriental culture; no. 18)

Bibliography: p.
Includes index.
1. Tz'u—History and criticism.   2. Chinese poetry—
T'ang dynasty, 618–907—History and criticism.   I. Title.
PL2341.W33   1984   895.1'104   83-20925
ISBN 0-231-04276-0

Columbia University Press
New York   Guildford, Surrey

*Clothbound editions of Columbia University Press books are
Smyth-sewn and printed on permanent and durable acid-free paper.*

To
Rich,
Kate, and Sarah

CONTENTS

PREFACE

I N his Preface to the first anthology of *tz'u* poetry by highly educated scholar-officials, the *Hua-chien chi* ("Among the Flowers"), dated 940, Ou-yang Chiung attempts to exalt the elite poetry by disassociating it from the lyrics currently being sung by local singing girls in the south of China. In his view, only the men of letters, *wen-jen* or literati, could compose poetry of high literary standards. He traces the origins of the *tz'u* to the famous High T'ang figure Li Po (701–762), whom he points to as the first court poet to write songs in the *tz'u* genre. According to Ou-yang Chiung, Li Po's example was followed by Wen T'ing-yün (812–870) and the contemporary Five Dynasties *tz'u* poets whose works make up the *Hua-chien chi*. Their poetry is of such high calibre that it will elevate the *tz'u* genre so it may be suitable for the entertainment of like-minded scholar-officials. Moreover, Ou-yang Chiung claims, the *tz'u* collected in the *Hua-chien chi* will provide a new model for the "Southern singing girls" who, when they learn this more refined style, will "stop singing songs of the lotus boat."[1]

However, it is my thesis that the *tz'u* actually did not emerge from court poetry, but rather grew directly out of those "songs of the lotus boat." Indeed, without the Southern singing girls' tradition, the development of *tz'u* poetry by literati would not have been possible. The popular songs from which *tz'u* originated were promulgated by courtesans and other musical entertainers. There is ample evidence that the literati learned the *tz'u* song form through prolonged and close contact with the singing girls who had mastered the popular style.

The fresh vitality of the popular style is captured in the following anonymous poem, the first of a series of three verses to the tune "Hsi chiang yüeh" ("Western Yangtze Moon").

#054 (S. 2607)

The girl and her companion together search for the misty water;
Tonight the moon on the river is clear.
The tip of the rudder moves effortlessly, the boat floats sideways;
On the surface of the waves a light breeze imperceptibly arises.

Rowing the oars and riding the boat, with no fixed destination,
The sound of fishermen's songs is heard here and there.
The river's waves stretch to the sky, soaking the autumn stars;
By mistake the pair enters the water smartweed thicket.[2]

This graceful poem uses a conventional situation (relaxed drifting with the flow), stock images ("the moon on the river is clear"), and fixed phrases ("rowing the oars and riding the boat") characteristic of poetry in an oral tradition. Yet it retains an immediacy of appeal even when isolated from its musical performance context. The expansiveness of the scene reinforces the leisurely mood, and the erotic innuendoes, particularly in the final line, enhance the charmingly playful tone.

Such unself-conscious lyrics were clearly the inspiration for early literati experimentations with the *tz'u* form. For example, Li Hsün (855?–930?), one of the contributors to the *Hua-chien chi* who served as an official in the Former Shu (Ch'ien Shu) dynasty, composed a series of ten poems to the tune "Nan hsiang tzu" ("Songs of the Southern Countryside"). These deliberate folksong imitations emphasize the flirtatious attractions of the conventional boating scene:

Riding the painted boat,
Passing the lotus banks;
The oars' song abruptly wakens the sleeping mandarin ducks.

Adorned with fragrance, the traveling girl leans toward her companion
    and smiles.
Incomparably lovely,
She picks a round lotus leaf to shade herself from the evening sun.[3]

Whereas the anonymous poem combined broad scenic description
with a brief narrative, the poem by Li Hsün emphasizes a static
scene, focusing on the figure of the lovely woman. Decked with
flowers in a painted boat, the girl in the literatus poem is more
elegant than her popular prototype. The poet's style is also slightly
more subtle: the sleeping mandarin ducks, a standard symbol of
marital fidelity, indirectly introduce the human lovers in the boat.
However, Li Hsün's setting and imagery explicitly draw on the
popular Southern tradition of "songs of the lotus boat." Then why
did Ou-yang Chiung, the author of the Preface to the *Hua-chien
chi*, as well as centuries of scholars and critics who followed him,
so disparage the quality of popular poetry?

The Confucian literati faced a double standard: on the one
hand, it was entirely acceptable, even institutionalized, for examination candidates, courtiers, and government officials to participate openly in the world of the entertainment quarters; on the other
hand, when it came to formal literary composition, one was expected to adhere to the classical norms of style and genre. Thus,
although an official might frequently exchange poems with a courtesan, and though these poems might be creative, thoughtful, sophisticated pieces, they were not considered part of his serious literary works because they deviated from the traditional subject
matter, tone, and form. Ou-yang Chiung's ambitious aspiration in
writing the Preface to the *Hua-chien chi* was to promote the acceptance of the *tz'u* in form and content as a respectable literary genre,
in spite of its inevitable associations with the entertainment world,
which he strove to downplay. Apparently he felt that in order to
advance the new genre he should argue for the acceptability of poetry treating the theme of love in a languid, sensory tone using
lines of unequal length—all of which phenomena had occurred
earlier in the history of Chinese poetry in isolated cases, but never
simultaneously and with such vigor as to establish a markedly new

poetic form. What Ou-yang Chiung could not do was to defend or give credit to the courtesan culture from which the new genre emerged, and thus he attempted to elevate the social status of the *tz'u* by denying its connections with the entertainment world, by declaring that the singing girls should adopt the literati style and discard their inferior "songs of the lotus boat."

In fact, the *tz'u* form was already accepted by 940; literati had by then been writing *tz'u* poems for at least two centuries, and the more idiomatic popular lyrics to *tz'u* song patterns had been in circulation even longer among merchants, artisans, professional musicians, and others. What was new in the publication in 940 of the *Hua-chien chi* was that poems by prominent members of the educated elite were published for the first time as serious literature with the authors identified by name and official position.

This innovation was made possible by various historical and social changes, not the least of which was the political transformation of China with the fall of the T'ang dynasty in 906. The centralized T'ang government, founded in 618, rose to a prosperous and magnificent peak in the seventh and eighth centuries, with its splendid capital in Ch'ang-an in the north; but it had been so beseiged by rebel invaders as well as internal conflicts for a century and a half that by the ninth century its orthodox foundation and political strength were increasingly eroded. The development of *tz'u* poetry in the north was reinforced by this foreign influence, for many *tz'u* tunes were imported from China's outlying regions. Meanwhile, the centers of power and cultural influence gradually shifted to the southern cities, the region called Chiang-nan, "south of the (Yangtze) river." The late T'ang urban culture which developed in the active port cities along the southern end of the Grand Canal such as Suchou, Hangchou, and Yangchou came to eclipse the decadent Ch'ang-an court culture. After the dissolution of the T'ang, rival political entities established their own local courts; the capital of the Later Shu (Hou Shu) dynasty in Ch'eng-tu and the capital of the Southern T'ang (Nan T'ang) dynasty in Nanching were particularly noteworthy as flourishing centers for the arts. This was a fortuitous geographical shift for the development of *tz'u* poetry, because the *tz'u* is ultimately derived from fourth- and fifth-century southern folk songs, and was fostered by the courtesan culture of the Chiang-nan region. (See map, pp. 16–17.)

Following this cultural movement toward the south from the middle of the T'ang period on, literati were infatuated with the Chiang-nan area. Its lakes and rivers were the most peaceful, its layers of mountains studded with pagodas were the most lovely, its mists and fogs the most romantic, its balmy climate the most favorable, its cuisine the most delicious, and above all its girls were said to be the most beautiful and talented in all of China. The many sensory attractions of the Chiang-nan region are captured in the image of the lotus boat. It is in the south that the lotus grows in lush profusion, with its deeply erotic associations—even the word lotus (*lien*) puns on a word for love (*lien*). It was on the southern waterways that the literati enjoyed the courtesans on their "painted boats." Even today, the most colorfully dressed and sensually attractive women I saw on a recent trip to China were in a traditional lotus boat on West Lake (Hsi-hu) in Hangchou (see Figure 1).

When Ou-yang Chiung suggests that the Southern singing girls "stop singing songs of the lotus boat," he is attempting to bring to an end an era of popular culture. Indeed, by the middle of the tenth century literati *tz'u* poetry had become so refined—for example, in the work of Li Ching (916–961), Li Yü (937–978), and Feng Yen-ssu (c. 903–960)—that it no longer relied on the popular tradition for inspiration. Courtesan culture remained extremely influential, and singing girls are mentioned explicitly in the *tz'u* of Sung poets such as Yen Chi-tao (1030?–1119?) and Liu Yung (990?–1050?), among others, but by the Sung dynasty the literati had become less dependent on the popular culture to nourish their own creativity.

The purpose of this study is to examine the preceding period of the T'ang dynasty, when we can find the origins of the *tz'u* in the popular song forms of the Southern Dynasties and in the foreign music imported during the Early and High T'ang eras. Because of the official Confucian prejudice against popular culture, manifested in their official repudiation of the music of the entertainment quarters, complete records of this material are lacking.

Figure 1. Young women in a "lotus boat" on West Lake (Hsi-hu) in Hangchou, 1982. *(Photograph by the author.)*

However, by a remarkable historical accident, manuscripts containing the texts of popular songs from the seventh through the tenth centuries were preserved in the Tun-huang caves, and it is to them that we will first turn our attention (chapter 2).

Most of the scholarly work which has so far been devoted to early *tz'u* poetry in the T'ang dynasty has been primarily research into dating and analysis of formal metrical development. Though these aspects are essential for understanding the evolution of a new form, in this study I add an emphasis on the social history of the text, exploring the cultural milieu from which it arose. I see a dialectical process at work, in which the popular tradition inspired the elite, who then adopted the style for court entertainment (chapter 3). But despite Ou-yang Chiung's rhetorical efforts to separate popular and elite strains, a cultural dichotomy does not occur: the street singers who perform in court learn new techniques from their palace training and professional contacts. Likewise, when scholar-officials visit the entertainment districts of Ch'ang-an or the southern cities, they participate with the courtesans in the composition of *tz'u* (chapter 4); as the singing girls learn refined diction and sophisticated rhyming techniques from the literati, the *wen-jen* in turn acquire a refreshingly simple directness and musical lyricism from their imitations of courtesan songs (chapter 5). The *tz'u* genre which is heralded in the *Hua-chien chi* has matured from several hundred years of continual social interaction and mutual literary influence (chapter 6). It is only through an understanding of this reciprocal process that we can truly recognize the achievement of significant individual poets such as Wen T'ing-yün and Wei Chuang (836–910), and that we can also give due credit to the generally anonymous courtesans and musicians and their popular "songs of the lotus boat."

To illustrate this poetic interaction, I have translated fifty-three anonymous popular T'ang songs and forty-two early *tz'u* by literati, as well as ten pre-T'ang precursors. Since my primary concern is with stylistic development, my translations attempt to reproduce, as accurately as English syntax and diction permit, the word

order and literal meaning of the original Chinese texts. The Tun-
huang manuscripts are notoriously problematic, for scribal errors,
local idioms, and textual lacunae abound; in general, I follow Jen
Erh-pei's interpretations, though I occasionally find it necessary to
modify his readings to achieve good English sense.

ACKNOWLEDGMENTS

DURING the period that I have been working on the preparation of this book, I have received support from many sources. For suggestions on translations and interpretations of individual poems I am grateful to members of the Chinese Poetry Group, especially Gloria Bien, Kang-i Sun Chang, Hans H. Frankel, C. T. Hsia, Yu-kung Kao, William Nienhauser, Nathan Sivin, and Hai-tao T'ang. For comments on an earlier version of this paper I extend my thanks to members of the Columbia University Seminar on Traditional China, especially Hans Bielenstein, Robert Hymes, Gari Ledyard, Christian Murck, Richard Vinograd, and Madeleine Zelin. My colleagues and students have made suggestions on the final version as well: I am particularly indebted to Victor Mair for his specialized knowledge of Tun-huang texts, to Tang Yi-ming, Burton Watson, and Wu Pei-yi for their poetic expertise, to Richard Sacks for his insights into oral poetic traditions, and to Amy Heinrich for her careful reading of the entire manuscript.

For assistance with research I am grateful to Philip Yampolsky, former Director of the Columbia University East Asian Library, New York; to Helen Spillett, Director of the East Asian Department of the Cambridge University Library, Cambridge, England; to Howard Nelson, Curator of Oriental Manuscripts in the British Library of the British Museum, London; and to M.-R. Guignard, Curator of the Oriental Division of the Département des Manuscrits at the Bibliothèque Nationale, Paris, France.

Locating the illustration for the dust jacket was a challenge which required the expert assistance of Alfreda Murck, of the Far East Department of the Metropolitan Museum of Art; Robert Mowry and Diane Cats, both of the Asia Society Gallery; and Wan-go H. C. Weng, President of China Institute. I especially appreciate Wan-go Weng's kind generosity in locating the Wang Hui painting from his collection and photographing the detail of the boat in the lotus pond which appears on the cover. I am also grateful to Virginia Bubek for designing the map on pp. 16–17.

I particularly wish to thank William F. Bernhardt of Columbia University Press, who has shown extraordinary patience and generosity since the inception of this project; and David Diefendorf for his meticulous and sensible editing, and for kindly designing the lotus leaf ornament found with each chapter title.

For generous support in the form of research grants during various stages of work on this study I wish to express my gratitude to the National Endowment for the Humanities, the American Council of Learned Societies, and the Columbia University Council for Research in the Humanities. The findings and conclusions presented here, however, do not necessarily represent the views of these organizations.

Finally, many friends—too numerous to list—have offered me the essential encouragement to complete this project. The friendly advice and intellectual companionship of Frances Schwartz and Michael Weinstein were immensely helpful. I am particularly grateful to Helen Allen for her cheerful assistance, to my parents for their timely support, and to my children for helping me to keep a sense of humor throughout. Above all, I wish to thank my husband, Richard McCoy, for his unwavering faith in me and in my work, for his generosity in allowing me the time to complete it, and for his love and understanding which carried me through the most difficult times and also enriched the periods of excitement and satisfaction.

CHAPTER ONE

Introduction

THE *shih* form, which dominates traditional Chinese poetry, has periodically given way to less regular forms of verse, such as the *tz'u* and *ch'ü*. This study examines one such period in Chinese history—the T'ang dynasty (618–906)—when the *tz'u* form emerged and developed. By the Northern Sung period (960–1126), the *tz'u* had virtually eclipsed the *shih* as the dominant poetic form. It had proved itself a vehicle of broad thematic variety, intense emotional expression, and charming lyrical beauty. Though the *tz'u*'s popularity diminished after the Sung dynasty, it remained a major genre of Chinese poetry until the twentieth century: indeed it was one of the favored forms in which Mao Tse-tung composed his own poems.

The outstanding characteristic of the *shih* form is its regularity. Employing the same number of characters in each line (usually five or seven) and an even number of lines, it typically develops in a rigid series of balanced rhymed couplets. Alternative forms like the *tz'u* break out of this regularity with lines of unequal length and a varying number of lines in a poem, with differently patterned rhyme schemes. The significance of the irregular form is suggested in the alternate term to identify the *tz'u* genre: *ch'ang-tuan chü* or "long and short lines." However, this is not to suggest that the *tz'u* genre is free verse; on the contrary, each *tz'u* is written to a prescribed tune pattern (*tz'u-tiao*), carrying a length, rhythm, tonal pattern and rhyme scheme which must be strictly adhered to.[1] But there are a large number of patterns among which

the poet can choose. The *Tz'u-lü*, a late seventeenth-century catalogue of *tz'u* forms with two supplements, lists 875 different basic
tune patterns *(cheng-tiao)* and 1496 recognized variant forms *(t'i)*
of those patterns.[2] In the early eighteenth century the K'ang-hsi
emperor commissioned a more inclusive catalogue: the *Ch'in-ting
tz'u-p'u* includes 826 basic tune patterns with 2,306 variant forms.[3]

Like the *shih*, the *tz'u* traces its origins to music. Each *tz'u*
pattern was originally a song, and the term *tz'u* itself simply means
"words," in the sense of "lyrics" to a song. During the T'ang dynasty the genre was called *ch'ü-tzu tz'u* or "words of songs." Gradually new words were written to fit the original melodic scheme
and the pattern was identified by the title of the tune *(tiao-ming)*.
Finally, even after the music was lost,[4] the pattern for that tune
title remained constant. For example, the basic pattern for the tune
"Keng lou-tzu" requires two stanzas of six lines each, with three
characters in lines 1, 2, 4, and 5, six characters in line 3, and five
characters in line 6 (i.e., 3-3-6-3-3-5), with a prescribed tonal pattern and rhyme scheme. Because the pattern requires such rigid
adherence, the process of writing a *tz'u* is called *t'ien-tz'u* or "filling in the words."

The endurance of the dominant *shih* form since the Han dynasty (206 B.C.–221 A.D.) indicates not only its suitability to Chinese
language and poetic temperament, but also its versatility and ca-
pacity for change. Why then, after several hundred years, was the
shih joined in the eighth and ninth centuries by a new poetic form
which would at least temporarily threaten to outshine it? The erotic
themes and casual, sensuous tones associated with *tz'u* poetry help
to explain its rise, as does its less regular form; but for a more
complete explanation of the place of the *tz'u* genre in the Chinese
literary scene we shall ultimately have to explore the social context
in which it grew. First, however, let us consider the available evidence from both elite and popular sources on the early history of
the *tz'u* form.

New Approaches to the History of *Tz'u* Poetry

An investigation of the emergence of *tz'u* poetry is problematic because its origins remain obscure—though less obscure than

they were a few decades ago.[5] It is well known that by the middle
of the ninth century, literati such as Wen T'ing-yün (812–870) were
writing great numbers of poems in the *tz'u* form. The *tz'u* was recognized as an established genre for literatus poetry with the publication in 940 of the first major anthology of *tz'u* poetry written
by scholar-officials, the *Hua-chien chi* ("Among the Flowers"). Until
recently, it was assumed by most scholars such as Hu Shih (1891–
1962) that the *tz'u* form was derived from the "new style" *shih* poetry *(chin-t'i shih)* of the T'ang dynasty, especially the *chüeh-chü* or
quatrain, with a few syllables added to or deleted from the basic
five- or seven-character *shih* lines to create lines of uneven length
which would fit new musical tunes.[6] The implication of this argument was that though common people, musicians, and singing
girls may have independently performed songs with lines of unequal length, the adaptations of *shih* to form *tz'u* were made by literati; Hu Shih dated the earliest *tz'u* creations to poets flourishing
during the Middle T'ang period (in the first half of the ninth century) such as Po Chü-yi (772–846) and Liu Yü-hsi (772–842), and
claimed that any attributions of *tz'u* poems of writers of the earlier
High T'ang period (in the first half of the eighth century) must be
false. Very few scholars challenged Hu Shih's views, with the notable exception of Wang Kuo-wei (1877–1927), who in a response
to an early draft of Hu Shih's article said, "I agree with you, that
tz'u poetry with lines of unequal length did not arise in the High
T'ang period, only in terms of the literati; [but] if we speak in terms
of musicians, this kind of song existed earlier."[7] Wang Kuo-wei's
insightful emphasis on songs being performed by professional musicians during the High T'ang period signals the beginning of the
recent debate over the origins of the *tz'u* form.

Twenty-five years later, Glen W. Baxter reopened the question in his study of the origins of the *tz'u*, in which he carefully
documented the succession of critics from the Sung dynasty scholar
Shen Kua (1030–1094) to Hu Shih and his Japanese contempor-
aries Suzuki Torao and Aoki Masaru, who all believed that *tz'u*
poems evolved from regular *shih* meters—primarily the *chüeh-chü*—
with interpolations gradually added to make them more singable
when set to music.[8] Baxter, like Hu Shih, named Middle T'ang
literati such as Po Chü-yi and Liu Yü-hsi as the first to write *tz'u*

poems with lines of unequal length; however, he emphasized that these Northern literati had personal contact with the popular music tradition in the South and he concluded suggestively that the prototypes of literary *tz'u* poems may in fact be these popular songs rather than aberrant forms of *shih* poetry.[9] Following Suzuki Torao, Baxter cited the various examples of poems of long and short lines which existed before the T'ang, and speculated that they were probably related to the popular Southern Dynasties Wu songs *(Wusheng ko)* which he showed were used in official performances in the seventh-century T'ang court.[10] However, Baxter found a puzzling gap in literary development: the Wu song tradition, he said, seems to have died out by the beginning of the eighth century, or at least poetry with long and short lines "was regarded as a subliterature and was not being preserved."[11] Was there a connection, then, between the fifth-, sixth-, and seventh-century folk song *(yüeh-fu)* tradition and the *tz'u* genre which emerged at the end of the eighth century?

The discovery of popular songs in the *tz'u* form dating from the early eighth century in the manuscripts found at Tun-huang, unavailable to Baxter and the earlier scholars, has revolutionized the study of the origins of *tz'u* poetry. The Tun-huang evidence helps to fill in the gap in literary history and confirms the intuitions of Wang Kuo-wei, Baxter, and others of the influence of popular song forms on the literati of the High T'ang period.

Before the publication in the 1950s of the pioneer work of two Chinese scholars, Wang Chung-min and Jen Erh-pei, only a handful of the *tz'u* poems recovered from Tun-huang were known. Writers like Liu Ta-chieh and Glen Baxter were aware of works such as Chu Tsu-mou's *Ch'iang-ts'un ts'ung-shu,* Lo Chen-yü's *Tun-huang ling-shih,* and Liu Fu's *Tun-huang to-so,* each of which transcribed about twenty individual *tz'u* songs from the Tun-huang manuscripts.[12] But the full extent of the Tun-huang *tz'u* materials was not recognized until the landmark publication in 1950 of Wang Chung-min's first annotated edition of 161 poems, the *Tun-huang ch'ü-tzu tz'u chi.*[13] Wang Chung-min had personally examined the Tun-huang manuscripts in Paris and London before World War II; after he returned to China as director of the National Library of Peking he wrote extensively on the corpus of Tun-huang *tz'u* poetry, culminating in the revised edition of his anthology of 162 Tun-huang *tz'u* in 1956.[14] At about the same time, Jen Erh-pei was completing a thorough study of Tun-huang *tz'u* poetry, which resulted in the publication in 1954 of his "preliminary investigations," *Tun-huang ch'ü ch'u-t'an*, and his comprehensive critical edition of 545 pieces, *Tun-huang ch'ü chiao-lu*, published the following year.[15] Jen Erh-pei demonstrated that the wealth of Tun-huang evidence shows many *tz'u* poems of popular origins flourishing as early as the High T'ang period.[16]

The significance of the Tun-huang *tz'u* in Chinese literary history was first articulated in English by Shih-chuan Chen in 1968, when he assigned about twenty-four of these songs, plus perhaps at least nine more, to the period of the High T'ang Emperor Hsüan-tsung's reign (712–755).[17] The methodology Chen used in making some of his attributions has been questioned, for example by Jao Tsung-yi, another Chinese scholar who studied the Tun-huang manuscripts in Europe.[18] Nevertheless, in a subsequent article Shih-chuan Chen argued more persuasively that "many men-of-letters practised *t'ien-tz'u* earlier than Liu Yü-hsi and Po Chü-yi," but that these High T'ang *tz'u* poets wrote "in private and kept their works anonymous."[19] Chen thus hinted that the social circumstances of composition influenced the literati poets' style and attitudes toward their work. Moreover, Chen followed Jen Erh-pei in finding much of the evidence that the *tz'u* form was thriving during the High T'ang period in the *Chiao-fang chi*, a record of music in Emperor Hsüan-tsung's court during the *k'ai-yüan* period (713–740). About two-thirds of the tune titles of poems in the Tun-huang manuscripts also appear in the list of tunes currently being performed in the court repertoire recorded in the *Chiao-fang chi*.[20]

Finally, in 1971 Jao Tsung-yi went a step further in filling in the gap which troubled Baxter by tracing the development of *tz'u* back to the Six Dynasties folk *yüeh-fu* tradition, with an emphasis on the role of Buddhist poetry used in eighth-century court ceremonials in the evolutionary process of the *tz'u*'s development.[21] The work of Jao Tsung-yi, which builds on the pioneer research of Wang Chung-min and Jen Erh-pei, marks a shift in the approach to T'ang dynasty *tz'u* poetry. Hu Shih and previous scholars had been most interested in the *tz'u* texts from the early ninth century which were the major ones extant before the Tun-huang finds, all of which were said to have been composed by literati. When the traditional scholars' pivotal question—could a High T'ang literatus poet such as Li Po (701–762) have written poems in the *tz'u* form?—was answered in the negative, it was assumed that therefore the genre did not exist in that period. Recent scholarship is less concerned with the *tz'u* poetry composed by literati, and focuses its attention instead on the hundreds of anonymous poems of popular origin unearthed at Tun-huang. This new material offers evidence of a thriving prototypical *tz'u* genre in the early eighth century and provides important clues to the understanding of a different social stratum of literary activity. It also demonstrates links between popular and elite cultures which indicate that a High T'ang literatus poet such as Li Po certainly could have written *tz'u* poems. Above all, the Tun-huang documents show that *tz'u* poems were not created by literati who made interpolations in their *shih* poems to fit musical tunes, but rather that a separate genre of *tz'u*, transmitted and performed at first by common people, musicians, and singing girls, was the model which the literati gradually emulated and adapted.

The Oral Origins of *Tz'u* Poems in the Tun-huang Manuscripts

The definition of the literary level of the Tun-huang poetic texts is highly problematic. The song words which survive in these manuscripts are written documents, yet they bear strong marks of oral origins. Characteristics of oral poetry such as repetition of images, colloquial diction, stock themes, straightforward expression of emotion, dramatic narrative, dialogue and direct speech, abrupt transitions, and fragmentary structure all abound in these texts. Clearly the written documents cannot be considered pure oral literature, yet they may come as close as possible in extant material to the oral culture. It is impossible to reconstruct T'ang oral literature precisely, but the Tun-huang texts at least provide a middle ground, for they are an unusual record of nonelite culture.

Distinguishing between oral and written literature is a vexing issue for the study of various national traditions. The early pioneering work by Milman Parry and Albert Lord attempted to establish a clear-cut dichotomy between "oral" and "written" genres. Parry and Lord demonstrated that Yugoslavian singers were able to produce long epics in oral performance not by memorization, but through an accumulated series of formulaic units; Parry and Lord then extended their analysis to claim that this style of formulaic composition in performance is a general, definitive characteristic of oral poetry and that the non-enjambement "adding style" of formulas is "one of the easiest touchstones to apply in testing the orality of a poem."[22] But there has more recently been dissatisfaction with this method of determining orality by quantitative analysis of formulas; indeed, many poems of oral origin have been shown to have survived in cultures which were not purely illiterate, and it is common for even highly formulaic texts to incorporate literary elements. Furthermore, formulaic lines, images, and motifs may also occur in explicitly written literature (consider, for example, the classical Japanese *waka* or literati *tz'u* poetry)—though Parry would term such a recurrence in a written text a "repetition" and not a "formula."

Most scholars now agree that it is not possible to determine fixed definitions of oral and written literature as mutually exclusive categories. On the contrary, it is necessary to treat texts such as Homeric epics as the *result* of an oral tradition; whether they were composed in performance or dictated or written, they were produced as "the culmination of perhaps over a thousand years of performance-audience interaction."[23] This accumulated tradition is currently the focus of scholarly investigation, and in a more recent article Albert Lord identifies the critic's main task as the determination of "how to read oral traditional poetry. Its poetics is different from that of written literature. . . . It cannot be treated as a flat surface. All the elements in traditional poetry have depth, and our task is to plumb their sometimes hidden recesses; for there will meaning be found."[24] The uncovering of traditional depth has proven a more fruitful scholarly endeavor than the quantification of formulas.

The layers of tradition can be approached from various perspectives. In terms of language, literature in an oral tradition is enriched by its accumulated density. As Leonard Muellner explains, "When a poet's units of expression are not single words but metrically fixed groups of words, and when these groups of words have existed before him in a tradition, any single word . . . [may have] maintained or acquired in time a sense which is more rigid, resonant, and intricate than it might be for a poet who lacks such a medium."[25] Other scholars, such as Gregory Nagy, consider theme the "overarching principle in the creation of traditional poetry." This approach, he explains, avoids the vexed question of the author's intent,

> that the artistic intent is indeed present—but that this intent must be assigned not simply to one poet but also to countless generations of previous poets steeped in the same traditions. In other words, I think that the artistry of the Homeric poems is traditional in both diction and in theme. For me the key is not so much the genius of Homer but the genius of the overall poetic tradition that culminated in our *Iliad* and *Odyssey*.[26]

But whether one emphasizes diction or theme, the tradition is particularly significant because it explains the reception and interpretation of the poem by its audience. The singer uses situations, themes, motifs, and phrases which everyone in his audience knows. When the audience is familiar with the conventions of oral performance, the poem resonates with the accumulated meanings of that tradition. Not only authorial intent but even the medium of composition are thus of subordinate importance to this traditional richness of association. It is less significant that Old English poems such as "The Wife's Lament" were written than that they used oral style for oral performance because that was the tradition known by the audience.[27] In *Oral Poetry: Its Nature, Significance, and Social Context*, Ruth Finnegan approaches oral literature as a social "communicative event," in which an understanding of the details and context of the performance and the nature of the audience are integral aspects of the text, its composition and transmission.[28] Moreover, she argues persuasively, most social contexts and performances mingle literate, semiliterate, and illiterate features. Therefore, we need a looser definition of oral poetry which will support "the continuity of 'oral' and 'written' literature."[29]

Finnegan's sociological insights into the mixed socioeconomic status of most audiences of orally performed literature are reinforced by the investigations of various anthropologists, historians, and literary critics. Recent students of China have been particularly concerned to qualify the traditional Confucian dichotomy between the culture of the highly educated minority and the culture of the uneducated peasant majority. Demonstrating that it is fallacious to identify government power, literacy, and the written text exclusively with the uban elite, Maurice Freedman, for example, argues that "elite culture and peasant culture were not different things; they were versions of each other."[30] David Johnson similarly shows that popular literature is not necessarily oral. Johnson asserts that literary works are created and performed to fill the needs and expectations of the audience, and therefore " 'elite literature' comprises all the creations of verbal art directed at an elite audience, and similarly for 'popular literature.' "[31] However, after the invention of printed texts in the Sung dynasty, there existed a "written literature aimed at a popular audience," or a "popular *written* literature."[32] The overlap of style and content which Johnson emphasizes is also a major theme in Patrick Hanan's study of vernacular fiction. Pointing to concurrent levels of style, Hanan stresses the plurality of literature.[33] Furthermore, this mingling occurs even before the advent of printing. Wang Ching-hsien, for example, finds in his study of China's oldest anthology of poetry neither purely oral nor purely written literature, but rather a transition "from an oral and perhaps very formulaic stage to what we see today, a version colored with scribal alterations and emendations."[34]

The development of T'ang *tz'u* poetry provides an illuminating illustration of the gradations within popular culture and elite culture and the frequent interaction between the two. The Tunhuang texts show the combination of oral style with written form.

These short lyric poems were probably all intended for oral performance—in tea houses or marketplace entertainments or elsewhere—but, as Finnegan points out, it is not unlikely that they
were deliberated on or composed and recorded long before the
performance.[35] Like "The Wife's Lament," a written poem which
draws heavily on the oral tradition, the Tun-huang poems are the
result of the accumulated layers of a long and complex tradition.
Moreover, the tradition from which the Tun-huang poems develop itself includes an interaction between oral and written elements.

   Approaching the Tun-huang texts as the outcome of a rich
tradition shifts our attention from their composition to their reception in performance by an audience familiar with that tradition.
Certainly the audience as well as the singers of T'ang *tz'u* included
members of various levels of society with various degrees of literacy, who would remember, repeat, and in some cases record the
songs they had heard perfomed in different ways. Accordingly, my
emphasis is on what we can discover and deduce of the social circumstances of the performance of the earliest *tz'u* poetry, especially the secular Tun-huang *tz'u*. Rather than concentrating on the
singer's mentality and means of composition (the older approach of
Parry and Lord), I am most concerned with how the *audience* responded, understood, and interpreted the songs.

   In this study I compare and show the gradations between two
bodies of material: the Tun-huang *tz'u* corpus of anonymous poems
in the style of the oral tradition, and the poems attributed to identified authors who were recognized scholar-officials which are collected in the *Hua-chien chi* anthology. The primary contextual difference between the Tun-huang *tz'u* and the literati poems in the
Hua-chien chi is that the former were primarily intended for performance wheras the latter can be read and deeply appreciated as
written texts without musical accompaniment. But even this distinction is not hard and fast. Though we may assume that the
poems attributed to literati were generally written compositions,
they were often intended for oral performance. A number of anecdotes from the period indicate that literati wrote compositions
on the spot for performance by singing girls. Conversely, the singing girls we tend to associate with the popular tradition were often

highly educated, and certainly exchanged written compositions with their scholar-official acquaintances, so it was not impossible that some of their poems were intended to be read as well as performed.

Throughout Chinese history, there has been a continuous overlap between written and oral cultures, and many degrees of education and literacy. Moreover, as we shall see, it was a common phenomenon before the T'ang dynasty for the aristocratic and literary elite to have frequent and close contact with the popular culture through the popular entertainers. However, the T'ang period saw more open acceptance of popular culture than ever before. Some of the factors in this expanded toleration include the encouragement of musical novelty and poetic experimentation at court under Emperor Hsüan-tsung, the increase in active court poets and entertainers before 755 and their subsequent displacement after the An Lu-shan Rebellion, and the cosmopolitan spirit and syncretistic ideology of T'ang culture. Therefore, though it was not new, the increased ease of interchange between literati and courtesans in the T'ang dynasty, and the burgeoning of the entertainment quarters, had widespread literary results. T'ang culture encouraged more open expression of what had formerly been relatively suppressed private styles and tastes.

Poetic Style and Audience Response

Given the extent of close contact between elite poets and professional entertainers, it may be fruitful to consider *tz'u* poetry attributed to scholar-officials as a sort of indirect audience response to popular songs with similar themes. Though the influence may not be direct, both levels of poetry participate, in different ways, in the same underlying tradition. For example, let us first examine a *tz'u* poem from the Tun-huang manuscripts for which the tune title is missing:

#212 (P. 3123)
Reed flowers turn white,
Autumn nights grow longer.

In front of my courtyard, the leaves of trees turn yellow,
Before the door it is cold.
Soon the grass will be covered with frost:
It will be time for winter clothing to come.
Husband and wife are in different places:
Tears fall in a thousand streams.

The emotion of this poem is conveyed through the series of traditional images associated with autumn and separation. The
speaker's point of view is consistently domestic, and the images
are tightly unified: the concern with the passing of time pervades
each line of the poem, and autumn's withering coldness and loss
of color and light not only discourage hope of reunion but also
represent the speaker's psychological desolation. The customary
human response to this seasonal inevitability is to send warm winter clothing. But the gesture of communication intensifies the separation: the emotional expression in the last line simply gives vent
to the dominant feeling sustained throughout the entire poem.
    Wen T'ing-yün, a ninth-century literatus who spent much time
in the entertainment quarters and may have heard this song or others
in the same tradition, composed a poem to the tune "Yü hu-tieh"
on a comparable theme:

The autumn wind bitterly cuts at her grieving isolation;
For the traveler it is not yet time to return.
Beyond the frontier, the grass has withered early;
South of the river, wild geese arrive late.
Like hibiscus fading, her delicate face;
Like willows falling, her newly painted eyebrows.
Their trembling makes one sad;
Broken hearted: who can know?[36]

Wen T'ing-yün's autumnal images come from a shared tradition: the
piercing wind, withered grass, and wild geese all represent the grief
of separation. But the point of view in this poem is more complex
than in the unified Tun-huang poem: the speaker views the for-
lorn woman and the traveling man from a distance, contrasting her
urgency with his delay, his premature autumn in the north with

her postponed reception of migrating messengers in the south. In Wen T'ing-yün's poem the woman is a static figure, whose face—like the flowers and branches to which it is likened—is an objective correlative of implicit emotion. The explicit grief is felt by the observer, though his feelings seem to merge ambiguously with hers as he wonders at the cause of her distress.

The Tun-huang poem presents a relatively straightforward correspondence between the natural scene and the human emotion. The tradition is so well known to the audience that there is no need to explain that the human separation is represented by the long cold nights of approaching autumn. The final couplet merely confirms the situation built into the poem's imagery by the accumulated tradition.

Wen T'ing-yün's poem, on the other hand, uses a similar constellation of images but with such a novel and complex treatment that the poet must give various signals to the reader/audience. For example, he indicates explicitly that the woman is suffering south of the river and the man is delayed north of the frontier. The subtle syntactic ambiguity of line 5 is clarified by the parallel construction of line 6. Finally, the open-ended references of the last couplet assume the rhetorical function of directing the reader's response.

Wen T'ing-yün's poem lacks the immediate accessibility of the Tun-huang poem. Since he expects his audience to read slowly and ponder the intricacies of the mood he evokes, he substitutes complexity for simplicity, ambiguity for clarity, multiple points of view for consistency. Yet fundamentally Wen T'ing-yün's poem demonstrates how an outside observer can imaginatively and empathetically participate in the sadness and despair depicted in the poem—and, by extension, in the conventional *tz'u* tradition. In directing our responses to this familiar poetic material, Wen T'ing-yün also expresses the experience of the recipient—the audience—of a longstanding oral tradition.

Throughout this study I shall consider the *tz'u* texts in their social contexts. It may be impossible to recover authorial intent, but analysis of poetic themes and techniques can be sharpened by an investigation of what the contemporary audience expected and needed. Preliminary research on early *tz'u* poetry has necessarily emphasized dating, attribution, and textual emendations. My study seeks to broaden the scope to explore the poetic style of compositions from various periods and social levels. An appreciation of the Tun-huang poems in their own context of performance is essential to overcome the traditional prejudice against popular lyrics as inferior to similar poems written in a highly sophisticated literary milieu. The popular texts must be evaluated according to their own criteria, rather than as crude precursors to a loftier elite model. Moreover, the understanding of literati poetry is also enhanced when it is regarded as another version of the same tradition.

The most promising clues to the origins of *tz'u* poetry are found among the Tun-huang manuscripts, though these documents still pose a number of difficult but intriguing questions concerning composition, transmission, and recording of the poems. To approach answers to some of these pivotal questions, let us begin by looking in more detail at the Tun-huang manuscripts themselves.

CHAPTER TWO

The Tun-huang Manuscripts

IN the extreme northwest of China, in present-day Kansu province which borders on the Sinkiang-Uighur Autonomous Region and Mongolia, lies the frontier town of Tun-huang (see map on following page). In 111 B.C., when the Han Emperor Wu (r. 140–86 B.C.) was expanding his empire in a series of campaigns against the Hsiung-nu and other outlying tribes, he established Tun-huang as a commandery (*chün*). Located near the end of the western extension of the Great Wall, with its series of watchtower signal beacons, Tun-huang guarded the Yang Pass (Yang-kuan) and the Jade Pass (Yü-men), the northwest gateways into China. It continued to be an important Chinese military post over the centuries, though it occasionally fell under the temporary rule of rival powers in the area, including the Tibetans, the Khotanese, and the Hsi-Hsia (Tanguts). Finally, after periods of domination by the Mongols and Manchus, Tun-huang was resettled by Chinese and made into a civil district (*hsien*) in 1760.

Coupled with its strategic importance for military campaigns, Tun-huang was significant as a flourishing center for traveling merchants and religious pilgrims, especially during the T'ang dynasty. Tun-huang—the name has been imaginatively translated "Blazing Beacon"—was the final stop in China proper for caravans heading westward over the old Silk Road across Central Asia to India and the Middle East. Expeditions leaving from the T'ang capital of Ch'ang-an (present-day Xi'an) would rest in Tun-huang

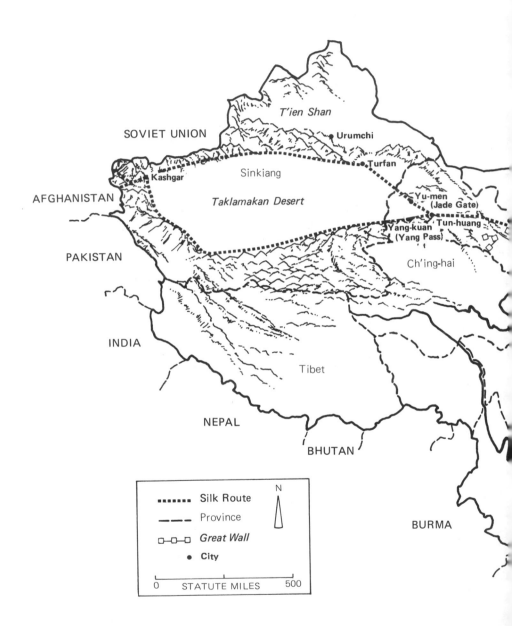

MAP OF CHINA

while stocking up on supplies, food, and water for their trip out south through the Yang Pass or north through the Jade Pass and around the formidable Taklamakan desert. Located at the intersection of the northern and southern branches of the Silk Route, and connected with roads to India, Tibet, Mongolia, southern Siberia, and the Middle East, Tun-huang was a unique juncture for the flow of peoples, cultural artifacts, and ideas. Buddhism was of course the primary cultural import from India, but Nestorian Christianity and Manichaeism also contributed ideological, artistic, and literary influence. Moreover, oases like Tun-huang became not mere stopovers, but important trading centers in their own right by the T'ang dynasty, and commercial enterprises were vigorously conducted.

According to legend, a monk who traveled to Tun-huang in 366 A.D. had a vision of a radiant golden cloud containing one thousand Buddhas, so he constructed the first of what was to become traditionally known as the "Caves of the Thousand Buddhas" (Ch'ien-fo tung) in the western hillsides of a steep river valley on the edge of the sand dunes at a small oasis fifteen miles southeast of the town of Tun-huang.[1] Apparently, travelers passing through Tun-huang followed his lead: as a last hopeful or pious act before entering the desert, the traveler would commission a local artist to decorate a cave for him, then dedicate it as a shrine to the donor's safe return. Conversely, travelers arriving at Tun-huang from the west after the arduous trip through the desert would establish similar shrines as acts of thanksgiving for their successful passage.[2] Construction continued from the time of the Northern Wei dynasty (386–534 A.D.) until the Mongols blocked the Silk Road in the fourteenth century. Gradually over one thousand caves were actually built in honeycomb layers, accompanied by numerous monasteries, though only 496 such grotto shrines remain today. Still, this intricate network, which is now known as the Mo-kao k'u caves at Tun-huang, forms the largest of China's rock temple complexes (see figures 2 and 3). The "Caves of the Thousand Buddhas" were visited by pilgrims from all over China, India, and Central Asia. The extraordinary frescoes painted over the centuries on the caves' inner walls and preserved by the dry climate are among the richest sources of early Chinese painting extant, and the caves housed fine examples of T'ang sculpture as well.

Discovery of the Tun-huang Manuscripts

But the most outstanding treasure of the Mo-kao k'u cave complex was the hidden library containing tens of thousands of manuscripts, which was not discovered until 1900.[3] Westerners as well as Chinese had visited Tun-huang in the late nineteenth century and knew of its exquisite wall paintings, but no one expected to find a cache of written materials there. It was only to examine the splendid art-historical specimens that the British archaeologist Marc Aurel Stein (1862–1943) trekked to Tun-huang in 1907. This was Stein's second expedition to Central Asia; in 1900–1901 he had already discovered the remains of several ancient towns and Buddhist centers buried by the sands of the Taklamakan desert after being abandoned when glaciers gradually withdrew and streams supplying water to these oases dried up. However, Tun-huang was not a buried site; not only was its water supply intact, but it had also been spared the Arab conquest which had destroyed many other Buddhist monuments in Central Asia. So it was much to Stein's surprise that soon after he arrived in the town of Tun-huang in March 1907, with no intention of excavating, he heard a rumor through an Urumchi merchant that Tun-huang had its own buried treasure: A Taoist priest named Wang Yüan-lu, who had fled Hupei to escape famine, had appointed himself guardian and restorer of the Mo-kao k'u caves. One day, while removing drifted sand from what is now called cave #16, Wang happened to notice a suggestive crack in the right-hand side wall, and upon further investigation discovered that the hollow area behind it was a small chamber (now designated cave #17), about five feet high and eight feet wide, literally filled with manuscripts. After rummaging through the piles of scrolls and ascertaining from exhibiting a few examples that the local government was uninterested in them, Wang Taoshih, or "Taoist Wang," as he was called, had fitted a locked door to the cave and kept the only key himself.

Figure 2. Honeycomb pattern of caves carved into cliff wall at Tun-huang. The caves in this photograph were generally used as monks' cells: since they have no murals and have not been restored, they indicate the original formation of caves cut into the desert sand hillsides. (*Photograph by the author.*)

Figure 3. View of the Mo-kao k'u Caves at Tun-huang, rich in Buddhist murals and sculptures, and the site of the discovery of the Tun-huang manuscripts. Facades have recently been repaired; stairs and walkways have been reconstructed to facilitate access and maintenance. (*Photograph by the author.*)

Stein was understandably eager to meet the Taoist, but he had to wait several weeks for Wang to return from a tour of neighboring oases where he was begging funds for future restoration work. Finally, in May, Stein and his interpreter Chiang Ssu-yeh approached Wang, who at first resisted not only selling manuscripts to Stein but even showing them to him. There followed a month of delicate and secret negotiations, in which Stein and Chiang continually pressed Wang, yet tried to downplay their keen interest in the hidden library and to avoid insulting Wang's piety by offering vast sums of money to purchase the manuscripts. Instead, they used a rather mystical approach which was in fact suggested by the nearly miraculous nature of the find itself. The key to achieving an understanding turned out to be the revered Buddhist pilgrim Hsüan-tsang (d. 664 A.D.), who had made a sixteen-year journey (629–645) along the Silk Road from China to India, bringing back to China Sanskrit sutras which he translated himself.

On their first meeting, Stein began by admiring Wang's dedicated if clumsy efforts at restoration of frescoes and statuary in the Buddhist chapel of cave #16; then, as he later wrote, he sought to establish a link with the monk through their mutual regard for Hsüan-tsang: "So surrounded by these tokens of lingering Buddhist worship, genuine though distorted, I thought it appropriate to tell Wang Tao-shih, as well as my poor Chinese would permit, of my devotion to the saintly traveler; how I had followed his footsteps from India for over ten thousand Li across inhospitable mountains and deserts. . . ."[4] Stein was immediately encouraged, first "by the gleam of lively interest which I caught in the Tao-shih's eyes, otherwise so shy and fitful,"[5] and then later that night by the arrival in his tent of Chiang Ssu-yeh "in silent elation with a bundle of Chinese rolls which Wang Tao-shih had just brought him in secret, carefully hidden under his flowing black robe."[6] By appealing to the memory of Hsüan-tsang, Stein had achieved his first goal: to see some of the actual manuscripts. Chiang studied these scrolls all night, and announced at dawn that they were Buddhist sutras which, according to the colophons, had been brought from India and translated by Hsüan-tsang himself. When Chiang reported to Wang this "auspicious omen," that the scrolls

Wang had happened to select to show Stein were the very ones transmitted by the same Hsüan-tsang, the priest was persuaded that Stein's visit was providential and he opened the locked door to the hidden chamber. Thus Hsüan-tsang had helped Stein achieve his second objective, and the results were well worth his patient perseverance:

> The sight the small room disclosed was one to make my eyes open wide. Heaped up in layers, but without any order, there appeared in the dim light of the priest's little lamp a solid mass of manuscript bundles rising to a height of nearly ten feet, and filling, as subsequent measurement showed, close on 500 cubic feet. The area left clear within the room was just sufficient for two people to stand in.[7]

Gradually, Stein and Chiang persuaded Wang to allow them to study a few manuscripts at a time in a nearby antechapel which they used as a "reading room." Stein immediately recognized the value of the cache. Whereas the priest Wang regarded the sacred Buddhist texts as the most important, Stein was particularly drawn to the more irregular bundles, containing miscellaneous secular writings along with Buddhist fragments, and particularly exquisite T'ang paintings on silk. But Stein felt he did not have the leisure to study these carefully: "My main care was how many of them I might hope to rescue from their dismal imprisonment and the risks attending their present guardian's careless handling."[8] Initially Stein selected the materials of special interest and obtained Wang's permission to take a few bundles at a time to his tent for what they euphemistically called "closer examination," which was the first step in removing them from the caves. But he still had to counteract "the Tao-shih's relapses into timorous contrariness."[9]

> Flushed as I was with delight at these unhoped-for discoveries, I could not lose sight of the chief practical task, all-important for the time being. It was to keep our priest in a pliable mood, and to prevent his mind being overcome by the trepidations with which the chance of any intrusion and of consequent hostile rumours among his patrons would fill him. With the help of Chiang-Ssu-yeh's genial persuasion, and what reassuring display I could make of my devotion to Buddhist lore in general and the memory of my patron saint in particular, we succeeded better than I had ventured to hope.[10]

Moreover, at the crucial third stage of negotiations, over the ultimate removal of the manuscripts from China, the precedent of Hsüan-tsang played a major role. Stein knew he could not have persuaded Wang with "unholy words of sale and purchase."[11] So,

> tired as we all were, I took the occasion to engage the priest in another long talk about our common hero and patron saint, the great Hsüan-tsang. What better proof of his guidance and favour could I claim than that I should have been allowed to behold such a wonderful hidden store of sacred relics belonging to his own times and partly derived, perhaps, from his Indian wanderings, within a cave-temple which so ardent an admirer of "T'ang-seng" [as Wang called him] had restored and was now guarding? Again I let the Tao-shih enlarge, as we stood in the loggia, upon the extraordinary adventures of his great saint as depicted in those cherished frescoes on its walls. The panel which showed Hsän-tsang returning with his animal heavily laden with sacred manuscripts from India, was the most effective apologue I could advance for my eager interest in the relics the Tao-shih had discovered and was yet keeping from daylight.
>
> The priest in his more susceptible moods could not help acknowledging that this fate of continued confinement in a dark hole was not the purpose for which the great scholar-saint had let him light upon these precious remains of Buddhist lore, and that he himself was quite incompetent to do justice to them by study or otherwise. Was it not evident, so Chiang pleaded with all the force of his soft reasoning, that by allowing me, a faithful disciple of Hsüan-tsang, to render accessible to Western students the literary and other relics which a providential discovery had placed so abundantly in his keeping, he would do an act of real religious merit? That this pious concession would also be rewarded by an ample donation for the benefit of the shrine he had laboured to restore to its old glory, was a secondary consideration merely to be hinted at.[12]

Stein's appeal to providential intention was again successful. That night and for the following seven nights Wang selected and passed on to Chiang, who secretly delivered them to Stein's tent, bundles of scrolls which could be shipped to London. By the time Stein left Tun-huang on June 13, he had packed up seven cases of manuscripts and five cases of paintings and embroideries, for which he rewarded Wang with four silver horseshoes.[13]

Sir Aurel Stein's clever manipulation of the semi-educated

Taoist priest Wang Yüan-lu, and his removal of the ancient manuscripts from the Tun-huang caves to the British Museum are, rightly, highly controversial issues. The Chinese today regard Stein as a "thief" and a "bandit" for having stolen their national treasures, and many Westerners are sympathetic to this view.[14] The British journalist Peter Hopkirk, who illuminates both sides of the controversy in his recent book, *Foreign Devils on the Silk Road*, reports after a discussion with Dr. Hsia Nai, Director of China's Institute of Archaeology, that Stein "is unquestionably regarded as the most villainous of the foreign archaeologists."[15] Hopkirk vividly portrays the "racc" among explorers from various nations for the treasures buried in Central Asia, and that Stein's motivations included a desire to be the first Westerner to stake a claim on the Tun-huang materials.[16] On the other hand, Stein's biographer, Jeannette Mirsky, points out in her subject's defense that Stein was naturally operating under nineteenth-century standards, and at the time "archaeology considered scientific validation as sufficient reason for removing the documents and relics to the West."[17] Moreover, she underscores Stein's attitude that the manuscript collection might not have been adequately cared for if left in the opened cave. From Stein's point of view, it was concern for the fate of these manuscripts, which were of such immense scholarly value, which induced him to negotiate so painstakingly with Wang Tao-shih, whom Stein and Chiang so deftly "gradually led from one concession to another, and we took care not to leave him much time for reflection."[18]

But though Stein was the first, he was by no means the last Westerner to retrieve treasures from the Tun-huang caves. The following year the French sinologist Paul Pelliot (1878–1945) spent three weeks in cave #17 carefully going over the thousands of manuscripts Stein had been unable to carry away. Pelliot, unlike Stein, could read classical Chinese and was therefore more discriminating in assessing the find. Wang Yüan-lu cooperated in allowing Pelliot to remove the majority of the most valuable remaining pieces to the Bibliothèque Nationale in Paris.[19] For this Pelliot is now regarded as a close second to Stein in shameless looting of China's history.[20] However, Pelliot reserved a box of sample manuscripts which he personally carried to Peking to show to Chinese scholars there. The government of war-torn China had not taken the Tun-huang materials seriously before, but when the astonished Chinese scholars alerted the Peking authorities to the significance of the claim, they immediately ordered Wang Tao-shih not to release any more materials to foreigners, and they had some of the remaining scrolls transported to Peking. Nevertheless, smaller bundles of manuscripts were occasionally purchased by various individuals; Stein obtained additional materials for the British Museum on his third expedition in 1916, and the same year a Japanese mission led by Ōtani Kōzui persuaded Wang Yüan-lu to hand over manuscripts which he had hidden from the Chinese government inside stucco Buddhist images. Others were procured by a Russian expedition led by Sergei F. Oldenburg.[21] In 1923 the American art historian Langdon Warner removed twelve frescoes and a three-foot T'ang statue to the Fogg Museum in Cambridge, Massachusetts.[22] But by 1925, foreign explorers were effectively banned from the Tun-huang site, and later expeditions by Chinese government authorities resulted in the relatively minor collections of the remaining materials now in the Peking Library, the National Central Library in Taipei, and elsewhere.[23]

Scope of the Tun-huang Manuscripts

The vast majority of the scrolls, folios, books, and fragments found in cave #17 is devoted to Buddhist subjects, but Confucianism, Taoism, and various other religions are also represented.[24] Documents include information on social institutions, history, politics, topography, and economics as well as ballads, stories, biographies, letters, and other literary works. Although most of the manuscripts are written in Chinese, there are items in Tibetan, Sanskrit, Sogdian, Khotanese, Uighur and Tocharian. The scrolls contain paintings, drawings, woodblock prints, and the world's earliest printed book, a copy of the *Diamond Sutra* (*Chin-kang ching*) dated 868.

The oldest pieces in the Tun-huang manuscript collection

probably date from the early fifth century, and the latest dates are the late tenth and early eleventh centuries.[25] The library chamber was apparently constucted in the last half of the ninth century, and it was subsequently filled with the scrolls and other materials.[26] The chamber seems to have been sealed up in the eleventh century, but the reason for hiding the manuscripts is unclear. Most scholars still accept the standard conjecture, that when the Hsi-Hsia tribe invaded the Tun-huang area in 1036, monks and priests hastily collected from the neighboring monasteries all the scriptures and paintings which they could not carry with them and buried them in the cave to protect them from the enemy.[27] However, this theory is currently being questioned by those who point out that the Hsi-Hsia were not particularly hostile to Buddhism.[28] Moreover, though Wang Yüan-lu disturbed the original order by rummaging through the manuscripts in search of valuable artifacts, he did acknowledge to Aurel Stein that when he found them they were all neatly arranged, which suggests that they were not hastily concealed. Stein's own theory was that cave #17 served "as a place of deposit for all kinds of objects sanctified by use but no longer needed in the various shrines." Calling attention to the many bags of fragments of sacred texts, he claimed "such insignificant relics would certainly not have been collected and sewn up systematically in the commotion of a sudden emergency."[29] Drawing on Stein's view of the cave's contents as sacred but discarded artifacts, Fujieda Akira describes the find as "a huge accumulation of waste" and hypothesizes that "when the printing of books became widespread in the tenth century, the handwritten manuscripts of the Tripitaka at the monastic libraries must have been replaced by books of a new type— the printed Tripitaka. Consequently, the discarded manuscripts found their way to the sacred waste-pile, where torn scrolls from old times as well as a bulk of manuscripts in Tibetan had been stored."[30] Though this theory is plausible, it does not fully explain why the texts and religious objects from many surrounding monasteries would have been collected in a central location or why they were so neatly arranged in this special chamber. Moreover, the presence of secular materials in the collection is further evidence that the chamber may have been used for many years as a place to deposit and store various items which were considered important enough to be preserved in the cave's ideally dry climate. It is likely that in a time when paper was scarce and the written word was esteemed, almost any written manuscript would be deemed worthy of preservation. In many cases the margins of scrolls which had been used primarily for formal documents are filled with miscellaneous writing samples, probably to aviod wasting paper. This may account for the presence in the collection of items such as invitations to club meetings, model letters, school primers, lists and contracts, and the words to popular songs.

The major literary significance of the Tun-huang manuscripts has been the recovery of narrative writing in the popular genres such as *chiang ching-wen,* or commentary on the sutras; and *pien-wen,* a particular form of storytelling during the T'ang combining prose and verse, closely related to the oral tradition, and found exclusively in the Tun-huang manuscripts.[31] The term *pien-wen* is ambiguous, and there are no commonly accepted guidelines for precisely defining the genre, but Victor Mair has recently isolated particular formal features to identify the *pien-wen,* which he translates as "transformation texts."[32] The *pien-wen* provide unique evidence for the early development of later narrative forms such as drama, the vernacular short story, and the novel. They are also invaluable as linguistic and social documents. Whereas most written records which survive from the T'ang dynasty represent the language and customs of the highly educated elite, the Tun-huang texts abound in colloquialisms and reflect the mores and attitudes of a less refined class, people who were able to read and write but did not share the rigid standards of the courtly elite. In Denis Twitchett's words, "the discovery of the Tun-huang MSS revealed a rich substratum of literature written by members of the large class of literate people who had not had a full classical education, but on whom depended to a large extent the day to day functioning of the Chinese state and society."[33]

Popular Songs in the Tun-huang Manuscripts

Though the early narrative texts from Tun-huang have received the most attention from literary scholars, the popular po-

etry found in the manuscripts stored in cave #17 is equally significant. One of the obstacles to the study of popular songs has been
their fragmentary arrangement. Whereas a *pien-wen* text might be
the primary or only material on a particular scroll, the words to
songs rarely appear in isolation. More often, a handful of popular
songs is interspersed among a wide variety of other writings on a
scroll. For example, six *tz'u* poems are embedded in a scroll catalogued in the British Museum's Stein Collection as S. 6537 which
has a Buddhist doctrinal treatise on the recto side, and the verso
begins with deeds and formal documents (copied by a monk), followed by the constitution of a benevolent club and the story of
Sakyamuni Buddha in verse, and after the six songs continues with
a collection of model letters for happy and unhappy occasions and
ends with three columns of a Buddhist text. In other cases, popular songs are written at the end of the verso side of a contract,
will, inventory, deed of sale, or scripture, perhaps as evidence that
the formal document is complete (e.g., songs to the tune "Wang
Chiang-nan'" appear at the end of a sutra in S. 3102 and other
songs are found at the ends of sutra commentaries in S. 3713 and
a manuscript from the Bibliothèque Nationale's Pelliot Collection
catalogued as P. 3128). There may have been legal or religious reasons for adding miscellaneous literary texts to the end of a formal
document: to give a Western parallel, the official Bologna list of
Criminal Accusations for the year 1317 uses verses of Dante's *In-
ferno* to fill up space at the end of the legal material in order to
prevent additions and to indicate that the document is complete
and has not been accidentally or deliberately fragmented.[34] However, it is more likely that these Buddhist scrolls were filled up
with writing of secular material less to insure legalistic authority
than because of a distaste for wastefulness—or, to put it posi-
tively, because of a desire to make full use of the precious com-
modity of paper or an eagerness for the opportunity to make any
kind of written records, regardless of the content.

Moreover, in some cases the songs do appear to constitute the
primary text of a manuscript—for example, in S. 4332 there are
songs to the tune "Pieh hsien-tzu" on the recto side and the verso
side is used for account notes regarding the purchase of wheat and
millet by monk Yüan-hsüeh of Lung-hsing Monastery (Lung-hsing

ssu). And there are a number of instances in which an entire small booklet is devoted exclusively to the recording—usually in very fine calligraphy—of *tz'u* songs (e.g., P. 3994 and P. 3911). Certainly at least some of these songs were written down simply because the scribes found them aesthetically pleasing or otherwise worthy of transmission and preservation.

But who were the scribes? A minority of the manuscripts are signed. Most commonly colophons to Buddhist pieces or deeds and formal documents give the names of clerks, monks, or lay devotees who copied them (e.g., S. 2925, S. 36, and S. 6537). It was usually a layman rather than a monk who did the copying.[35] Scrolls were written out for various reasons. Colophons indicate that one could commission the copying of a sutra as an act of piety or repentance, or as a filial act to help one's deceased parents accumulate merit, to reduce their "suffering in any subsequent state of existence and to expedite them on the path to Nirvāna."[36] Nor were all motivations purely religious ones: the colophon to scroll S. 87 is signed by an Assistant Commissioner who had the *Diamond Sutra* copied out as an act of thanks for his official promotion.

Since the production of written religious materials was thought to improve a person's good luck or hope of salvation, the individual who initiated the project was eager to receive personal recognition for it. This is the case for a few of the popular songs. For example, the set of three Buddhist song sequences in fixed form in S. 5549 is said to have been copied by six individuals, whose names are listed. But in contrast to formal Buddhist sutras, the poetic material frequently appears in the hand of a schoolboy (S. 5477) or in an otherwise casual or careless style. In some cases ballads are signed by the lay student (*hsüeh-shih-lang*) who copied them (e.g., S. 5441, S. 692). Many of the songs are interspersed with pieces which are clearly writing exercises, such as the child's primer, the "One-thousand-character Classic" (*Ch'ien-tzu wen*, e.g., S. 7273), and many texts have been copied and recopied several times. It seems clear, then, that a significant motivation for recording songs and ballads was to practice writing, and that many of the song words were copied out by lay students connected to the monasteries which were the primary institution for teaching reading and writing. Tun-huang contained nearly twenty monasteries and convents during the eighth to tenth centuries, and each one had a school to educate lay children.[37]

Arthur Waley has suggested that the long pieces of popular literature preserved in the Tun-huang manuscripts may have been based on orally transmitted stories but in written form they were composed "by people of the scribe or village schoolmaster class" who were literate enough to write them down.[38] I believe that in the case of short lyrics it is not necessary to make a clear-cut distinction between an oral version and the written text—and indeed it is not unlikely that some of these texts do in fact represent records of actual performances, or the writer's memory of songs he had heard. However, it is useful to emphasize Waley's notion of a secular scribal class "who could read and write, but had not the sort of higher literary education that would have enabled them to join the regular Civil Service."[39] These scribes might also include the students of village schoolmasters as well as lay students being educated in the surrounding monasteries. Nevertheless, it must be emphasized that the materials found in cave #17 at Tun-huang in no way constitute a homogeneous corpus, and many of the manuscripts were in fact copied out in many different areas of China and carried to Tun-huang by traveling merchants or religious pilgrims. Therefore, the manuscripts do not merely represent local culture of the Tun-huang area. Furthermore, some manuscripts—particularly those small booklets in fine calligraphy such as P. 3994 (see below)—may have been written out specifically for the purpose of spreading a cultural form from one area to another, or as a merchant's or traveler's souvenir of the songs he had heard in a particular city he visited.

How the scribes chose which song words to record, and under what circumstances they had heard them, are questions on which only speculation is possible. No doubt the materials deposited in cave #17 of the Mo-kao k'u complex represent only a fraction of the entire corpus of written materials in circulation during the T'ang dynasty, and there may be a certain random selection to the ones which happen to have been preserved so fortuitously. It is fascinating that the *tz'u* songs contained in the manuscripts unearthed at Tun-huang present such a heterogeneous collection. Some are apparently written by traditionally educated and aristocratic literati (see chapter 3), though they are recorded as anonymous works in the Tun-huang manuscripts. Most of the songs, especially the secular lyrics, bear marked characteristics of folk songs, including colloquialisms, dialogue, formulaic phrases, sequential narrative, direct expression of emotion, and abrupt fragmented structure.[40] Moreover, as opposed to early literati *tz'u* which are devoted almost exclusively to the theme of unrequited love, the Tun-huang poems exhibit such a wide variety of subject matter that Jen Erh-pei has formulated twenty categories, ranging from songs of soldiers' loneliness and complaints against war to recluses' songs, young scholars' songs, heroes' songs, and doctors' songs, as well as the various Buddhist themes.[41] Some of these songs also appear in an extremely simple, unpolished style. The broad range of content has led various critics to emphasize that the poems reflect the contemporary social and historical circumstances.[42] However, it is difficult to determine the degree to which the songs are direct expressions of the common people's fundamental desires and grievances, as opposed to more refined versions of some of these sentiments as modified and adapted by musical performers. As Jen Erh-pei states, it is tempting to conclude that soldiers' songs were composed by soldiers, students' songs by students, Buddhists' songs by Buddhists, and doctors' songs by doctors, but in fact literary history is not so simple.[43] Although critics differ in their estimation of the social class of the composers and performers of these songs, the consensus seems to be that they originated among people with some training, at least in poetry and music, but who lacked the thorough education of literati.[44] Nevertheless, many questions remain open: were the songs originally oral or written (*k'ou* or *shou*) compositions? Were they composed spontaneously, or commissioned for particular occasions? Were they transmitted spontaneously, or under more formal circumstances of performance? Since we do not have complete records of T'ang cultural activities, many of these questions will have to remain unanswered; others will be treated in chapter 4. Moreover, since the poems contained in the Tun-huang manuscripts are so varied, I do not believe that a single set of answers will be appropriate to all the poems; indeed, each of the alternatives may apply to one or more of the different texts.

Certainly, there is no unified corpus of popular songs from the Tun-huang manuscripts. As mentioned in chapter 1, the first edition of Tun-huang songs by Wang Chung-min in 1954 contained 162 poems, but was quickly followed in 1955 by Jen Erh-pei's collection of 545 poems. Some of the discrepancy arises over the content of the poems: if Buddhist songs are added to the secular ones, the total number swells. Moreover, there is a question about what constitutes a complete song, especially when series of verses are often joined in a sequence. Jen Erh-pei's numbering system is sometimes dubious or misleading because he tends to assign a new number to each consecutive stanza of a linked series of verses. Even the formal features of the songs are quite diversified, and they are referred to by various terms, especially *ch'ü* ("songs"), *tz'u* ("words"), and *ch'ü-tzu tz'u* ("words of songs"), indicating that there was no consistent distinction made between the performed song and its written text. Furthermore, the terms *tz'u* and *yüeh-fu* ("music bureau songs") were used interchangeably throughout the Sung dynasty.[45] This indicates T'ang and Sung Chinese may not have regarded the *tz'u* as an absolutely distinctive and unified genre.

Classification of Popular Songs in the Tun-huang Manuscripts

"Miscellaneous common songs" (*p'u-t'ung tsa-ch'ü*)

Jen Erh-pei divides the popular poems in the Tun-huang manuscripts into three main categories. His first section, "miscellaneous common songs" (*p'u-t'ung tsa-ch'ü*), comprises the largest number of independent songs. Most of these consist of a single isolated stanza, and by Jen's count there is a total of 227 poems of this form (#001–227). Most of these poems are also secular in content. The majority are love songs, but they cover a broad range of styles, from simple folk songs to more ornate poems; three of the former are illustrated by the following examples.

The first song is a lover's pledge of fidelity, using the trope identified in Western rhetoric as adynaton or "impossibilia":

#041 (S. 4332)
Tune: "P'u-sa man"

Over the pillow I made a thousand kinds of vows:
If you want me to stop loving you, then you must wait until the green
    mountains crumble,
Until iron floats on top of water,
Even until the Yellow River becomes dry.

Until Orion appears in broad daylight,
Until the Big Dipper points south;
If you want me to stop, I cannot stop yet,
You must wait until the sun is seen at the third watch of the night.

The second song shows the narrative element underlying many of the Tun-huang *tz'u;* the most common situation presented is that of the warrior fighting at the frontier and his lonely wife lamenting his absence:

#040 (P. 3251)
Tune: "P'u-sa man"

Yesterday morning I went early to bid farewell to the traveling man,
The fifth watch was not yet over; the golden cock crowed.
We parted, and he passed beyond the river bridge.
The sound of water: hearing it broke my heart.
I recall only the grief of separation,
And how hard it was for him to set off on the long road.
He stopped his horse, then again plied the whip,
To send me one hundred thousand words.

The third example is a straightforward folk song on the theme of mutability, which centers on the contrast between the brevity of man's life and the constant renewal of the moon.

#126 (P. 2809)
Tune: "Yang-liu chih"

Spring goes, spring comes, spring again turns to spring.
The cold and the heat often alternate.

The moon waxes, the moon wanes, the moon is always new,
But man is pressed by old age.
Just look at the thousand-year-old moon in front of the courtyard:
It has always been here, it will always remain.
But I do not see a hundred-year-old person before the hall:
All people ever do is merely become a bit of dust.

In addition to the numerous poems in which young lovers vow eternal fidelity, or lonely women and homesick frontier soldiers lament their plights, however, there are also a variety of other personae represented in the secular "miscellaneous common songs." I will present three examples of these varied personae: the traveling merchant, the loyal subjects of Tun-huang, and the recluse.

The first song gives three aspects of a merchant's life; for considerations of authorship and transmission of these songs it is important to note that if he is rich, the merchant is said to frequent the entertainment quarters and thus he would be familiar witth current popular music. If he is poor or sick, however, the merchant is lonely and forsaken:

#110–112
Tune: "Ch'ang hsiang-ssu"

A traveling merchant in Chiang-hsi:
His riches and honor are rare in this world;
All day he stays in the red chambers
. . . * dancing and singing.

He continues to fill his cup until he's drunk as mud;
He lightly exchanges golden goblets.
The whole day he pursues pleasure and seeks joy:
This is a case of not returning due to wealth.

A traveling merchant in Chiang-hsi:
So lonely only he knows it;
His face is covered with dust and dirt,
All day he is cheated by others.

Morning after morning he stands to the west of the market gate,
The wind blows tears which fall from both eyes.

*Ellipses indicate a lacuna in the original manuscript.

He gazes into the distance toward his native home, far away:
This is a case of not returning due to poverty.

A traveling merchant in Chiang-hsi:
He has fallen sick and lies within an inch of death.
He searches everywhere, asking for the latest news,
It seems this is his end.

The villagers drag his corpse to the west of the side of the road,
His father and mother do not know about it.
On his body is attached a tag with written characters:
This is a case of not returning due to death.

Another song is also apparently of local origin, and Jen Erh-pei dates it to the government of Ts'ao Yi-chin of the later Chin dynasty, approximately 943–945.[46] The inhabitants of Tun-huang pledge their loyalty to the conquered T'ang empire, hoping the rightful Emperor will soon be restored:

#082 (P. 3128)
Tune: "Wang Chiang-nan"

Tun-huang prefecture
Surrounded on all four sides by six barbarian tribes;
Only Heaven sees it when living souls are so bitterly humiliated.
For several years the route has been cut off: we are absent from court
    ceremonies.
We gaze from afar toward the imperial palace.

A new favor will descend
All plants and trees will receive its splendor;
If we cannot depend from the distance on the awesome power of the Em-
    peror,
Then we must fear that the Yellow River and the Huang River will sub-
    mit to barbarians.
But sooner or later the Sacred One will know it.

Finally, a song in the persona of a recluse scholar is stylisti-cally closer to the plain diction and simple parallelism of popular songs than the sophisticated techniques which might be expected in a refined literatus poem of reclusion, suggesting the *wen-jen*'s versatility in adapting his style to suit the genre. On the other hand, the conventional stance and imagery indicate the author's familiarity with courtly eremitic poetry. This diversity is characteristic of the wide range of thematic content, stylistic refinement, and apparent social origins among the poems grouped under the category "miscellaneous common songs."

#068 (P. 3821)

Tune: "Huan hsi sha"

Behind the mountain I cultivated a garden and planted herbs and sunflowers;
In front of the cave I dug a pond for fish and stocked it.
On a single frame of purple vines, flowers cluster;
The rain is light and fine.

Sitting I hear the gibbons cry, I sing an old rhapsody;
Walking I see the swallows chattering, I recite a new poem.
Since I have no affairs, I return to my library,
And close the wicker gate.

Although the majority of the "miscellaneous common songs" are isolated verses, almost one-third (79 out of 227) in Jen Erh-pei's first section belong to formally structured sequences of from five to fourteen poems (#141–205, #214–227). Thus, there are in the entire collection only 148 independent secular lyrics, the form of poem which was the prototype of later *tz'u* poems written by literati. Most of the longer sequences in Jen's first section consist of a series of verses telling stories on Buddhist themes, especially recounting various episodes in the life of Buddha and focusing on Chinese versions of the legend of Siddhartha's "Great Departure" from his early life as a prince to his renunciation of worldly ambition for the spiritual pursuits which eventually led to his Buddhahood. But one sequence of twelve verses (#141–152) is devoted to Confucian material: entitled "The New Summary of the Eighteen Chapters of the Book of Filial Piety" (*Hsin-chi hsiao-ching shih-pa chang*), it was probably written during the reign of Emperor Hsüan-tsung.[47]

"Song sequences in fixed forms" (ting-ko lien-chang)

Jen Erh-pei's second category is "song sequences in fixed forms" (ting-ko lien-chang), in which from 5 to 134 stanzas (which Jen numbers as individual poems) are linked to form a set or series of songs on a fixed chronological topic such as the five watches of the night, the twelve hours of the day, the one hundred years of an individual's life, or the twelve months of the year. By Jen's count there are 298 poems in this form (#401–698); however, there are only eighteen separate cycles. Most of these sets are Buddhist in subject matter, with titles like "The twelve hours of meditation" (Ch'an-men shih-erh shih, #455–466), or "The twelve hours of the law" (Fa-t'i shih-erh shih, #635–646), in which a rule of conduct or meditation practice is presented in each sequential verse. But there is also a Confucian cycle on the twelve successive stages of practicing filial piety through study (#467–478), and several sequences on common folk song themes, such as the ten decades of suffering in the life of a man (#657–666) or a woman (#667–676), or the "Twelve months of longing" (Shih-erh yüeh hsiang-ssu) of a lonely woman whose husband is absent on a military expedition. Most of these "song sequences in fixed forms" are too long to translate here,[48] but one of the shorter sets, on the secular topic of the lonely wife and organized around the "Five Watches" of the night, will indicate the form in spite of its fragmented condition:

#406–412 (P. 2647)
Tune: "Wu-keng chuan"

At the first watch, the beginning of the night, I sit and play the ch'in;
I would like to convey my thoughts to him, but it breaks my heart.
Whenever I think of him, I resent my wild husband's footloose behavior;
Once he goes, he abandons me for many years and months.

Since you left, many springs have come and gone;
I have not received a letter, news is cut off.
I want to change myself into a wild goose at the edge of the skies,
Crying mournfully over ten thousand li, seeking to visit you.

At the second watch, under the lonely boudoir canopy I prepare to play
　　the cheng;
Which of its strings will not produce a sound of grief?

Suddenly I remember my wild husband fighting in the sandy desert:
This sends me into anxiety and sorrow; my eyes fill with tears.

At the beginning, you only said you would return within a year;
Who could know that once you had left, news and letters would be so
    scarce?
I am like Ch'ang O, goddess of the moon,
With all my chaste heart, alone I stay in my empty room.

At the third watch, sad and lonely, I pick up my *k'ung-hou;*
I lament my wild husband . . .*
. . .
. . .

You are serving your sovereign with loyalty and fidelity,
It is all for fame and profit, seeking to be enfeoffed;
I wish you would soon ascend to the rank of prime minister,
Then I would also be able to stay alone for one hundred autumns.

At the fourth watch, I prepare the bamboos to play *kung* and *shang* tones;
I deeply resent my good husband at Yü-yang,
In the pond the amorous fish play around,
Sea gulls . . .*

In the original eight-stanza poem, two four-line stanzas corre-
sponded with each of the five nocturnal watches (periods of approximately two hours each from dusk to dawn). The structure is
further reinforced by the incremental repetition of the musical elements, from *ch'in* (lute) to *cheng* (zither) to *k'ung-hou* (harp) to *kung*
and *shang* (pentatonic) tones; the movement from third- to second-
person address, and the apparent increasingly positive or forgiving
attitude toward the husband as the night progresses.

"Grand songs" *(ta-ch'ü)*

The *ta-ch'ü* or "grand songs" are also sets of verses but their
sequential unity is defined less by narrative content or by prosodic
repetition than by their performance context. The *ta-ch'ü* was actually a dance performance including singers and musicians as well

*Ellipses indicate a lacuna in the original manuscript.

as dancers, consisting of a prelude, a set of three to six songs separated by instrumental interludes, and a finale. It could be used
for lavish entertainment of a large audience. Jen counts twenty verses
in this form, which make up five separate cycles or medleys (#1001–
1020). Only the first of these is Buddhist in subject matter; the
last one, to the tune "Chien-ch'i tz'u" ("Songs of swordsman-
ship") apparently praises the Emperor Hsüan-tsung and his subjects for their martial valor.[49]

I shall present two other examples of the "grand songs." The
first shows that although the verse form and performance context
may vary, certain themes—particularly the lonely wife—remain
popular. Several lines of this *ta-ch'ü* medley echo almost verbatim
certain lines of the previous set of *ting-ko lien-chang* verses in the
"Five Watches" form:

#1011–1013 (S. 6537)
Tune: "A ts'ao p'o"

Last night the spring breeze blew into my door,
It moved as if it would open.
I saw in front of the courtyard flowers about to blossom,
Only half open.
Solely on account of thinking of you my countenance changed:
A soldier fighting at the Lung-hsi barracks.
Then I saw in front of the courtyard a pair of magpies for good luck:
You are beyond the frontier, will your expedition return?
Dreams come first.

Alone I sit in my secluded room, my thoughts multiply.
What do I think about?
The autumn night lengthens so it cannot be endured;
I love him still.
Whenever I think of him, I resent my wild husband's footloose behavior;
Once he followed the army out to fight, he was gone.
Solely on account of thinking of him, my countenance changed:
From the outermost borders return . . .*

At the beginning, you only said you would return in three years;
Anxiously I've waited so long.

*Ellipses indicate a lacuna in the original manuscript.

From dawn until dusk much weeping saturates and weakens my eyes;
Letters and news are scarce.
In my empty room, I constantly sleep alone;
North of the frontier, you also must know.
Sad and anxious, I have no words to show my innermost feelings;
Keep hope in our hearts that we will be able to meet again in better times.
. . .*

The second example of a "grand song" indicates a popular subtheme, the husband who is assigned to frontier duty. But in this case the four songs are not tightly unified except in form, and it is likely they were performed by different singers, showing various aspects of the frontier life. We have a portrait of the gallant warrior in the first song, his lonely wife's lament in the second, a colorful scene of hunting in the frontier area in the third, and a rather ambiguous song of return at the end.

#1014–1017
Tune: "Ho man-tzu"

At midnight the autumn wind, cold and bleak, is high;
At the Great Wall the warrior displays his valor.
In his hand holding a steel knife, as sharp as frost and snow,
At his waist always hanging a sword so sharp it could cut a hair blown
     against it.

The autumn waters, clear and still, are very deep;
They resemble my heart, in the cold of the year (like an evergreen);
At the river stop I am lonely, no news or letter;
At dusk I only hear the cries of birds coming from the frontier.

Beside the wall hunters ride swiftly,
Sitting sideways on golden saddles, they urge the horses with whips.
Barbarian words and Chinese language are quite seldom heard together;
Listening to barbarian songs—very charming.

Once the gold river flows, it goes on forever;
When it reaches the edge of the sky, then there is another horizon.
On horseback I am unaware of changes on the calendar,
But when I have made not yet half of my return journey, already a year
     has passed.

*Ellipses indicate a lacuna in the original manuscript.

These selections can only suggest the tremendous variety of songs in the *tz'u* form contained in the Tun-huang manuscripts. They indicate the diverse social levels, literary themes, and religious or secular purposes which influenced T'ang popular entertainment. The complexity and mobility of cosmopolitan T'ang culture favored the development of a diverse musical repertoire, and as we shall see the changing historical circumstances fostered poetic innovations based on this dynamic popular song tradition.

Popular and Elite Materials in the Tun-huang Manuscripts

The juxtaposition and blending of popular and elite styles in the Tun-huang poems are beautifully illustrated by a single manuscript in the Paris collection, P. 3994. This four-page booklet, executed in neat calligraphy, records six anonymous poems. However, the first three of these poems are elsewhere attributed to literati authors; one other poem resembles the ornate *Hua-chien chi* style; while the last two poems are fragmented and rough, as is characteristic of the unrefined popular style. How these particular poems came to be combined in this way is a fascinating area of speculation.

Fujieda Akira describes the construction of the four-page booklet from the Tun-huang finds: a piece of paper originally measuring approximately twelve inches by eighteen inches was cut into three sheets, each one measuring fifteen centimeters by thirty centimeters. When one such sheet was folded in the middle, it made a four-page booklet. Sometimes several folded sheets were pasted or stitched together, but a single folded sheet could also be used alone, as in the case of P. 3994. The result was a compact handsize booklet, about six inches square, easy to hold and to carry. "A large number of these [booklets] date from the first half of the ninth century, while we hardly find an earlier sample, although the type must have been introduced into Tun-huang during the preceding century." [50]

The first poem in P. 3994 is nearly identical to the poem attributed to Ou-yang Chiung in the *Tsun-ch'ien chi;* an anthology of early *tz'u* poems by literati:

#140 (P. 3994)

Tune: "Keng-lou ch'ang"

In the thirty-six palaces, the autumn night is endless.
Dewdrops fall drop by drop in the tall *wu-t'ung* trees.
Drip by drip, the jade waterclock gurgles in its bronze container.
The bright moon rises over the golden bed.

A red fiber rug,
A Bo-shan-style incense burner.
The fragrant breeze subtly touches the curtain tassles.
The goat carriage, once it has gone, will leave the road filled with long
    green grasses.
In the dusty mirror, a multicolored phoenix all alone.

One of the most striking characteristics of this poem is its lack of narrative content. Though a resting palace woman is implied by the golden bed in line four, and the brilliantly colored phoenix represents a lovely woman, no human presence is explicitly asserted. The poem presents the evocative setting only, with no animating figure. All of the emotional force of the poem is contained in the objects. Without doubt, the drops of water in the first stanza and the dusty mirror in the last line suggest tears and neglect; the road where grasses grow because the carriage no longer comes by reinforces the conventional situation of the abandoned woman. However, a poem with no human emotional focus is still unusual, if not obscure, in the Tun-huang corpus, and represents the extreme end of the spectrum moving away from dramatic or narrative popular poetry.

The second poem is recorded in P. 3994 with no tune title, but it differs in only four characters from a poem to the tune "Keng-lou tzu" attributed to Wen T'ing-yün in the *Hua-chien chi* anthology.

#139 (P. 3994)

[Tune: "Keng lou tzu" I]

The fragrance from a golden duck-shaped censor,
The tears of a red candle,
Shine right on the autumn longing felt within the painted chamber.

Her eyebrows of kingfisher are faded,
Her temple-cloud hairdo is becoming thin.
Night comes, making her quilt and pillow cold.

The *wu-t'ung* trees,
Rain at the third watch,
They do not tell the true suffering of the separated heart.
Leaf after leaf,
Sound after sound,
Continue to fall on empty steps until dawn.

This poem, like the previous one, is also notable for its vagueness. The mood is evoked with the conventional images of the neglected woman whose grief keeps her awake at night. Yet the references to her situation are oblique. The elegance of the objects in the woman's chamber suggest her beauty, and the relentless dripping of the raindrops suggests her tears. Otherwise this poem is a delicate depiction of passing time and continual neglect. Like the first poem, this one is also closer to the refined and evocative literati style than the straighforward popular style.

The third poem in this elegantly inscribed booklet is a song which is also identified elsewhere as having been composed by Ouyang Chiung. The song describes a banquet, specifically placed in Lo-yang by the street name in the final line. Significantly, the social context of this poem as described internally is a feast at which aristocrats and courtesans share wine and song:

#053 (P. 3994)
Tune: "P'u sa man"

The red stove warms the room where a beautiful woman sleeps,
Beyond the curtains flying snow increases the coldness.
In the small garden, they are playing mouth organs and singing,
The fragrant breeze gathers robes of silk and gauze.
Wine is poured, the golden cups are full;
Amidst orchid musk, the feast is offered again.
The young gentleman is as drunk as mud,
On the Avenue of Heaven his horse is heard neighing.[51]

This poem does have narrative content, and it provides a direct insight into the literati's indulgence in the entertainment quarters. The imagery emphasizes aristocratic opulence, with the silk robes and golden cups. The poem also closes with restraint characteristic of refined public poetry: the only direct expression of emotion is projected onto the horse.

The next poem in the booklet is more difficult to place than the first three, for it does not appear elsewhere with a specific attribution. However, the tone of this fourth poem is nevertheless quite elevated. It may represent the kind of courtesan poem which directly inspired literati compositions, or was inspired by contact with literati. On the other hand, it is also possible that it was composed by a man of letters but anonymously transmitted. The onomatapoeic reduplicated syllables at the beginning of each line show the profound concern with refined style, and specifically with the musicality of this performed verse:

#036 (P.3994)
   Tune: "P'u-sa man"

Drop by drop and drip by drip, rain on the winding banks,
Pair by pair and one by one, mandarin ducks chatter.
Lush, lush, the fragance of wild flowers,
Soft, soft, the yellow of the golden willow-threads.
Lovely, lovely, the girls on the river,
Two by two, dancers beside the stream.
Bright, bright, the gleam of silk and gauze robes,
Dainty, dainty, the adornments of cloud hair-dos and cosmetics.

With the exception of the silk robes and cosmetics in the final couplet, the imagery of this poem is natural. However, the festivity being held on the river banks suggests an ambience of leisure and pleasure not so different from that of the entertainment quarters. Though anonymous, this poem approaches the *Hua-chien chi* in imagistic richness.

The last two poems in P. 3994 are a pair of anonymous verses to the tune "Yü mei-jen." These poems are altogether different in style, for they lack the coherence and the tonal richness of the preceding poems in this series. However, they do share with the other poems in booklet P. 3994 an elevated diction which suggests a similar social ambience in spite of the relative deficiency in artistic craft.

#034 (P. 3994)
Tune: "Yü mei-jen"

The East wind blows, making the crab-apple blossoms open,
Fragrant musk fills the chamber tower.
Fragrance and red beauties pile up together,
And when they are picked by the lovely woman,
She drops her golden hairpin.

#035 (P. 3994)
Tune: "Yü mei-jen"

Golden hairpin: flowers attached to the hairpin,
A branch of crab-apple flowers.
Just now butterflies are flying all around her,
She brushes off the accumulated red flower centers:
"They dirty my clothes."

The mutual associations between the beautiful woman and spring flowers are reiterated in this pair of poems, and the elegant detail of the pivotal golden hairpin enhances the sense of refined aestheticism. However, the emotional level of these verses is banal. Moreover, the narrative inconsistencies and abrupt shift in speaker and point of view suggest that perhaps the audience knew more about the tradition of these poems than the information in the extant texts indicates. Perhaps these songs were accompanied by a dramatic enactment or were performed by two singers. In any case, whereas the preceding poems in the P. 3994 booklet may be read and appreciated as autonomous literary works, these poems seem to need the support of a performance context, to participate in an oral traditional depth known to the contemporary audience but not to us.

The neat calligraphy of booklet P. 3994 suggests that this handbook was not the exercise of a schoolboy. It was perhaps copied out by an educated man as a memento of a visit, perhaps to a Chiang-nan entertainment center. Or it may have been intended as an art object for trade. Whatever its purpose, it includes a wide stylistic range, from an abstract and evocative elite poem to a concrete and flat popular verse, with several intermediate gradations between these two extremes. The interaction and cross-fertilization of the elite and popular traditions is here tangibly demonstrated: whoever designed this lovely little booklet preserved a striking record of the continuum of literary styles and techniques.

CHAPTER THREE

The Rise of *Tz'u* Poetry
Before 755

CONFUCIAN Chinese ideology has always assumed two levels of culture, the "Great Tradition" of the highly educated and the less significant popular tradition. The reverence accorded the texts of the elite culture, coupled with a general respect for antiquity, account for the remarkable length and continuity of the Chinese literary tradition. For hundreds of years schoolboys read the same books and later passed civil service examinations by thorough familiarity with the standard canon. After achieving official positions, they in turn made classical allusions to the same texts in their own writings and thus perpetuated the stability of the tradition. Popular or heterodox culture was regarded with condescension, if not scorn, and only rarely was it deemed worthy of written preservation. Thus the *Chiao-fang chi* records the titles of songs performed at Emperor Hsüan-tsung's court as a history of that aspect of elite life, yet it does not include the song texts themselves because, due to their popular origins, they were considered too crude or trivial to be worth recording.

In fact, the popular tradition has been highly influential in all genres of Chinese literature. In recurrent cycles an elite literary form tended to lose its vigor, to become superficial and merely conventional or even mannered and decadent. At these times the form was often revitalized by inspiration from the popular culture. Thus the poetic tradition—which began, after all, with the folk songs collected in the *Shih ching (Book of Songs)*[1]—was set on a new path when literati of the second and third centuries A.D. began writing *shih* poetry in the five-word-per-line meter of the anonymous *yüeh-fu* songs collected by the imperial music bureau. *Tz'u* poetry likewise originated as a popular genre when, about five hundred years later, the *shih* form was beginning to suffer from redundancy and overextension.

This pattern of the influence of popular literature on the elite mainstream, in poetry, fiction, and drama, has often been noticed, but it has rarely been studied in any depth because the folk materials were unavailable. Specifically, scholars generally gave only cursory mention to the debt of later literati *tz'u* poetry to its oral origins, until the discovery of the Tun-huang manuscripts provided unique evidence of some of the actual contents of that influential popular culture. However, the Confucian condescending attitude toward nonelite literature, which was maintained well into the twentieth century, was still an obstacle to scholarship, and critics continued to dismiss folk songs or poetry popular among the unlettered masses from the serious study of Chinese literary history. Liu Ta-chieh is only one of the many scholars who could be mentioned who repeats the familiar evaluation that the songs are "vulgar" *(ts'ang-ning)* and "unrefined" *(pu-ya);* although he indicates that the poems have features characteristic of folk literature and that they were influential precursors of later literati *tz'u*, he stresses their technical faults and literary shortcomings from the point of view of the elite tradition.[2] Even Jen Erh-pei himself apologizes that the content of some of the songs, especially those concerning philanderers from wealthy families and singing girls who "sell smiles," does not accommodate itself to the refined Confucian tradition; he adds that such poems do not represent the wide variety of the songs, and that even though they are not necessarily trite or unfeeling, still he cannot resist adopting a defensive posture on this point.[3]

On the other hand, recent mainland critics attempt to reverse this trend; however, their praise of popular literature suggests that its superiority is a consequence of its proletarian class origins rather than inherent literary qualities. Chang Hsi-hou, for example, criticizes Wang Chung-min for justifying the importance of popular songs only because they led to the development of "elegant" literati *tz'u* poetry; instead, Chang advocates the position of "taking popular songs and raising them to the same high level as literati songs, completely destroying the incorrect traditional attitude of condescension toward 'vulgar songs' and 'small tunes.' "[4] Nevertheless, it is remarkable that the persistent primary issue for most students of the development of *tz'u* poetry has been not the nature of the folk song origins of the *tz'u* but rather the date when the literati first began writing in that form (see chapter 1).

Because of the ambiguity of dating poems which were recorded as "anonymous" or attributed to particular poets centuries after their deaths, it is impossible to say with precision when the literati began to write poetry in the *tz'u* form. Furthermore, as I will argue in detail in the following two chapters, there was so much interaction between T'ang scholar-officials and professional musicians and singing girls who had only moderate education that it is indeed false to make a clear-cut distinction between "elite" and "popular" *tz'u* poetry. One is directly confronted with this problem when studying the Tun-huang manuscripts. Though it is true that the materials found in cave #17 come as close as possible to representing the contemporary oral popular literature, that is not all they represent. Along with the Buddhist sutras and historical records, and interspersed among the apparently genuine anonymous folk songs, are a handful of poems which have been associated with well-known aristocratic authors. Two poems (#046–047, S. 2607) are nearly identical to those said to have been composed by the T'ang Emperor Chao-tsung, named Li Chieh (r. 888–904), as recorded in anthologies such as the *Ch'üan T'ang shih*.[5] And as discussed above (chapter 2), three poems which are recorded without attribution in the Tun-huang manuscripts are also included with slight variations in tenth-century anthologies of early *tz'u* by literati. One poem to the tune "Keng-lou tzu" (#139, P. 3994) is virtually the same as a poem by Wen T'ing-yün in the *Hua-chien chi* anthology.[6] Two poems attributed to Ou-yang Chiung, who wrote the Preface to the *Hua-chien chi*, in the *Tsun-ch'ien chi*, an anonymously compiled anthology of *tz'u* poets from the eighth to the tenth centuries, are likewise recorded as anonymous works in the same Tun-huang manuscript (P. 3994): one to the tune "P'u-sa man" (#053) and one to the tune "Keng-lou ch'ang" (#140).[7] Other poems found in the Tun-huang manuscripts which are not attributed to particular authors are often written in a relatively refined style—for example, all thirty-three of the anonymous but polished poems in the *Yün-yao chi* anthology of 922 are included in the Tun-huang manuscripts (#001–033, S. 1441, P. 2838).[8]

Though the point at which literati began writing in the *tz'u* form is unclear, there is no question that *tz'u* poetry was recognized as a genre suitable for literati with the compilation of the first major anthology of *tz'u* by scholar-officials, the *Hua-chien chi*, which contains five hundred *tz'u* poems by eighteen authors, edited by Chao Ch'ung-tso, himself a minor official of the Later Shu (Hou Shu) dynasty (934–965). The Preface to the *Hua-chien chi*, dated 940, by Ou-yang Chiung (896–971), who served in the Later Shu court both as an official and as a poet, is almost a manifesto for the recognition of *tz'u* by literati. It identifies the authors of the poems specifically as poets *(shih-k'o)*. Extolling the virtues of the Chinese song tradition by mentioning prominent legendary and historical figures who composed songs, Ou-yang Chiung—in the best Confucian manner and the elevated "parallel prose" *(p'ien wen)* style—labored to distinguish the elite *tz'u* of the *Hua-chien chi* from popular *tz'u* songs, which he condemned: "Not only were the words vulgar, but the content though pretty had no substance."[9] Ou-yang Chiung also indirectly acknowledged the interaction between scholar-officials and popular entertainers, though he gave priority to the elite poets by suggesting that the contents of the *Hua-chien chi* might provide a model which "Southern singing girls" *(nan-kuo ch'an-chüan)* could use to improve the quality of their own compositions, so they might "stop singing songs of the lotus boat."[10]

Although I intend to show that Ou-yang Chiung's strict polarization between popular and elite poetry is historically inaccurate and that in fact the two modes were mutually influential, it must be acknowledged that the majority of the *Hua-chien chi* poems are stylistically more subtle and elevated than their popular counterparts. As Kang-i Sun Chang points out, though absolute ge-

neric boundaries are impossible to establish, the literati *tz'u* of the
Hua-chien chi may be generally contrasted with the popular *tz'u*
found in the Tun-huang manuscripts. Following Jen Erh-pei, Chang
contrasts subject matter and techniques, finding the Tun-huang
poems more narrative and more dramatic, and also more likely to
use dialogue, interrogative openings, emotional straightforwardness, and emotional diction.[11] The "stylistic common denomina-
tor" which generally distinguishes the *Hua-chien chi tz'u*, according to Chang, is their similarity in theme and conventions to the
Palace Style poetry of the sixth century A.D.[12] The treatment of
love in the *Hua-chien chi* and in the Liang dynasty (502–557) anthology of Palace Style poetry, *Yü-t'ai hsin-yung (New Songs from
a Jade Terrace)*, is indeed in many ways strikingly similar, but there
are also important differences. Moreover, an examination of the
influences of sixth-century poetry on the development of the *tz'u*
form also requires consideration of the contemporary Southern
Dynasties popular song tradition.

Poetry of the Southern Dynasties Period

In the Preface to the *Hua-chien chi,* Ou-yang Chiung defensively denied any links between the literati *tz'u* and sixth-century
Palace Style or popular love poetry. He first described the elegant
ambience of court poetry, extravagantly praising the social settings
in which poetry was composed:

> Poets competed for precedence before their patrons as in the story of
> "the three thousand guests and the tortoise shell pins." They strove
> to outdo each other at their feasts, as did the rivals with their "coral
> trees." There were gentlemen on the silken mats, and ladies behind
> ornamented curtains. Page after page, they passed around the flow-
> ered paper, and their literary offerings were like beautiful embroi-
> deries. The women raised their delicate fingers and beat time with the
> fragrant wood. There was no lack of splendid lines to enhance the
> graceful postures of the singers."[13]

However, Ou-yang Chiung concluded, in the fifth and sixth centuries the influence of popular songs from the Pei-li—literally, the

"Northern lanes," which signified the pleasure quarters—contaminated the elegance of court poetry: "The Palace Style of the Southern Dynasties was fanned by the singing girls' air of the Pei-li. Not only were the words vulgar, but the content though pretty had no substance." [14]

There were various reasons Ou-yang Chiung took pains to make this disclaimer. One is simply class bias: the highly educated elite looked down on the "crude" colloquial language and "unrefined" manners of professional entertainers, and Ou-yang's goal in the Preface was to elevate the *tz'u* to a level of respectability among the literati. Second, Ou-yang Chiung may have been aware of formal and geographical similarities between Southern Dynasties love poetry and early T'ang *tz'u* poetry, which he wanted to downplay. Third, both the popular songs and the Palace Style court poetry were considered too hedonistic in theme and decadent in style for proper Confucian society. Finally, Ou-yang Chiung was defensive because love was not one of the major traditional themes of classical Chinese poetry, and its dominance in the *Hua-chien chi* would naturally invite comparison with two related groups of love poems: popular songs and the *Yü-t'ai hsin-yung*, the only other extant anthology of love poetry. As Hans Frankel has explained,

> Love between the sexes is not as preponderant a poetic theme in China as in the West. This is because Confucian moralists discouraged the open expression of erotic sentiments in literature. Love, in their view, is essentially a private affair and therefore not a proper subject to be communicated by the man of letters to his public audience. Thus love poetry, by and large, is outside the mainstream of Chinese literature, and is to be found in certain types of popular and semipopular poetry, such as the anonymous *yüeh-fu* songs of the Southern Dynasties (fourth to sixth centuries) and the anonymous *tz'u* songs preserved in Tun-huang manuscripts. [15]

Though over one-third of the folk songs in the *Shih ching* concern courtship and marriage, love was not a predominant theme in the Han dynasty *yüeh-fu* tradition. These early, anonymous poems, which generally followed a five-word-per-line meter, more typically consisted of laments over the hardships of war, poverty, loneliness, illness, and death. Throughout the four centuries of disunity after the Han dynasty, when empires rose and fell in quick succession and capitals moved from north to south due to continuous pressure by northern invading tribes, literati poets imitated *yüeh-fu* themes of suffering, travel, and homesickness, writing new words to *yüeh-fu* titles like "The weary road," "Breaking a willow branch," and "Moon over the mountain pass."

The period known as the "Southern Dynasties" or "Six Dynasties" covers the years after the fall of the Han dynasty, when six ruling houses—the Wu (222–258), Eastern Chin (Tung Chin) (317–420), Liu Sung (420–479), Ch'i (479–502), Liang (502–551), and Ch'en (551–589)—consecutively established their capitals in the southern city of Chien-k'ang, now known as Nanching. During this time two groups of popular songs developed in the south: the *Wu-sheng ko* or Wu songs were sung around the capital city of Chien-k'ang, while the *Hsi-ch'ü ko* or Western songs flourished farther up the Yangtze River around Chiang-ling (in modern Hupei) to the west. Both groups of songs tend to follow the four-line or *chüeh-chü* form, with four or five characters per line, and both focus on love. The Western songs often have outside settings and deal with the life of the traveling merchant. The Wu songs emphasize the woman's point of view and often describe her boudoir, furnished with "silk curtains, lattice screens, jeweled vanity cases, and embroidered robes."[16] Both groups of songs employ a conventional set of puns, which tend to center around the activities of sericulture and love. For example, *ssu* means both "silk thread" and "love thoughts" and *p'i* means both "piece of cloth" and "pair."[17] An entire song may be structured around such puns; for example in a recurrent motif, threading the loom represents an emotional receptiveness to love:

Tzu-yeh Songs of the Four Seasons: Summer

Spring is over, the mulberry leaves are consumed;
Summer begins, the silkworms' work is done.
Day and night I arrange threads (love) in my loom,
So you will know I hope to make a piece (pair) soon.[18]

Many of these Wu songs are titled "Tzu-yeh ko" or "Song of Tzu-yeh." Tzu-yeh was apparently the name of a well-known local singing girl during the Eastern Chin dynasty (317–420). It is unclear whether or not she herself composed the dozens of extant songs with her name in the title; it is more likely that some or all of these titles refer to songs in imitation of the Tzu-yeh style, for several examples are attributed to aristocratic male authors.[19] The "Tzu-yeh songs" provide a fascinating parallel to the Tun-huang *tz'u* in this interaction between singing girls and literati. In addition to using clever puns, "Tzu-yeh songs" characteristically treat situations of lovers' meetings and separations with a direct and earthy charm. Many associate the seasons of the year with the course of a love affair through witty wordplay. In the following song the repetition in the first three lines of *ch'un* ("spring") and *to* ("many, full") shows the singer's obsession with the emotions suggested by the season:

Tzu-yeh Songs of the Four Seasons: Spring

The spring forest is full of flowers,
The spring birds are full of feelings.
The spring wind also is full of desire:
It blows my thin silk skirt open.[20]

The Wu songs are significant influences on early *tz'u* poetry because of their quatrain form, simple diction, and associations with singing girl performance. They are also thematically influential, for they develop fresh poetic approaches to love, including the early stages of attraction, as well as separation. Though courtship is an important theme in the *Shih ching*, that classic also contains many poems which treat lonely women longing for their lovers. Most *yüeh-fu* poetry and early *shih* poems by literati avoided the celebration of love and emphasized instead the theme of the neglected wife.[21] One of the poems most often imitated during the Six Dynasties period was the last of the anonymous *Nineteen Old Poems (Ku-shih shih-chiu shou)* of the late Han dynasty:

The bright moon is gleaming:
It shines on my thin silk bed curtains.

I am so unhappy I cannot sleep
So I gather up my clothes, get up and walk back and forth.
Though people say that travel is pleasant,
It's not as good as a quick return.
I go out the door and stand hesitating, alone.
To whom can I tell my sad thoughts?
Gazing ahead, I go back inside:
Falling tears wet my robe.[22]

The conventions of nocturnal loneliness and insomnia under a bright moon became hallmarks of the Six Dynasties *shih*, whether written from a male or a female point of view. The variations on this theme which suggested a woman persona focused on the furnishings of her bedroom and many male poets wrote "boudoir laments" (*kuei-yüan*) from the point of view of a female poetic speaker. A large number of the Southern Dynasties *yüeh-fu*, especially the "Tzu-yeh songs" associated with autumn and winter, illustrate this theme of the neglected woman longing for her absent lover and resenting her cold bed, with more straightforward language than most of the literati poems. Notice in the following poem the conventional elements, established in the *Nineteen Old Poems*, of looking at the moon through the window of the boudoir with its gauze bed curtains:

Tzu-yeh Songs of the Four Seasons: Autumn

The autumn night enters my window,
The thin silk curtains rise and blow around in the breeze.
Looking up, I see the bright moon:
I send my love across a thousand *li* of moonlight.[23]

In the Southern Dynasties songs the absent lover was often a traveling merchant, or simply a wanderer. But another variation on this theme which emerged in this period and flourished in the T'ang specified that the traveling lover was away on a military assignment: the boudoir laments of soldiers' wives thus formed a complementary pair with the frontier laments (*cheng-jen yüan*) of the soldiers themselves.

The "Tzu-yeh songs" date from the fourth and fifth centuries. The sixth century saw a revival of court poetry, centered in the literary salons of the ruling family of the Liang dynasty. In this opulent and self-contained elite society, a coterie poetry emerged which is known as Palace Style poetry *(kung-t'i shih)*. About 544 Hsiao Kang, who was Crown Prince of the Liang dynasty from 531 until 549, and then ruled as Emperor Chien-wen for only two years (549–551), commissioned a court poet named Hsü Ling (507– 583) to compile an anthology of love poetry. The result, entitled *Yü-t'ai hsin-yung*, included 655 poems dating from the second century B.C. until the middle of the sixth century, with a strong emphasis on the more contemporary works.[24] In his Preface, Hsü Ling praises the beauty and poetic talents of the women kept in special apartments for the pleasure of kings and emperors. But he points out that their lives are often tedious, and suggests that reading this volume of poetry may help them pass the time. Significantly, Hsü Ling assumes the conventional Confucian attitude toward love poetry, and claims that these poems are not intended for a male audience of highly educated officials and refined aristocratic gentlemen, but passes them off as a second-class works, fit only for women's entertainment. Similarly, he acknowledges that the poems of the *Yü-t'ai hsin-yung* are inferior to the odes and hymns of the canonical *Shih ching,* but, he argues, like the turbid Ching and the clear Wei rivers, which flow in the same channel without mixing, this lesser poetry for entertainment can coexist with the purer classical poetic tradition without contaminating it.[25]

In fact, though Hsü Ling's disclaimers, like Ou-yang Chiung's in the Preface to the *Hua-chien chi,* may be necessary according to traditional Confucian disparagement of love poetry, they do not reflect the actual climate of the Liang court. It was the courtiers themselves who were most enthusiastic about Palace Style poetry, and they wrote the poems for each others' entertainment.[26] Indeed, seventy-six of the poems in the *Yü-t'ai hsin-yung* are composed by the Crown Prince Hsiao Kang himself. In the literary salons poets displayed their courtly accomplishments by dashing off verses with apparent ease and *sprezzatura* in order to impress their patrons. They demonstrated their virtuosity through clever conceits and mannered diction in courtly poetry contests. Because this was a coterie style, it was highly conventionalized, and the exclusive audience shared an intimate familiarity with the themes, imagery, and nuance which defined the genre. Palace Style poetry characteristically presents the poignant ennui of a beautiful but lonely palace woman immured in her elegantly furnished boudoir.[27] The conventional poetic imagery is highly evocative: dust and spider webs suggest neglect, curtains and screens suggest confinement, mirrors and cosmetics suggest narcissistic self-absorption due to isolation, and artificial or embroidered flowers and birds suggest the unnatural surroundings of the secluded palace lady.

It is not difficult to trace the origins of Palace Style poetry, for the *Yü-t'ai hsin-yung* includes a number of anonymous *yüeh-fu*, including some of the *Nineteen Old Poems*, and many literati imitations of folk songs. The last chapter of the anthology is devoted to poems in the popular quatrain form. Here the emphasis is on the lovers' separation, with a merging of class attributes; many poems reflect a delicate blending of the peasant girl who picks mulberry leaves and weaves cloth and the palace lady who applies make-up and arranges hair ornaments. In the following poem, Hsiao Kang's father Hsiao Yen (464–549), who founded the Liang dynasty and ruled as Emperor Wu for almost five decades during the height of its literary productivity (502–549), makes graceful courtly gestures. He uses folk song motifs but suggests an opulent palace setting through metaphors, and ends with a subtly evocative question.

   Summer Song

Within the boudoir, flowers like embroidery,
On the curtains, dew like pearls.
If you want to know if she's thinking about her lover,
Just notice how she stops weaving and simply stands hesitating.[28]

This poem demonstrates the art of courtly reversal: whereas the palace lady's embroidery and pearls would be fabricated to resemble real flowers and dew, the peasant weaver's actual surroundings are poetically elevated. A related technique more characteristic of literati than popular poetry is understatement. The following qua-

train, also attributed to Hsiao Yen, which combines the frontier
and boudoir themes, emphasizes emotional restraint:

Hsiang-yang Shining Hooves of Bronze

At the ends of the paths, soldiers march off;
Within the boudoirs, women step down from their looms.
Filled with emotion, they cannot speak:
The farewell has dampened their silk clothing.[29]

The Palace Style poetry which developed out of this popular
tradition extends the courtly reversals and emotional restraint of
the folk song imitations to a virtuoso display which excels in the
stylized description of objects. Witty wordplay gives rise to cir-
cumlocutions and poetic tours de force; in the language of Palace
Style poetry, the crescent moon is a "jade hook" (*yü-kou*) and tears
are "pearls" (*chu*) or "jade" (*yü*). Poets would strive to outdo each
other in hyperbolic imagery, resulting on occasion in the excessive
embellishment for which the style was condemned by moderate and
conservative critics. A typical illustration of this effete hyperbole
is found in the closure of a poem by Hsiao Kang, where streams
of tears are depicted as "jade chopsticks":

Sighs of a Lady of Ch'u

Boudoir stillness: the water-clock drips on and on,
Flowing endlessly in the evening loneliness.
Fireflies flit through the night door,
Spiders entwine on autumn walls.
Her thin smile does not turn to joy;
Her faint sigh becomes sorrow.
Golden hairpins hang drooping from her coiffure;
Jade chopsticks drip on the front of her gown.[30]

On other occasions, instead of accumulating a series of separate
images, poets would elaborate on a given theme, such as the conventional "cold bedroom" motif. The following example creates an
indirect emotional intensity through the concentrated imagery of
congealment and frigidity in almost every line. It was composed

by Liu Huan, who served as secretary to Hsiao Kang's younger brother Hsiao I (507–555), the Prince of Hsiang-tung and later Liang Emperor Yüan (r. 552–554):

Cold Bedroom

After we parted the spring pool looked different,
Lotus withered, ice began to form.
In the sewing-box my scissors felt cold,
On the dressing table my face-cream froze.
My slender waist has become so frail
I'm afraid it cannot bear the coldness of my clothes.[31]

Lois Fusek has shown that in the figure of the beautiful, solitary, inaccessible palace lady we see the convergence of two of the most enduring and powerful images of women in Chinese poetry, the neglected wife and the goddess, who derive, respectively, from the traditions of the *Shih ching* and *yüeh-fu* and the *Ch'u Tz'u* (*Songs of the South*) and *fu* ("rhyme-prose"). Moreover, as Fusek and others point out, the lonely despair of the palace lady is often a metaphor for the frustrating position of a courtier, who longs for recognition by his ruler as the abandoned woman yearns for the return of her absent lover.[32] The interpretation of the palace lady as a metaphor for the courtier is useful, for it helps explain why literati poets were attracted to this theme for centuries, and why they wrote poems from the neglected woman's point of view with such sensitivity. On the other hand, the limitation of the metaphoric interpretation is that it overlooks the popular origins of the theme: to a large extent, the melancholy palace lady is a variation on the lovesick mulberry girl, dressed in finer clothing for presentation at court.[33] Furthermore, when we acknowledge the extent to which Hsiao Kang's literary salon received inspiration from folk literature, we come to understand the elitist motivations of contemporary critics who condemned it as excessive and decadent.

The fifth and sixth centuries were a period of lively critical debate. Conservative scholars such as Chung Hung (fl. c. 500) felt literature should imitate the ancient classics, while more moderate thinkers such as Liu Hsieh (sixth century) acknowledged the value of modern innovations as well, and the avant-garde, led by Shen Yüeh (441–513), attempted to codify some of these innovations into a new set of principles for writing poetry. Hsiao Kang's brother Hsiao T'ung (501–531) tended toward the conservative side: he felt that only the best works of literature were worthy of preservation, and these should serve as models for imitation. Therefore he compiled the *Wen-hsüan,* an anthology arranged by genre of what he and later generations until the twentieth century considered the greatest works of Chinese literature, from which he deliberately excluded all erotic and Palace Style poetry. Hsiao Kang reacted against his elder brother's elitist and didactic impulses when he compiled the *Yü-t'ai hsin-yung.* In opposition to the formal standards of the more conservative critics, Hsiao Kang believed poetry should provide for emotional expression and should be entertaining rather than morally instructive. Soon after Hsiao T'ung's death, Hsiao Kang wrote to his son, Hsiao Ta-hsin, "The principles for developing your personal character and for writing literary compositions are not alike. In personal conduct, you first should be cautious and serious. But in literary composition, you should be free and unrestrained."[34] As we shall see, a similar reaction against courtly formality occurred during the T'ang dynasty with the development of *tz'u* poetry. But whereas Hsiao Kang's innovations took place within the courtly context, in the T'ang the new style emerged primarily outside the court after the An Lu-shan Rebellion of 755, and was adopted by disaffected literati who were searching for alternatives to regulated *shih* poetry.

Musical Developments in the Early and High T'ang Periods

Before considering how *tz'u* poetry was disseminated outside the T'ang imperial capital, we must look at the evidence of its existence inside the court. Scholarly debate has been perpetuated by the vagueness of this evidence; since changes occur gradually, it is often difficult to pinpoint precise moments in poetic development. The clearest records for the early T'ang period concern court music, which was radically changing during the Sui (589–618) and T'ang dynasties. Due to military, religious, and commercial expansion, foreign music entered China through troops stationed at the frontiers, foreigners who gained footholds on Chinese soil, religious pilgrims and traveling merchants. New tunes and metrical styles circulated, and as foreign instruments such as the four-stringed *p'i-p'a* became popular in China, music designed for the traditional seven-stringed *ch'in* was revised to fit the specifications of the modern instruments.

An index to the rapid changes can be found in the historical records of the formal classifications of court music. Though music of foreign origin (*hu-yüeh*, literally "barbarian music") was used in court at the end of the Six Dynasties period, it was not officially recognized until the Sui. The first Sui ruler, Emperor Wen, took stock of the musical variety in the *k'ai-huang* period (589–600) and classified seven types of music, all of them named after foreign territories surrounding China except *ch'ing-shang yüeh*, which referred to native music including the Southern Dynasties Wu songs.[35] Soon thereafter, in response to the importation of still more new styles, Sui Emperor Yang in the *ta-yeh* period (605–615) reclassified music into nine categories, with instruments and costumes added accordingly. The second T'ang Emperor T'ai-tsung (r. 627–649) substituted a new category for one of Emperor Yang's nine and added a tenth, *yen-yüeh*, which means music for entertainment. Only *ch'ing-shang yüeh* and *yen-yüeh* were native to China, but by T'ai-tsung's time the other styles were sufficiently assimilated that they could all be loosely referred to under the general rubric *yen-yüeh* or entertainment music, to distinguish them from *ya-yüeh*, the music derived from antiquity which was reserved exclusively for formal imperial ceremonies.[36] By the period of Emperor Hsüan-tsung (r. 713–755), the category *yen-yüeh* designated popular songs of foreign origin which dominated court music, *ya-yüeh* referred to the ancient formal music for state occasions, and *ch'ing-shang yüeh* indicated music of the Han, Wei, and Six Dynasties periods such as *yüeh-fu*.[37]

The native *ch'ing-shang yüeh* was generally neglected in the High T'ang; the *T'ung-tien* states that only eight tunes were known, and the original versions were corrupted.[38] Baxter and other scholars have assumed that the Southern Dynasties song tradition died out in the northern capital of Ch'ang-an, though "it is at least conceivable that popular songs with some irregular line-lengths continued (though no doubt with changes of style and convention) in an unbroken stream in the South until the *tz'u* itself emerged as *ch'ang-tuan chü* [lines of unequal length] in the ninth century."[39] However, it is not necessary to search for a separate southern tradition to find the origins of the *tz'u* in the ninth century, for there is ample evidence, confirmed by the Tun-huang manuscripts, that poetry with lines of unequal length was being composed to "fill in" song tunes throughout the eighth century, and this form flourished in Hsüan-tsung's court. Southern Dynasties songs probably did not die out, but rather became mixed with music of foreign origin. The Sung scholar Shen Kua explained, "Foreign music (*wai-kuo chih sheng*) had since previous dynasties been distinguished as music from the bordering states in all four directions (*ssu-i yüeh*). After the thirteenth year of the *t'ien-pao* period [754], the Emperor ordered that 'proper songs' (*fa-ch'ü*) be played together with 'barbarian categories' (*hu-pu*). From this time on, the music played has completely lost its ancient purity (*ku-fa*)."[40] Not only were the native styles readily combined with foreign music, but the new songs were eagerly taken up by the literati. Shih-chuan Chen cites a quotation by another Sung writer, Wu Tseng, which makes this point: "Emperor Ming [Hsüan-tsung] was very fond of the *Hu* music. It soon became a vogue of his time. The gifted scholars wrote Tz'u of long-short lines in accordance with the beats of the tune practiced by instrumentalists."[41] Hsüan-tsung encouraged local popular music (*su-yüeh*) as well as foreign music (*hu-yüeh*), and the two styles gradually fused. The "Treatise on Music" (*Yin-yüeh chih*) of the *Old T'ang History* (*Chiu T'ang shu*) states, "since the *k'ai-yüan* era, singers used foreign music mixed together with songs of the streets."[42]

Tz'u poetry was probably popular in the imperial court before the reign of Hsüan-tsung; certainly *tz'u* songs were performed "in the streets" in the seventh century, and some of the Tun-huang poems may date back to the seventh century.[43] But though the rise of the *tz'u* was a gradual process which began earlier, Hsüan-tsung is regarded as the one most responsible for it both because of his general enthusiasm for music which motivated his generous patronage of the arts, and because of the institutional changes he initiated. He significantly expanded the training and repertoire of contemporary performers and promoted musical diversity. In 714 Hsüan-tsung established a separate government office to accommodate these new popular musical styles, which were not controlled by the *t'ai-ch'ang ssu-pu yüeh*, the office for formal Confucian ritual music (*ya-yüeh*) of the *t'ai-ch'ang-ssu*, the Ministry of Rites and Music. The new office was called the *chiao-fang* or palace music school on the left and on the right (*tso-yu chiao-fang*), and here hundreds of singing girls (*chi-nü*) and male musicians (*yüeh-kung*) were trained for performances in popular music which became the center of the musical activities in the High T'ang court. The very best three hundred performers from both the *t'ai-ch'ang ssu* and the *chiao-fang* were selected to become members of the elite imperial Pear Garden Conservatory (Li yüan).[44] The *Chiao-fang chi*, a record of court music during the *k'ai-yüan* period, lists titles of 343 *tz'u* tunes which were performed at that time; Jen Erh-pei has shown that about two-thirds of these titles are also found in the Tun-huang manuscripts, and with the information now available there is no reason to doubt, as Hu Shih did, the authenticity of the *Chiao-fang chi*.[45] Moreover, the *T'ang hui-yao*, compiled in the tenth century, which presents further subdivisions of the ten categories of music defined by Emperor T'ai-tsung, also records 242 tune titles known in the Early and High T'ang periods and their alternate names after they were changed under Emperor Hsüan-tsung in 754.[46]

Having determined the existence of *tz'u* music in the Early and High T'ang courts, let us now turn to the evidence of the literary content of the song-words of these performances. Again we shall see a blend of the popular and the elite traditions, producing a variety of styles.

Early *Tz'u* Poetry by Literati

The records of literati compositions in the *tz'u* form for the Early and High T'ang periods are even more fragmentary and controversial than the records of developments in T'ang music. We know that by the High T'ang many hundreds of different tunes of diverse geographical origins were being composed and performed in Hsüan-tsung's court. We do not know to what extent these songs were created and transmitted by the common people ("songs of the streets"), foreign entertainers ("barbarian songs"), or trained court musicians ("music for entertainment"). We also do not know how much the literati themselves actually contributed. I suspect that the literati were much more involved than the written records indicate, and that the interaction between elite court poets and un-lettered musicians and singers began even earlier than the High T'ang.

Certainly, in the sixth century and earlier, aristocrats eagerly imitated folk songs. As we have seen, Liang dynasty Palace Style poetry indirectly developed out of the tradition of popular south-ern songs; the *Yü-t'ai hsin-yung* includes an entire chapter (ch. 9) of explicit folk song imitations, many of them in irregular meters. A long list could be compiled of poems in lines of uneven length written by literati of the Southern and Sui dynasties.[47] Ch'en Shu-pao (553–604), the last emperor of the Ch'en dynasty (r. 582–589), wrote the following poem, for example, to the tune pattern "Ch'ang hsiang-ssu" in the form 3-3-7-3-3-5-5-5-5, which cannot be con-sidered merely a variation on the regular quatrain form:

Forever longing for you,
Always thinking of you,
At the pass in the mountains the frontier garrison troops, when will they
    be finished?
Gazing at the wind and clouds,
All news broken off:
In Shang-lin Park letters do not come back.
Though my fabric contains poetic messages, I weave by myself in vain.
I am ashamed that my appearance is so altered that after this separation
Your return will seem like meeting for the first time.[48]

Here the poet uses the persona of the lonely woman longing for her husband who is away on a frontier assignment with all the standard cliches of the popular song tradition. Yet he slightly elevates the tone with an allusion in line 6 to Su Wu, who sent letters by carrier birds, and in line 7 to women who sent palindrome messages woven into cloth: but with courtly reversal, both these means of communication are then denied.

The influence of Southern Dynasties songs and Liang court poetry in the Sui and Early T'ang periods has generally been underestimated. Poetic development was in fact "a gradual process involving no major or abrupt changes."[49] Southern songs were still popular at court in the Early T'ang dynasty, though they tended to occur in regular forms, especially quatrains with a consistent number of characters in each line. It is well known that there was a common practice of composing new words to fit a given tune. Many of these composition activities were probably so casual they were not documented. But an anecdote in the *Pen-shih shih* describes an occasion on which poets composed new words to the tune "Hui-po yüeh" in an attempt to please Emperor Chung-tsung (r. 705–710):

> Shen Ch'üan-ch'i [c. 650–713] once had been exiled for wrongdoing and subsequently forgiven. He had been recalled to the official ranks but his red ceremonial robes of office had not yet been restored. One time at a palace banquet all the ministers sang "Hui-po yüeh." They composed new words (*tz'u*) and got up to dance. Many took advantage of this occasion to ask for a transfer or promotion. Shen Ch'üan-ch'i's poem said:
>
> "Hui-po" this time it's Ch'üan-ch'i's turn.
> I was exiled to the south beyond the mountains, now I have returned.
> My person and name have already been restored to the ranked list of officials,
> But I have not yet recovered my red robe and ivory tablet of rank.[50]

Apparently moved by Shen Ch'üan-ch'i's clever poem, the account continues, Emperor Chung-tsung immediately restored to him the appropriate signs of office. Two other poems to the tune "Hui-po yüeh" are recorded, including Li Ching-po's attempt to impress the Emperor with his moral judgment:

"Hui-po" this time it's about wine cups.
Your humble minister's duty is to admonish and advise:
We at this feast have already passed three pitchers of wine;
This excess I am afraid is not proper.[51]

That this series of "Hui-po yüeh" poems represents the earliest examples of T'ang literary *tz'u* is somewhat debatable because of the poems' regular quatrain form, with six characters in each line. However, since early *tz'u* generally have a form which resembles regular *chüeh-chü*, we must look for distinctive qualities in the performance instead. *Chüeh-chü* could also be sung, but the words to a *chüeh-chü* were fixed and the musical setting could vary. In the case of the *tz'u*, on the contrary, the tune was fixed—and identified by the tune title—and the words could vary. The circumstances of composition described in the anecdote as well as the extant texts themselves show that the courtiers used the given tune pattern to fill in their own words appropriate to the particular occasion. These poems are hardly worthy of preservation in literary terms, though they were apparently well received in performance. But they are historical landmarks indicating the activity of *tz'u* composition at court in the Early T'ang period.

Other early literati *tz'u* are also composed to tune patterns with regular meters, but likewise suggest the primacy of musical performance rather than purely literary expression. For example, we have six surviving stanzas composed by Chang Yüeh (667–730) for an annual performance on Emperor Hsüan-tsung's birthday of a ballet of one hundred lavishly decorated horses. The horses were rigorously trained to move in time to a particular tune, called a *tz'u* in the title, "Wu-ma tz'u" ("The Song of the Dancing Horses"). Chang Yüeh's first verse to this tune emphasizes the splendid spectacle in which the handsome equipage of the horses represents the official insignia of the Emperor's loyal subjects:

The ten thousand jade honor the phoenix screen;
The thousand gold follow the dragon leader.
Attending to the drums they stop with dignity and step in time,
Listening to the songs they play with their shadows and trot back and
        forth.[52]

Chang Yüeh's own "Wu-ma tz'u" lyrics reveal a striving to display courtly erudition in composing appropriate occasional lyrics to the set tune. Thus they illustrate the literary refinement that could be superimposed on an art form with popular origins.

However, poets with courtly training cultivated a stylistic versatility which enabled them to imitate folk songs as literary exercises or for pure enjoyment. It is safe to assume that it was quite common for them to write words to tunes such as this very early "Willow Branch" song ("Liu chih") by Ho Chih-chang (659–744), which combines a light musical charm with an implicit erotic metaphor suggesting the pathos of a young maiden's loss of youth and innocence:

Green jade grows to a tree's full height;
Ten thousand tendrils hang down, green silk ribbons.
One does not know, these fine leaves, who cut them off:
By the second month the spring wind is like scissors.[53]

There exist today very few examples from the High T'ang period of poems which are both written by literati to known *tz'u* tune titles and also contain lines of unequal length, but as presented above there are several extant texts which meet the first condition. Moreover, the two significant instances of poems which meet both conditions, the song words discussed below by Emperor Hsüan-tsung and Li Po, suggest that the popular *tz'u* forms with lines of unequal length were known and imitated within the High T'ang court.

Among the anthologies of *tz'u* poems by known authors, the earliest one which includes poems written before 850 is the *Tsun-ch'ien chi* ("In front of the wine-jug"), which is generally assumed to have been compiled about 900, though some scholars date it as late as the Ming dynasty.[54] The *Tsun-ch'ien chi* includes several hundred *tz'u* poems, mostly from the Late T'ang, Five Dynasties (Wu-tai, 906–960), and early Sung periods. It begins, however, with a poem attributed to Emperor Hsüan-tsung (Li Lung-chi) himself. The "Brilliant Emperor" of the High T'ang period is said to have personally composed several *tz'u* poems, but this is the only one which is extant:

"*Hao shih-kuang*" ("*Good Time*")

Your treasured hairdo is just fitting for the palace fashion,
Your lotus face is tender;
Your body is pink and fragrant,
Your eyebrows are so dark they do not need Chang Ch'ang style paint-
　　ing:
They are naturally long enough to extend to your temples.

Do not rely on your beauty which could overthow a country,
Get married to a man
Who will be a devoted husband.
This is the period when you both are young:
Do not neglect your good time.[55]

In its catalogue of the conventional attributes of a beautiful woman, and the direct simplicity of its message, this poem is clearly indebted to the popular song tradition. On the other hand, the tone is elevated by the reference in line one to "palace fashion" and the allusion in line four to Chang Ch'ang, a respectable Han dynasty official who personally painted his wife's eyebrows. Thus we have an early instance of a *tz'u* poem by an elite author and evidence that even the Emperor himself set an example by participating in the *tz'u* performances at his court. "Hao shih-kuang" is also important because it is one of the earliest datable T'ang literary poems with lines which are definitively of unequal length (6-3-3-7-5 5-3-3-5-5).

　　The *Tsun-ch'ien chi* is also an important early record of the much-disputed *tz'u* poems attributed to Li Po. The *Tsun-ch'ien chi* includes twelve poems to four different tunes assigned to Li Po; later the *Ch'üan T'ang shih* gave him credit for fourteen *tz'u* to six tunes.[56] The scholarly debate has centered on the issue of when the literary *tz'u* form emerged, and the most controversial poems were the ones with the most irregular meters. Critics were willing to accept Li Po as the author of three poems to the tune "Ch'ing p'ing tiao," for example, because even though it was known as a song, the form was that of a regular quatrain, 7-7-7-7. The less regular poems were generally considered to be Li Po's through the Sung. But ever since Hu Ying-lin (1551–1618) of the Ming dynasty, many scholars have claimed that the poems to the irregular tunes "P'u sa man" (7-7-5-5 5-5-5-5) and "Ch'ing-p'ing yüeh" (4-5-7-6 6-6-6-6) must be forgeries because literati did not write words to songs with lines of unequal length before the ninth century. The skeptics pointed out that only the *tz'u* to the regular "Ch'ing-p'ing tiao" meter were included in Li Po's complete works and in the *Yüeh-fu shih-chi*, but this argument is circular, for it merely confirms that the bias against the *tz'u* influenced the selections of poems by T'ang and Sung editors. As Kang-i Sun Chang has mentioned, the relevant chapters of the *Yüeh-fu shih-chi* tend to include only the *tz'u* of a more regular quatrain form with five or seven words per line, thus giving later generations a distorted picture of poetic development.[57] The partial selection reflects Kuo Mao-ch'ien's own neglect of *tz'u* in irregular forms and perhaps suggests why other records of Early and High T'ang *tz'u* of long and short lines are so sparse. For example, T'ang poets' "complete works" also tended to exclude poems written in irregular meters as too frivolous or merely experimental. No one doubts that Po Chü-yi and Liu Yü-hsi actually wrote *tz'u*, but these poems are not included in their collected works, either.

On the other hand, a number of scholars believe that it is quite possible that a poet like Li Po could have written words to the "P'u sa man" tune as early as the High T'ang period, and evidence from the Tun-huang manuscripts confirms this view that literary *tz'u* in irregular meters existed in the early eighth century. In 1947 Yang Hsien-yi, without access to the Tun-huang findings, stated that the "P'u sa man" dance song entered China from Burma in the seventh century, before the reign of Hsüan-tsung, and that since Li Po's native Szechwan province lay on the trade route between China and Burma, he had ample opportunity to be familiar with this tune since his childhood. Yang not only accepted Li Po's *tz'u* with long and short lines as authentic, but he even assigned the date of 726 to his "P'u sa man" poems.[58] Later, Chang Wan, who was aware of the Tun-huang evidence, agreed that historically speaking Li Po might have written all twelve or fourteen of the *tz'u* attributed to him, but on the basis of a rather impressionistic stylistic analysis Chang argued that of the two poems to the tune "P'u sa man" translated below, Li Po was the author of the second, but the first—mistakenly attributed to Li Po—was actually composed by Wei Chuang (836–910).[59] This is a plausible theory, but it is of course unverifiable, and finally the historical continuity it implies is more significant than the precise identification of authorship.

A reading of two of the famous "P'u sa man" attributed to Li Po shows that if indeed they were composed in the High T'ang, then they are transitional works which announce a new phase in the history of the *tz'u*. Numerous poems by literati of the Middle T'ang period (from the end of the eighth until the beginning of the ninth centuries) praise the joys of the Chiang-nan area (the southern Yangtze region), seductively mild and beautiful, and particularly known for its pleasure quarters filled with "flowers and willows" (euphemisms for courtesans):

Tune: "P'u sa man" I

Travelers all say Chiang-nan is wonderful,
But travelers only should go to Chiang-nan and stay until they are old.
Until you are old, do not go home:
Going home would simply break your heart.

Embroidered screens, golden folded screens:
Drunk, enter the flower clusters to spend the night.
Spring water is bluer than the sky,
In a painted boat, listen to the rain while sleeping.

Tune: "P'u sa man" II

A stretch of woods, misty, as if woven in haze;
A strip of cold mountains, heartbreakingly blue.
Evening colors enter the tall tower,
Someone in the tower is grieving.

On jade steps, I stand aimlessly;
Nesting birds fly home urgently.

Where is my road back?
Long stops follow short stops.[60]

The theme of the lonely woman grieving for her absent lover echoes
the long tradition of neglected-wife poetry, yet in this poem the
conventional aesthetic distance between reader and immured woman
is reduced by the figure of the poetic speaker, who identifies his
plight with hers. The "long stops" and "short stops," which refer
to wayside resting places with long and short intervals between them,
suggest the perceived endlessness of the journey home in both spatial and temporal terms, and thus imply the perpetual waiting for
reunion, with artful economy and grace.

It is not necessary here to pursue questions of authorship.
Rather, we should note two aspects of the style of these two poems
which were feasible, if precocious, in the High T'ang period. First,
it was clearly possible during the first half of the eighth century
for educated men to write artful and sophisticated poems to *tz'u*
tune patterns. Most literati preferred to use the *shih* form and the
number of High T'ang song-poem masterpieces is relatively small,
but poets such as Li Po—who was himself best known for his *yüeh-
fu* and songs—did produce original and skillful song lyrics.[61] In
the above "P'u sa man," the subtle parallel between the woman in
the tall tower and the speaker on the jade steps, both constrained
in contrast to the homing birds, illustrates the imaginative vitality
a High T'ang poet like Li Po could bring to a song form.

Second, the "P'u sa man" poems which could be High T'ang
products reveal the contemporary interest in metrical experimentation. Li Po himself was in the vanguard of this movement, but
the increasing use of heptasyllabic songs and irregular *yüeh-fu* patterns in the eighth century indicates a general tendency to move
away from the rigid pentasyllabic *shih* form which dominated Early
T'ang poetry.[62] Indeed, by the High T'ang period generic distinctions among song categories such as *yüeh-fu, ko-hsing, ch'ü, tz'u,*
and *tiao* were quite vague, thus preparing an open field for metrical experimentation and innovation in the next two generations.

Interaction Between Popular and Elite
in the High T'ang

Additional evidence of the flourishing of the *tz'u* genre in the early eighth century is found in anthologies which include anonymous poems from that period. The *Yün-yao chi*, which was probably compiled about 922, is a collection of thirty-three poems in lines of unequal length set to thirteen different tunes, preserved in the Tun-huang manuscripts P. 2838 and S. 1441.[63] Since twelve of the thirteen tune titles occur in the *Chiao-fang chi*, it is likely that some or all of the *Yün-yao chi* poems date back to the High T'ang period.[64]

The loose generic term *yün-yao*, "cloud song"—or sometimes *pai-yün-yao*, "white cloud song"—has a long history. It may be derived from the title of a legendary song sung by the Taoist goddess Hsi Wang Mu (the Queen Mother of the West) to Mu T'ien-tzu (King Mu), an early Chou ruler (1001–947 B.C.), when he visited her at the Yao Pond (Yao Ch'ih, present-day T'ien Ch'ih) in the Heavenly Mountains (T'ien Shan):

White Cloud Song

White clouds in the sky
Emerge from the hills.
The road is long and far,
Mountains and streams separate us.
I hope that you will not die,
So you can come again.[65]

It is significant that Hsi Wang Mu's "White Cloud Song" concerns separated lovers, for most of the poems in the *Yün-yao chi* anthology focus on the conventional popular themes of the hardships of frontier life and the loneliness of the neglected woman. The colloquial language of the anonymous *Yün-yao chi* poems is characteristic of the language of other popular texts in the Tun-huang manuscripts. However, the *Yün-yao chi* poems tend to be longer and more polished in form. Kang-i Sun Chang argues persuasively that the emergence in the eleventh century of the literary *man-tz'u* form of *tz'u* poetry—distinguished by its greater length (70 to 240 characters) from the shorter *hsiao-ling* form (fewer than 62 characters)—can be traced back to popular prototypes of the *man-tz'u* in the *Yün-yao chi*.[66]

Though the style and diction of the poems in the *Yün-yao chi* clearly indicate popular origins, some scholars believe that the polished form, longer length, and aristocratic references of these poems may suggest literati authorship or editing.[67] It is quite possible that poems recorded anonymously were compositions of well educated poets in imitation of the popular style, just as courtiers wrote "Tzu-yeh songs" in the fifth and sixth centuries. By the second half of the T'ang dynasty, the term *yün-yao* was commonly used to refer to poems written in imitation of the popular style.[68] The following quatrain by the T'ang poet Ts'ao T'ang indicates a practice, apparently common among the literati, of discreet or anonymous composition and circulation of their own casual *yün-yao* poems:

Ninety-eight Little Roaming Spirit Poems, #33

Herbal grasses and fragrant flowers in bright spring,
Auspicious incense, mist and dew permeate my clothing.
The Jade Fairy clandestinely shows off my written work:
In private I write *yün-yao* songs and secretly present them to people.[69]

The triple reiteration in the last couplet of the avoidance of public acknowledgment of the activity of writing *yün-yao* style poetry is further confirmation of the Confucian double standard, which overtly disparaged popular literature while covertly finding it an appealing pastime.

Poems in the *Yün-yao chi* provide an excellent illustration of the wide range of social levels represented in the Tun-huang materials. The following poem, for example, indicates familiarity with both the popular and the elite cultures:

#021 (S. 1441, P. 2838)
Tune: "Ch'ing pei le"

Graceful and delicate,
Her loveliness surpasses all others';

Even a beauty who could overthrow a country could hardly compare with
　　her.
Over her body hangs a thin silk gown,
One wonders if she came from heaven.
Her face is like a flower, naturally abundant in charm,
With green willows her eyebrows are painted,
Her sideways glances are like autumn floods;
Her skirt is a lovely pomegranate red,
Red as blood her silk blouse.

Her appearance so lovely, her straightforward speech and gentle words
　　so tender,
A jade hairpin dangling a white tassle ties up her dark cloud hairdo.
She is sixteen, for a long time she has been concealed in her fragrant
　　boudoir,
She loves to lead her dogs and parrots in play.
Her ten fingers are as white as jade and as slender as scallions,
Her soft frail form glistens like snow through her silk dress.
She is a worthy match for young nobles and sons of aristocrats;
A youth of Wu-ling should be her fashionable husband.

The area of Wu-ling, around the ancient tombs of five Han emperors, was the place for fashionable young noblemen to strut about,
showing off their finery. The woman described in this poem is
suitably beautiful and elegant to join them, and she has likewise
been pampered since childhood.[70] But these aristocratic references, and even the tightly unified construction of the poem, do
not necessarily indicate elite authorship, and in fact they are coun-
terbalanced by the unadorned style (such as the list of similes) and
the earthy diction (literally, "blood dyed her silk blouse," l. 10;
and "ten fingers like jade, like scallions," l. 15) characteristic of
popular poetry. The Tun-huang manuscripts probably represent
the culture of the semiliterate, a group of people who fell some-
where between the uneducated and the elite. The *Yün-yao chi*
poems, among the most refined of the Tun-huang *tz'u* corpus, then
illustrate the expression of a middle group of society, perhaps those
aspiring to social mobility. The above poem reflects an intense
consciousness of the external signs of class in appearance, attire,
and speech. It also demonstrates stylistic refinement in maintain-

ing a consistent descriptive point of view and beginning with a phrase used in the first poem of the canonical *Book of Songs* (*yao-t'iao*, "graceful"). However, the poetic style is still bound by conventional imagery ("her face like a flower," 1. 6), and it is constrained by the emphasis on physicality ("her soft frail form glistens like snow through her silk dress") which an elite poet would avoid. But though the poem achieves no technical subtlety or metaphoric resonance, it has a readily accessible appeal. It may well be the work of highly trained and artistically sophisticated musicians and singers, whose performances would attract a socially mixed audience.

Thus we have seen many examples of the influence of the folk song tradition on literati poets, and we have considered evidence that the scholar-officials often experimented privately with imitations of popular songs. Contemporary accounts suggest that even Li Po probably composed more songs which circulated during his lifetime than are now extant. The style of such early literati *tz'u* poetry was not fixed; it varied from simple lyrics which captured the charm and directness of folk songs (e.g., Ch'en Shu-pao, Ho Chih-chang) to the superimposition of various types of elevated allusions or references to courtly occasions on the original popular forms (e.g., Shen Ch'üan-ch'i, Li Ching-po, Chang Yüeh, Hsüan-tsung), to artistically sophisticated and poignantly personal expressions of emotion set to tune patterns (e.g., Li Po). This blend of popular and elite material in poetry naturally followed the same process of assimilation as the history of Sui and T'ang court music, which combined foreign tunes, Southern Dynasties songs, and popular contemporary melodies with traditional elite forms and conventions.

Moreover, the use of popular song material by highly educated poets was by no means new. When in the sixth century Hsiao Kang and his circle sought freer emotional expression, they also turned to local lyrics for inspiration. They merged the popular mulberry girl figure with their refined palace lady, drew on long-standing traditions of the unattainable goddess and the neglected wife, and produced a courtly style of strained subtlety, excessive conceits, and mannered hyperbole. Perhaps some of the decadent excesses of Liang dynasty Palace Style poetry can be attributed to the intense, ingrown, and competitive circumstances of writing within the insulated world of a royal court facing political threats on all sides. In any case, when T'ang dynasty literati poets participated in the vogue of composing songs based on popular *tz'u* forms, they achieved more literary success when writing outside the court.

In the following chapter we will explore the ways that T'ang poets of the late eighth and ninth centuries used popular *tz'u* tunes and styles to develop a new elite literary genre. Like the Liang dynasty poets, they relied on many aspects of folk songs, including the melodic form, the point of view of the woman in her bedroom, and the focus on the early stages of love as well as the aftermath of neglect. Also like the Liang courtiers, T'ang *tz'u* poets refined the diction, made the presentation more subtle, replaced straightforward puns and folk culture wordplay with luxurious conventional images carrying metaphoric force, such as gossamer curtains and embroidered quilts. However, the Liang poets finally lived in a rarified world utterly cut off from the experience of singing girls such as Tzu-yeh whose songs originally inspired their poems. The T'ang *tz'u* writers, on the other hand, created a genre of poetry which, though stylized and conventional, did not reach the effete and mannered excesses of the sixth-century pieces in the *Yü-t'ai hsin-yung*. As we shall see, the Mid-T'ang and Late T'ang scholar-officials, often separated from the imperial court, participated in an alternative lifestyle among musicians and singing girls in the Chiang-nan region of China, and their work more closely reflects the popular song origins which so directly influenced their poetry.

CHAPTER FOUR

Popular *Tz'u* Poetry in the Entertainment Quarters After 755

T HERE are many and complex reasons for the literary changes which occurred after the An Lu-shan Rebellion of 755. One factor is poetic form. The five- and seven-character "old style" (*ku-t'i*) *shih* of indeterminate length had been eclipsed at the beginning of the T'ang dynasty by the increasing dominance of the more tightly constructed, shorter "recent style" (*chin-t'i*) *shih*. During the century before 755, three generations of talented and rigorously trained court poets had exploited the suggestive economy and subtle compression of expression made possible by the *shih* form. Composition of appropriate occasional poetry was an obligatory part of their function as government officials, and public ceremonies and poetry contests encouraged the development of technical skill, impersonal decorum, and courtly wit and sophistication. The reign of Emperor Hsüan-tsung witnessed numerous highly talented poets whose prolific creative work has fixed this period as the golden age of Chinese poetry. The era saw the individual geniuses Li Po and Tu Fu (712–770), great recluse poets like Meng Hao-jan (689–740) who wrote under the shadow of the conventions of capital poetry, and exalted court poets like Wang Wei (701–761) who developed the austere but evocative "grand style" of High T'ang poetry.[1]

Naturally, after the climactic achievement of the High T'ang there was a sense of decline. The redundancy of perpetuating the

High T'ang style was demoralizing, especially when the poetry represented a glittering court culture and confidence in imperial order which had been devastated by the An Lu-shan Rebellion. Though the *shih* form was by no means abandoned, poets apparently felt that the rigid "recent style" court poetry had been extended to its peak, and there was a general movement back to the more leisurely "old style" *shih* forms and to more personal themes and relaxed moods in reaction against the public formality and decorous regularity of High T'ang "recent style" verse. At the same time, keen interest developed in alternate forms. In terms of literary development, the time was ripe for the introduction of a new literary genre and popular *tz'u* songs were conveniently available for this purpose of revitalizing the poetic repertoire.[2] Traditional Chinese literary historians have treated the development of *tz'u* poetry as a gradual modification by literati of *shih* forms such as *yüeh-fu* and *chüeh-chü*.[3] Consideration of the degree to which *tz'u* poetry was already known in Hsüan-tsung's court and popular culture, as indicated by the Tun-huang manuscripts, and the nature of the social context in which literati composed *tz'u*, show that rather than evolving as a variant *shih* form, the *tz'u* was a popular form adopted as an alternative by literati.

Coupled with this literary transition, the period after the An Lu-shan Rebellion saw profound social and political changes as well. When the rebels led by An Lu-shan captured Ch'ang-an in 755 and forced the Emperor and his entourage to flee to Szechwan, members of the *chiao-fang*, the imperial palace music school of which Hsüan-tsung had been the ardent patron, were likewise dispersed from the capital. Many of the highly trained former *chiao-fang* singing girls and male musicians gradually resettled in entertainment halls (*chi-kuan*) in urban centers, where their cosmopolitan backgrounds added prestige as well as talent and skill to the local musical entertainment. These private and commercial courtesan houses were in fact closely modeled on the self-contained and hierarchical structure of the *chiao-fang*, and they thus provided the professional musicians with an institutional alternative to the court.[4] Increasingly, new songs were produced and performed.

Entertainment halls had begun in Ch'ang-an, but in the ninth century they also flourished in the Chiang-nan area, particularly in Yangchou, Suchou, and Hangchou (see map, pp. 16–17). At this time, the imperial court was besieged by internal political and economic conflicts and external military threats. No longer able to sustain a consistently prosperous intellectual and artistic community, it lost some of its former attraction for many literati. Disaffected scholar-officials increasingly went to the Chiang-nan region, due to official appointment, exile, or in search of pleasure. For example, Wei Ying-wu (737–792?) became Governor of Suchou in 785, Po Chü-yi assumed the position in 825, and Liu Yü-hsi followed as Governor of Suchou in 832. These and many other literati spent much time in the *chi-kuan* of the southern cities. At the same time, scholar-officials were frequenting the entertainment quarters in the capital. There, in the company of courtesans, they searched for alternatives to courtly formality not only in literary genre but also in subject matter and tone.

The Courtesan Culture

Interaction between singing girls and the educated elite dates back to the beginnings of Chinese history. Certainly in the Chou dynasty and probably earlier, princes and high officials kept their own troupes of trained singing girls and female musicians (*nü-yüeh*), who performed at official banquets and private parties, and were also available as bedpartners for their master, his retinue, and his guests.[5] These entertainers could be sold, resold, or given as gifts, particularly as diplomatic tokens. The possession of one's own *nü-yüeh* became a status symbol. In the Han period, the emperor, members of the royal family, and high officials still kept their own private troupes of female musicians, but the institution of commercial, public brothels also began. Emperor Wu (r. 140–86 B.C.) allowed the establishment of "barracks prostitutes" (*ying-chi*) near army camps, under direct government control. This was accompanied by the rise of urban brothels, called "houses of singing girls" (*ch'ang-chia*) or "towers of singing girls" (*ch'ang-lou*).

During the Six Dynasties period, the well-known courtesans,

such as Yao Yü-ching and Su Hsiao-hsiao, noted primarily for their poetic talents, were *chia-chi*, private singing girls, kept in groups of dozens or hundreds by rich members of the elite.[6] However, a shift occurred in the T'ang dynasty, and public singing girls, called *kuan-chi* or *min-chi*, available to the less prominent men, gained increasing social significance. By the time of Emperor Hsüan-tsung, there existed four basic groups[7] of female entertainers: 1) The singing girls of the imperial court, *kung-chi*, lived in one of the two capitals, Ch'ang-an and Lo-yang, and served the Emperor as instructors in the *chiao-fang*, performers in the Pear Garden Conservatory (Li yüan), or entertainers at state ceremonies. They could be purchased as concubines by the very rich. 2) Imperial princes and high officials of the fifth rank or above owned private troupes of singing girls, *chia-chi*, and the maximum size of these troupes was determined by rank in imperial decrees. Some members of the royal family had several dozen musicians; a high official named Li Yüan (d. 825) is said by Meng Ch'i to have had "more than one hundred extraordinarily talented and extremely beautiful" singing girls in his household.[8] These entertainers could also be sold or given as gifts. 3) The government provided "official singing girls" (*kuan-chi*) for provincial officials who served outside the capital; if these entertainers were located in military camps at the frontiers, they were called *ying-chi* like their Han prototypes. These government-provided provincial courtesans entertained at local official functions and they were sexually available to the provincial governor, who could take them or leave them when his local assignment was over. 4) Finally, in the urban centers official courtesan districts housed brothel singing girls, *min-chi*, on various social levels. The government controlled these establishments, registered the courtesans, and restricted them from traveling outside the official entertainment district, except for special occasions. These entertainers could also be purchased as secondary wives or concubines. The brothels were known as *ch'ing-lou*, "blue mansions" or "green bowers," and the courtesans were called *lü-ch'uang nü*, "women of the green windows," because of the colorful shutters which advertised the services offered within these establishments.

Details of the lifestyle of the courtesans in the entertainment quarter of ninth-century Ch'ang-an are presented in a contemporary description, *Pei-li chih*, or *Records of the Northern Ward*. This work was probably composed by a scholar-official named Sun Ch'i, known also by his *hao* "Master Non-action" (Wu-wei Tzu).[9] The account consists of a Preface, an introductory chapter which provides a general overview of the "Northern Ward," and twelve chapters giving incidents in the lives of famous courtesans known personally by Sun Ch'i and his colleagues during the period 869–881, including poems written by and for these entertainers. Five brief chapters in the Appendix, perhaps supplemented by another author, add anecdotes and poems concerning courtesans primarily from the period 838–876. Despite the claim in the Postface that these are cautionary tales to alert future generations to beware of the seductive dangers of the pleasure quarters, the author's actual intention seems to have been, as stated in the Preface, to preserve his memories of this glamorous and pleasant world as it was before it was lost in the overthrow and occupation of the T'ang capital by the rebel Huang Ch'ao on January 8, 881. The Preface of this nostalgic account is dated 884, and the book was probably substantially completed by 885.[10]

Sun Ch'i explains that the entertainment quarter occupied about one-fourth of P'ing-k'ang fang, one of the walled districts in the symmetrical checkerboard layout of T'ang Ch'ang-an. This was the most fashionable area of the capital, located directly Southeast of the imperial palace, and bordering on high-class residential districts, the East Market center of commercial enterprise, and the busy road leading into the gate called Ching-feng Men, the most active entrance into the palace.[11] The Northeast quadrant of P'ing-k'ang-fang, the courtesans' area, was divided into three sections (*san ch'ü*); the highest class courtesans resided in the south and middle sections (*nan-ch'ü* and *chung-ch'ü*), and the lower class establishments were located along the northern wall in *pei-ch'ü*.[12] From Sun Ch'i's account it is evident that the entertainment quarters were well situated to promote ready access by the distinguished officials who lived nearby, and that visits to the courtesans were socially acceptable.

It was extremely common for men of Sun Ch'i's acquaintance

to spend much of their time in the "Northern Ward," and he does not hesitate to identify them by name. The attraction of the courtesans transcended sexual favors. Van Gulik, who stresses that by the eighth century "the courtezan had become a social institution, an indispensable part of elegant life both in the capital and in the provinces," claims that "there can be no doubt that [the role of the courtesans] was primarily a social one, its sexual aspects being of secondary importance," and he goes on to cite their functions as congenial company in whose presence to facilitate business deals or make an introduction to a well-placed superior who might arrange a promotion.[13] In other words, relations with the courtesans were open and public. Van Gulik goes on to argue persuasively that the primary social function of courtesans explains why their biographers praise them more for their artistic skills than for their beauty, and also why the stories of scholar-officials' relationships with courtesans are often so protracted, complex, and sentimentalized. Men who had several wives and concubines at home with whom they had a Confucian obligation to produce sons, Van Gulik claims, "frequented the company of courtezans often as an escape from carnal love, a welcome relief from the often oppressive atmosphere of their own women's quarters and the compulsory sexual relations."[14]

Qualifying Van Gulik's observations, I would emphasize that even more important than their social functions were the courtesans' specifically literary roles. Though most of the Pei-li courtesans originally came from humble families, they were purchased at an early age and many of them had received rigorous training in poetry and music by the time they began to receive guests at age twelve or thirteen. Since the majority of Chinese women were only minimally literate, the courtesans were often the only female companions available to literati who shared their interests in music and verse. Indeed, I believe the singing girls were significantly instrumental in promoting the popularity and acceptance of the relatively new *tz'u* genre. Moreover, the mutual respect between the literati and the courtesans as poets, and their practice of frequently composing poems together and reciprocally, was directly responsible for the elevation of the *tz'u*, by the end of the T'ang dynasty, to a position of respectability, as presented in the Preface to the *Hua-chien chi*.

Furthermore, the social interaction between courtesans and literati was not merely voluntary, not merely a pleasurable escape from official routine, but it was instead often integrated into the very public activities expected of scholar-officials. Most conspicuously, relations with the courtesans were even institutionalized as an obligatory rite of passage for examination candidates. In his Preface, Sun Ch'i describes the ceremonial festivities to honor the candidates who had successfully passed the official *chin-shih* degree examination that spring. After formal honors at the spring festival in the palace, the new degree-holders would continue to celebrate for several weeks. Recently, he comments, the festivities have been prolonged even until the second month of summer. There were ongoing parties with singing girls in the *chiao-fang*, as well as visits to the courtesans in the Pei-li. A grand royal banquet was held at the Ch'ü-chiang Pavilion (Ch'ü-chiang t'ing-tzu) on the banks of Ch'ü-chiang Pond (Ch'ü-chiang ch'ih) in the southeast corner of the city of Ch'ang-an. Scholars were expected to arrive prepared for a protracted celebration, carrying their own knapsacks filled with gifts, money, wine cups, and bedding.[15] The scores of courtesans assembled to perform and entertain at these festivities are praised by Sun Ch'i for their particular sensitivity to the entire range of official titles. "In their ability to distinguish among social classes, to assess the quality of a personality, and to know the proper response to a superior, even well-bred young men could not equal them."[16] Clearly it was necessary for these facilitators of social relations among the elite classes to cultivate a specialized knowledge of official hierarchy and protocol. Their skill at achieving such a rapport led to the social integration of courtesans and literati. The scholars and officials accepted the courtesans as sophisticated companions in social and literary terms. Moreover, the nature of the celebration of achieving *chin-shih* status immediately socialized the new elite literati into the expected mode of intimate relations with the courtesans.

Further evidence of the primacy of the literary attraction of the courtesans is the large number of poems quoted in the *Pei-li chih.* In the Preface, Sun Ch'i states, "I have often heard people talking about the talent and eloquence of the Szechwan courtesan Hsüeh T'ao [768–831], but I certainly consider it an exaggeration. Now that I have seen two or three young courtesans from the Pei-li, I realize that Hsüeh T'ao's merits were far inferior to theirs."[17] The fact that the poems quoted by Sun Ch'i, and the poems by T'ang courtesans included in the *Ch'üan T'ang shih*, are in the *shih* rather than the *tz'u* form, reflects, I believe, only the author's and editors' generic bias. Certainly *tz'u* poetry was flourishing by the end of the ninth century among courtesans and literati, though it was still regarded as less respectable than the *shih*. The frequent and prolonged literary contact between literati and courtesans provided the catalyst for the development and acceptance of the *tz'u* genre.

Fortunately, though the official anthologies and collected works of poets may exclude early examples of *tz'u* lyrics, the Tun-huang manuscripts do contain them. The literati of the eighth and ninth centuries must have been familiar with popular songs performed by courtesans which had been transmitted among the common people, or at least among trained but semiliterate musicians. Some of the secular lyrics in the Tun-huang manuscripts were in all probability composed by the singing girls themselves, or adapted from singing girls' songs—particularly those simple laments from the courtesan's point of view, such as the following striking song which uses the conventional image of the willow to represent the courtesan, but adds poignancy with a first-person speaker:

> #086 (P. 2809, P. 3911)
> Tune: "Wang Chiang-nan"

Do not pluck me,
Plucking me is too unfair.
I'm a willow near the pond by the Ch'ü River.
This man broke me, that man plucked me:
Each one's love lasted only a moment.[18]

It is likely that a large number of the Tun-huang secular songs were performed in the local Kansu province entertainment quarters or

by itinerant musicians. However, a number of the songs preserved
in the Tun-huang manuscripts may also have originated in Ch'ang-
an or the large southern urban centers of China and were somehow transported to the far west, either by singers or perhaps in
written form. The booklet P. 3994 (see above, chapter 2) is an excellent example of poems which traveled in written form from major urban centers to the Silk Route oasis of Tun-huang, either as
souvenirs or as art objects for trade. Moreover, the poems written
by literati in the P. 3994 booklet, combined with the above poem
from the point of view of the courtesan directly, indicate the rec-
iprocity of the poetry which survives from the culture of the entertainment quarters. The integration of literati poems among otherwise less refined Tun-huang folk song material shows that the
elite and popular styles were by no means separate. The kind of
tz'u poetry which was promoted by the *Hua-chien chi* is a direct
result of the cross-fertilization which occurred when scholar-officials and courtesans wrote verses together and learned from each
other. Poetic styles moved smoothly among various social levels.

Further evidence of the social mobility of the *tz'u* form can
be inferred from numerous accounts of the social mobility of the
courtesans who performed these songs. Though the classes of singing
girls ranged from illiterate prostitutes to highly skilled entertainers, it is clear from the above summary of the four groups of
courtesans that all of them could be purchased as secondary wives
or given to individuals as private musicians and concubines. Many
contemporary anecdotes focus on the theme of abrupt changes in
status, including both upward and downward mobility.

Sun Ch'i is apparently moved by the pathos of courtesans who
have outlived their prime. Many of the women described in the
Pei-li chih, after having tasted luxury and riches, were finally neglected, and finished their days bitter, destitute, and nostalgic for
the glamor of their youths. The courtesan Yü Hsüan-chi (c. 843–
868), for example, well known for her fine poetry, suffered such
vicissitudes during her short lifetime. She was a singing girl in the
capital purchased by a man named Li Yi who later abandoned her
in the south. She eventually returned to Ch'ang-an, lived in poverty, and then became a Taoist nun, but continued to receive vis-

itors. One of her short-term relationships was with Wen T'ing-yün. Her sad, brief life ended when she was executed by police, perhaps for having beaten a maid to death.[19] Apparently the dismissal of courtesans was almost as common as the acquisition of them. Po Chü-yi, for example, conducted the expected affair with "Peach Leaf," the official singing girl attached to the Suchou Governor's office, while he was posted there from 824 until 826, but he left her behind when he returned to the capital. In 840, when he retired, he dismissed his private courtesan "Willow Branch"—so nicknamed because of her skill in singing the popular song of that title—though she had served him for about ten years.[20]

On the other hand, since most of the courtesans had been originally procured from poor families, being purchased by a wealthy or prominent man represented an awesome gain in stature within the generally rigidly stratified T'ang society. These courtesans' meteoric ascent from rags to riches must have provided a sensational inspiration to women of humble background, and their good fortune was the subject of numerous anecdotes in circulation at the time. In fact, some courtesans did achieve lasting respect and material comfort. Hsüeh T'ao, mentioned above as Sun Ch'i's model of the exemplary courtesan poet, was the daughter of a Ch'ang-an government official who followed her father when he was transferred to a post in Ch'eng-tu, Szechwan. Soon thereafter her father died, leaving her in poverty and without protection, and she had no choice but to become registered as a singing girl. However, Hsüeh T'ao's considerable poetic talents did not go unrecognized, and she also became famous as the favorite concubine of Wei Kao (745–805), the Governor of Szechwan, who even appointed her to an official government position as "collator" (*chiao-shu*). She met many famous poets who traveled to Szechwan, including Po Chü-yi and Yüan Chen (779–831). Though she outlived Wei Kao, she was well provided for and continued her artistic pursuits until her death at age sixty-three, remaining highly respected as a literary figure. She liked to write love poetry on a kind of specially decorated note paper which is still named for her (*Hsüeh T'ao chien*). Hsüeh T'ao was a prolific writer, but only about ninety of her poems have been preserved.[21]

Liu Yü-hsi wrote a ballad recounting the rapid fortunate and unfortunate changes in status of a Miss T'ai (T'ai-niang), a native of Suchou, who had been the primary singer in the household of Grand Secretary Wei (Wei Shang-shu) when he served there. Wei had musicians teach Miss T'ai the arts of playing the *p'i-p'a*, singing, and dancing, in which she excelled, and when he returned to Ch'ang-an he took her with him. "In the capital there were many artists skilled in the new styles, so Miss T'ai again rejected her old techniques and took up the new styles of singing in accordance with the tunes. Then the name of T'ai-niang became known everywhere among the company of the highest class of people," Liu Yü-hsi explains in his Preface to the ballad. But early in the *yüan-ho* period (806–821), Grand Secretary Wei died and Miss T'ai was sent out to live among the common people. Eventually she was obtained by Prefect Chang Sun of Ch'i-chou, whom she accompanied when he was banished to Wu-ling. When he died, she was left alone with no place to return to, and far away from anyone who could appreciate her beauty or artistic talent. Liu Yü-hsi heard about her downfall, and wrote a ballad describing her glamorous rise and subsequent decline.[22] Though a singing girl could win fame for her talent, she was ultimately dependent on her attachment to a man for her social status and welfare, and consequently even the most accomplished musician potentially had the same helpless vulnerability as a palace lady confined to the emperor's harem or a peasant woman abandoned by her husband. It was usually the pathos of a woman's insecure status which captured the attention of literati who wrote many stories and ballads and short poems—and later, dramas— on this theme.

The mutual interaction between sophisticated literati and professional entertainers is beautifully illustrated in the symmetrically balanced plot of the prose story "Li Wa chuan" by Po Chü-yi's brother Po Hsing-chien (d. 826). Li Wa is a lovely courtesan who raises herself from humble origins to wealth through her series of liaisons with men of the most prestigious families, and she is finally accepted as the proper daughter-in-law of a prominent family. Conversely, one of her lovers, a talented and well-to-do scholar, squanders his fortune on Li Wa and is then forced to make his way as a funeral singer. Eventually this man of means who fell to the level of a street musician is saved from poverty and shame by Li Wa's compassionate intervention and she manages his career rehabilitation for a conveniently happy ending.[23] However, although this account of rapid upward and downward mobility is probably somewhat exaggerated, it does make its point of illuminating a fact of ninth-century social life in China. For an aspiring literatus a fortuitous liaison with a well-connected courtesan could be the avenue of social success. Likewise, when a talented courtesan was recognized and purchased by a member of the elite, her fortune could also be dramatically improved.

The ease with which a poor singing girl from the streets could enter the halls of aristocrats, and there participate in musical exchange, is also illustrated in another late T'ang anecdote:

> In the *ta-li* era (766-779) there lived a talented singer named Chang Hung-hung. Originally she had sung with her father on the highways and byways to beg for food. Once they passed by the residence of General Wei Ch'ing in the Chao-kuo Ward near the south gate. Through the window, Ch'ing heard her singing in deep, clear tones, and because she was also beautiful he at once received her as a concubine; he had her father live in the rear house, where he was generously recompensed. When Hung-hung demonstrated her artistic talent, her versatility was beyond comparison.[24]

The account goes on to emphasize Chang Hung-hung's remarkably high status, describing how after the death of Wei Ch'ing and her father, she was recognized in an audience with the Emperor himself, who conferred on her the posthumous title of *chao-i*.[25]

But the significance of an individual courtesan's social mobility is that it suggests the fluidity with which a song or poem could pass from one level of society to another. The following story, also concerning Chang Hung-hung, indicates this cultural intercourse:

> Once there was a musician who had composed his own song to the old tune "Ch'ang-ming Hsi-ho nü." He had varied its meter and here and there revised the melody. Before he was brought for a hearing, his song was first performed for Wei Ch'ing at a banquet. Ch'ing summoned Hung-hung, who was behind a screen, to listen to it. Hung-

hung then took some small beans and counted out and marked the rhythm. When the musician finished the song, Ch'ing went in to ask Hung-hung her response. She said: "I have already learned it." Ch'ing went out and said, "I have a female student who has known how to sing this song for a long time—it's not a new song." Then he ordered her to sing it from behind the screen. Not one note was incorrect. The musician was very surprised and astonished; then he asked to meet her and admired her unceasingly. Hung-hung spoke again: "in the previous performance there was one note which was not sung right; this time I have corrected it." [26]

The primary point of this anecdote is to show Hung-hung's particular talent for memorizing a poem on the spot. However, it is significant for my thesis of the social mobility of popular music that Wei Ch'ing can use Hung-hung to embarrass the musician by suggesting the alternative possibility, that he is a plagiarist trying to pass off a commonly known popular song as an original composition at an aristocratic banquet.

Thus, the courtesan culture of the late T'ang dynasty presents an unusual context in which the integration of men and women, of aristocrats and commoners, is reflected in the merging of elite and popular literary styles. In China, elite culture is generally associated with the educated minority in the cosmopolitan court, while the heterodox popular culture is located among the peasantry in the countryside. But in the case of early *tz'u* poetry we find an extraordinary situation of *urban* popular culture, where the traditional sexual, social, and geographical boundaries are transcended. Consequently, what began as an oral or semiliterate genre gradually entered the written culture. For the analysis of this process of the merging of popular and elite we shall have to use a methodology which goes beyond the conventional dichotomy between "oral" and "written" categories. Instead, we find gradations along a continuum of constant interaction.

The Performance Context of Early *Tz'u* Poetry

As discussed in chapter 1, the difficulty of distinguishing between "oral" and "written" literature can be avoided by emphasizing instead the audience and their understanding of the poetry. Mid-T'ang *tz'u* by literati and *tz'u* from the Tun-huang manuscripts both reflect the performance context. These poems should be read as occasional pieces, composed for public performance or addressed to particular individuals.

We must assume that the extant *tz'u* in the Tun-huang manuscripts represent only a small portion of the larger body of popular songs being performed during the T'ang dynasty. The audience as well as the composers of these songs shared familiarity with a common repertoire which might vary according to social class, occupation, or region, but which nevertheless established certain conventions and criteria for the creation, performance, transmission, and reception of new songs. Some of these conventions may be related to other subgenres of Chinese poetry: interrelations may be found between some of the Tun-huang *tz'u* and T'ang literati frontier poetry, for example, just as characteristics of the Tun-huang love poems may be traced to southern songs or Palace Style poetry of the Liang dynasty. Sometimes we even have explicit narrative contexts for *tz'u* poems, as in the case of the verses embedded in Tun-huang *pien-wen* stories. Another example of a poetic tradition in which the poetic material gradually diminished as the audience familiarity with the narrative context became more widespread and certain is the series of *yüeh-fu* songs concerning Ch'in Lo-fu. The late Han dynasty song "Mulberries by the Path" (*Mo-shang sang*) was widely imitated through the Six Dynasties period and into the T'ang dynasty, but the later versions of the song were generally shorter than the original 53-line *yüeh-fu* because the audience knew the tradition.[27]

Therefore, it is difficult to isolate single texts even of the most nonsequential and nonnarrative of the Tun-huang lyrics. Among the extant 148 secular lyrics which are not part of sequences of five or more poems, for all their diversity there are numerous recurrent motifs—both on the smaller scale of standard colloquial diction and conventional imagery and on the larger scale of stock poetic speakers, situations, and attitudes. Some of these devices recur so often that they may be considered formulaic, and the appreciation of a certain song often depends on a knowledge of other songs which employ the same conventions. Moreover, our understanding is limited by lack of a more complete corpus of contemporary popular lyrics. Indeed, the Tun-huang *tz'u* are so much a part of the social setting in which they were composed and performed that it is misleading to remove any single item from its context. Thus, the generic norms of individual Tun-huang *tz'u*, the codes which guide audience (or reader) expectations, are defined by a larger body of similar poems, many of which may no longer exist. Julia Kristeva has called this process intertextuality, which she defines, following Baxtin, as a phenomenon by which "every text takes shape as a mosaic of citations, every text is the absorption and transformation of other texts."[28] This essential intertextuality is an outstanding feature of the popular songs which at least partially distinguishes them from literati *tz'u*, particularly from literati poems intended to be read individually rather than performed in a group.

Not only is it difficult to distinguish "oral" or "folk" songs from "written" or "literatus" songs in the Tun-huang manuscripts; it is also sometimes difficult even to interpret apparent structural connections among preserved texts. Jen Erh-pei's numbering system is highly disputable, for the run-on manuscripts frequently do not indicate where one poem ends and the next one begins: the result is that there is often no formal difference, for example, between two separate poems and a single two-stanza poem. Moreover, many of the poems are part of longer narrative sequences, but they sometimes seem to present incomplete stories, perhaps because other stanzas, accompanying poems, or surrounding narrative, have been lost. Alternatively, these hypothetical missing links may well have been part of the shared knowledge of the T'ang audience, not directly available to us; the story may have been so widely known that the singer could present only a few details and the listeners would automatically supply the context.

An example of a small group of poems appearing in the Tun-huang manuscripts which may represent only a fragment of what was once a longer sequence, or may have circulated independently because the story was so well known, is the songs to the tune "Tao lien-tzu" under the title "Song of Meng" ("Meng Ch'ü-tzu"), which concern the legendary heroine Meng Chiang-nü. Jen Erh-pei groups

four songs together under this title, but manuscript evidence of
their relationship is more ambiguous.

The Meng Chiang-nü poems occur three times in the Tun-
huang manuscripts. The most incomplete version, P. 3319, appears to be a writing exercise, for it contains only short fragments
in a rough hand: it begins the Meng Chiang-nü set twice, first ending
abruptly in the middle of line 3 of the first poem, then starting
again and continuing into a second column, this time ending in
the middle of the third line of the second poem. In the other two
manuscripts which contain Meng Chiang-nü poems, P. 3911 and
P. 2809, all four of the songs grouped together by Jen are recorded in the same sequence, but in each case the first two are
written together as one (under the title "Meng Ch'ü-tz'u" in P.
3911) and the last two are likewise paired, with the heading *t'ung-
ch'ien* ("same [tune] as above").[29]

First let us consider the thematic content of the poems. The
story of Meng Chiang-nü, the faithful wife of Ch'i Liang, is one
of the best-known Chinese legends, dating back to origins in the
third-century-B.C. *Tso-chuan*. As Demiéville points out, it may have
had renewed popularity during the late T'ang dynasty when again
large numbers of war widows were in mourning.[30] A longer but
still fragmentary *pien-wen* version of the story in prose and verse
is also recorded in the Tun-huang manuscripts.[31] The story typically includes an account of Ch'i Liang's having been sent off to
build the Great Wall, and his faithful wife's making him winter
clothes and pursuing an arduous journey to deliver them in person
only to find he has died and been buried in the wall, whereupon
the intensity of her grief causes the wall to collapse, enabling her
to find her husband's bones and bring them home for a proper
burial.[32]

The first two songs—or two stanzas—clearly follow the beginning of this narrative outline:

#127 (P. 3911, P. 2809, P. 3319)
Tune: "Tao lien-tzu"

Meng Chiang-nü,
Ch'i Liang's wife.

Once he went to the Yen Mountains, he did not return.
She made him clothes for the cold, but had no one to deliver them,
So she had no choice but to deliver his war clothing herself.

#128

The road to the Great Wall,
Is indeed difficult to travel.
At Ju-lao Mountain snow falls profusely.
She drank wine, but only to avoid sickness from doing without rice;
She wanted her body to be strong, so she could soon return.

But the last two songs, or stanzas, are either flashbacks to Ch'i
Liang's farewell to his parents and his wife before his departure,
or perhaps even part of another narrative sequence altogether:

#129

Standing before the hall,
He bowed and bid farewell to his mother,
Unaware of the thousand streams of tears falling from his eyes.
"I urge you, father and mother, to dispel your anxiety:
Since I am in official service, we depend on the state for clothing and
    provisions."

#130

After he had bid farewell to his father and mother,
He entered his wife's chamber:
"Do not be disobedient to my father and mother."
"You are going; for your future advancement I will work with all my
    effort,
I would not dare to neglect my duty toward my husband's father and
    mother."

Most scholars would agree that the versions of the Meng
Chiang-nü songs we have available are probably incomplete.[33] We
may assume that the original audience had a more thorough understanding of the context—either from intimate familiarity with

various versions of the stories or from other texts now lost—than the limited material transmitted in the extant texts. For example, poem #127 might have been a prologue, or a refrain interspersed among multiple verses. Moreover, the manipulation of direct speaking voices in the use of dialogue and shifting points of view, particularly in the second pair of poems, indicates the performance style. Jen Erh-pei calls attention to this characteristic narrative quality of the Tun-huang *tz'u,* which he terms *yen ku-shih,* or "performing a story"; Jen points out that the technique avoids a detached narration or description of the story but rather involves direct speech, dialogue, and shifts in point of view.[34] Although all forms of address may be used in oral poetry, a mixture of third-person and first-person narration and the use of dialogue are often characteristic of the oral mode.[35] It is even conceivable that dramatic clues in the performance itself were sufficient to establish the context of these poems for the audience, and they were not presented in a more fully coherent, logical sequence. But although the original relationship between the two pairs of poems included under the "Song of Meng" title may remain ambiguous, the very problem alerts us to the possibility of various other codes available to the audience—including, perhaps, other songs, dramatic presentation, prose storytelling, and visual illustrations.

The Social Quality of Popular *Tz'u* Poetry

One of the most outstanding characteristics of the Tun-huang *tz'u* is the preponderance of dialogue. This is not surprising in a genre which arose and flourished in a social context. Dialogue often occurs within a single poem, though intertextuality is more clearly demonstrated by question-and-answer coordination between different poems.

An often cited example of a single poem which can be understood only as a verbal exchange between two speakers is the following charming song:

#115 (From Lo Chen-yü, *Tun-huang ling-shih*)
Tune: "Ch'üeh t'a chih"

"I cannot bear the magpie's many lies:
He brings good news but when does he ever have evidence?
Many times he flew by, then I caught him alive
And locked him up in a golden cage to stop his chattering."

"I intended to bring good news in good faith;
Who would have thought she would lock me up in a golden cage?
I hope her husband will soon return from war,
So she will set me free to soar into the blue clouds."

The poem is structured on simple repetition with dramatic variations due to the shift in point of view. According to popular belief, it was auspicious to hear the magpie's song. This poem's intensity is derived from the woman's sense of having been betrayed not only by her lover who has not returned, but also by the unreliability of the magpie's message. It is particularly striking that the lonely woman is answered by the magpie himself, a clever literary conceit which distances the audience from the lovers' plight. Despite the antagonistic confrontation, this poem has a sense of resolution, both in the balanced dialogue and in the witty tone, characteristic of many of the Tun-huang songs for secular entertainment.

As an extension of the dialogue technique, questions raised in Tun-huang poems are often provided with responses, if not within the same poem then in an accompanying poem—in contrast to the typical open-ended closural questions of literati poetry. Jen Erh-pei has pointed out[36] that the following two *Yün-yao chi* poems to the tune "Feng kuei yün" form a sequence because the second poem answers the question posed in the last line of the first poem:

#003 (S. 1441, P. 2808)

I am fortunate because on this day
I was able to gaze at a lovely girl.
Her eyebrows like the new moon,
Her eyes alluring with sidelong glances.

Her white breasts, like the last snow before it melts,
Visible through light silk.
. . . *

In her red mouth, teeth of jade,
Her cloud hairdo sways gracefully.

My neighbor to the east had a daughter:
She was enticing, which made loving her hard to overcome.
Her silk gown covered her sleeves;
She had an undulating walk.
Whenever people she met asked her anything, she was bashful and lan-
     guid;
Her alluring charms were many.
A handsome young man with brocade robes saw her:
He dropped his whip and stopped his horse.
Do you know why my heart is broken?

#004 (S. 1441, P. 2808)

My family has always been thus:
For successive generations we have worn official hat pins and tassels.
All my male relatives served
Aiding the country as good officials.
In my childhood I was raised in the women's quarters,
Deep in the inner chambers.
I had an ample education in rites and ceremonies:
The three obediences and four virtues;
My fine needlework was distinguished.

I was married to my husband;
On behalf of his country he was willing to go far away to war.
Contending for fame is bound to be difficult,
But still he has had no return trip home.
Vain labor breaks the heart of a young man,
But do not worry about me.
My body is like pine or cypress:
I'll preserve my determination and resist betrayal.
A woman of Tseng is chaste and virtuous.

---

*Ellipses indicate a lacuna in the original manuscript.

Structurally, the two poems make a well-matched pair. The other two poems in the Tun-huang manuscripts of the *Yün-yao chi* to this title, #001 and #002, also have rhetorical breaks after lines 9 and 15, but use a single woman's speaking voice which is sustained throughout. In this pair, however, the speaker of the first poem is a man, and a woman speaks in the second poem. Moreover, there is a shift in stance after the first half of each poem: in the first poem the catalogue of the woman's charms in the first stanza is replaced by a formulaic narrative account in the second stanza which splices together phrases from circulating ballad literature.[37] Similarly, the catalogue of elements of the girl's upbringing in the first half of the second poem is followed by an account of her marital circumstances after line 9. In both poems, the reliance on literary formulas and the patchworklike juxtaposition of the various components suggest oral composition. However, each poem is in fact tightly unified, and the content of the first half (the girl's beauty and her proper upbringing, respectively) ultimately establishes the basis of each closing sentiment (the lover's longing and the wife's fidelity). The pair provides a fine example of the blend of the material of popular songs with the craftsmanship of sophisticated singer-composers. Like other poems in the *Yün-yao chi*, this set reflects aspiring social mobility in its awareness of the customs and attributes of the upper class, though the treatment is relatively naïve. Due to its combination of dramatic question-and-answer dialogue with lyrical expression, this pair of poems offers for Jen Erh-pci the earliest example in Chinese literature of a dramatic song set, prefiguring later such sequences in Yüan and Ming drama.[38]

Another pair of poems in question-and-answer form, to the tune "Nan ko-tzu," is even more clearly coordinated. Here the tone is much rougher, for the absent lover has returned to angrily accuse his wife of infidelity; she responds defensively to his charges in the second poem:

#121 (P. 3137)
Tune: "Nan ko-tzu"

You stand leaning within the red curtain;
In affairs of the heart, with whom are you intimate?

Clearly on your face there are new scratch marks,
The lovers' knot on your silk belt: who has tied it up?
What man has stepped on and torn your skirt?

Your cicada hair, why is it in disarray?
Your gold hairpin, how was it broken in half?
Through red makeup, falling tears: which man do you long for?
In front of the palace, tell the truth clearly:
Do not try to hide anything.

#122 (P. 3137)

Ever since you left,
I cannot love another man.
In my dreams, my face got new scratch marks,
The lovers' knot on my silk belt I've tied up myself.
My skirt has been stepped on and torn by a monkey.

My cicada hair is in disarray from the red curtain,
My gold hairpin has been broken in half since long ago.
Through red makeup, falling tears: weeping for you.
My trust is a pine or cypress of South Mountain:
I cannot love another man.

Unlike Palace Style poems in the elite tradition, in which the poet's scrutiny of the delicate external appearance of a lonely woman leads him to wonder about her inner feelings, this set of poems presents a direct confrontation, in which evidence of passion suggests actual sexual involvement. As opposed to the ambiguous open-ended quality of literati style poetry, there is another kind of appeal in the straightforwardness of the popular song: the intimacy of the dramatic encounter, in which the woman is apparently surprised by the unexpected return of her lover, heightens the tension in this pair of poems. Although the woman's excuses in #122 may seem rather feeble, the pair of poems must have been entertaining in performance because the confrontation required wit and clever wordplay in her formulation of a response to her husband's interrogation in the same tune pattern, rhyme scheme, and level of diction.

Poems #121–122 may be regarded as a paradigm representing an aspect of the intertextuality of the Tun-huang songs. Either of the poems could stand alone, and indeed many Tun-huang lyrics are similar to #122, although the violent effects of passion are usually softened by lingering melancholy: personal, direct explication and expression of emotions from the woman's own point of view are quite common in the popular tradition. But the existence of poems such as #121 which provide the context of apparently rhetorical questions to be answered in the second verse is highly significant for it provides a sort of code for reading the less explicit poems, and indicates that the T'ang audience had a rather precise sense of the range of appropriate answers to such questions. Just as they probably filled in details when only part of a narrative sequence was presented, the contemporary audience can be presumed to have understood the broader context of individual poems of various thematic subgenres—such as those spoken by homesick travelers, smitten suitors, or lonely women.

From its inceptions, elite Chinese poetry has been occasional. Candidates for public office demonstrated on the civil service examinations their poetic abilities, and after they assumed official positions they were regularly required to commemorate social and political occasions with appropriate poems. Messages of invitation, gratitude, farewell, congratulation, and condolence abound in T'ang court poetry, and it is not surprising to see this custom extended to private exchanges between literati and courtesans. However, in the case of actual poetic correspondence between lovers, we see an interesting blend of the conventional stance and imagery of anonymous popular poetry and the personalization of the actual individual situation.

Most private poems between literati and courtesans have not been preserved, but the following pair is noteworthy not only for its wit but also as a historically significant case of early *tz'u* poetry in a social context by a man of education. Han Hung (fl. 750), after a period of estrangement from his former lover, wrote a poem in long and short lines to reestablish contact. He addresses the courtesan by a conventional euphemism, "Willow," which is particularly appropriate since her surname was apparently Liu ("willow"). Chang-t'ai or Chang Terrace was the name of a courtesan establishment in Ch'ang-an.

> Tune: "Chang-t'ai Liu"
> *Sent to Miss Liu*

Chang Terrace Willow
Chang Terrace Willow
Your beauty was so green and fresh, is it still thus?
Even though your long tendrils hang as before,
They must have been plucked by other men's hands.

In response, "Willow" or Miss Liu (Liu Shih) indicates that the painful quality of her personal experience is to her more significant than the social and literary conventions she is expected to yield to. Her tune title means "willow branch."

> Tune: "Yang-liu chih"
> *Response to Han Hung*

Willow branch
In the fragrant and lovely season.
How hateful that year after year it is presented as a token of departure.
One leaf following the wind suddenly announces autumn;
Even though you come, how can I bear to be plucked?[39]

The conventional witty personification of the willow as courtesan, and its inevitable loss of springlike youth when facing autumnal aging, provide material for Miss Liu's response. But she laces her poem with an emotional intensity which, like the opening outbursts of the speakers of Tun-huang poems #086 and #115 (see above), protests against these conventions. Courtesan poetry has been praised for its sincerity and openness.[40] The personal lyric voice, which is first heard in such early popular *tz'u* of lament or protest, was after the T'ang to become the outstanding achievement of masterpieces of elite Five Dynasties and Sung *tz'u* poetry.

The dramatic dialogue pair of Tun-huang poems #121–122 and the poems to and from Courtesan Liu indicate the social quality implicit in the T'ang popular songs. This tradition of early *tz'u* poetry was indeed, as Ou-yang Chiung said in his Preface to the *Hua-chien chi*, "fanned by the singing girls' air of the Pei-li." The poetry of courtship, love, and separation obviously arose in a social situation; furthermore, it was presented and received in a public performance, which set the stage for the adoption of the *tz'u* genre by the literati who participated in such popular entertainment. The frequent and customary social contact between elite scholar-officials and performing musicians and singing girls is directly responsible for the poetic developments which were becoming crystallized by the end of the T'ang dynasty.

CHAPTER FIVE

T'ang *Tz'u* Poetry by Literati After 755

POETIC interaction between literati and singing girls did not simply begin after 755. It probably dates back to the Chou dynasty, and there is clear evidence of its vitality in the fifth- and sixth-century literati imitations of songs by the courtesan Tzu-yeh (see chapter 3). But with the flourishing of cultural exchange in the T'ang dynasty, the amount of social and literary contact between literati and courtesans certainly increased.

A famous anecdote from the High T'ang period describes the experience of three well-known poets, Wang Ch'ang-ling (698?–c.756), Kao Shih (706?–765), and Wang Chih-huan (eighth century), who went out drinking one evening at Ch'i Pavilion (Ch'i-t'ing). Along came a group of about ten actors from the imperial Pear Garden Conservatory to attend a banquet upstairs. The three poets concealed themselves behind a brazier to watch. Soon four beautiful singing girls arrived to join the festivities. When they all began to perform the most famous contemporary music, the three poets secretly agreed to determine the relative quality of their own poetry by counting who would have the most of his pieces set to music and performed that evening. First an actor sang a *chüeh-chü* poem by Wang Ch'ang-ling, then another performed a poem by Kao Shih, and finally a third presented another by Wang Ch'ang-ling. Wang Chih-huan, who had been a famous poet for a long time, said to his companions: "This is a miserable bunch of musicians. The songs they sing are vulgar verses from the countryside. How could they know songs of the quality of 'Yang-ch'un ch'ü' and 'Pai-hsüeh ch'ü'? The presumption of such philistines!" Then Wang Chih-huan pointed out the most beautiful of the singing girls and said, "Wait until we hear what this one sings. If it is not one of my poems, then I will never again presume to compete with you. But if it is my poem, then you will all have to honor me as the master." Soon the lovely courtesan did perform one of Wang Chih-huan's *chüeh-chü* poems, and so Wang Chih-huan won the wager.[1]

Though this anecdote may not be completely reliable in detail, it does reflect cultural attitudes. For Wang Chih-huan and his companions, the singing girls were granted relatively more prestige than the actors, and their selection of poems determined the winner of the competition. However jovially Wang Chih-huan disparages the actors who performed his friends' poems as philistines (literally, "commoners," *su-wu*), he accurately predicts that the courtesans are more likely to demonstrate more sophisticated training and taste, so they would know refined songs like his own, which he compares to the "Spring Song" ("Yang-ch'un ch'ü") and "White Snow Song" ("Pai-hsüeh ch'ü"), music from antiquity which was considered so beautiful that few musicians were capable of mastering it. In the hierarchy of the entertainment world, as we have seen, the singing girls approached the literati in erudition and talent, and were accordingly regarded with great respect.

The Wang Chih-huan anecdote also provides evidence that during the High T'ang period, the *chüeh-chü* poems written by literati had "trickled down" to the level of professional entertainers, who set them to music and performed them publicly. At the same time that poets like Li Po were writing new words to popular *tz'u* tunes, actors and courtesans were composing music to accompany the words of elite poems. This activity of cross-fertilization had profound effects on the stylistic development of poetry during the following century. If there were isolated cases of words to *tz'u* tune patterns being composed by members of the elite in the High T'ang period, as shown in chapter 3, by the Mid-T'ang literati imitations of popular *tz'u* became a widespread vogue. After the An Lu-shan

Rebellion in 755, poets writing in the *shih* form became more conservative, and "there was a nearly universal retrenchment in postrebellion poetry."[2] However, the *tz'u* was available to fill the vacuum created by this retrenchment, and particularly the poets who fled or were sent to the southeast in the late eighth and early ninth centuries actively experimented with the alternative *tz'u* style. Even given the reigning prejudice against the *tz'u* genre which excluded examples of it from most written records, we still have numerous extant texts which suggest the vast appeal of the new poetic form.

Mid-T'ang *Tz'u* by Literati

Wei Ying-wu (737–792?) is an interesting transitional figure, whose work bridges the High T'ang and Mid-T'ang periods. Born in Ch'ang-an, he served in his youth as an imperial guard in the retinue of Emperor Hsüan-tsung. Later, after holding several positions in Ch'ang-an and Lo-yang, he was appointed to three prefectships in the south, which he held from 783 until 790. Because of his final position as prefect of Suchou, Wei Ying-wu is often called "Wei Su-chou."

Though he is best known for his tranquil, contemplative *shih* poetry, Wei Ying-wu was well versed in music and wrote a number of pieces in song form, often describing the chaotic social conditions after the An Lu-shan Rebellion. Two surviving poems to the *tz'u* tune "T'iao hsiao," with lines of radically unequal length (2-2 6 6 6 2-2-6), treat the age-old themes of the loneliness of the frontier guard and the neglected wife:

I.

Tartar horse
Tartar horse,
Let free far off below Yen-chih Mountain,
Runs on the sand, runs on the snow, neighing alone;
Looking east, looking west, lost his way.
Lost his way

Lost his way,
The frontier grasses extend without end, the sun sets.

II.

Milky Way
Milky Way,
At daybreak hanging over the autumn city, ever so dim.
The grieving one rises and gazes off with longing;
South of the river, north of the border: separation.
Separation
Separation,
Milky Way: although the stars are the same, the road is cut off.[3]

It is unknown whether Wei Ying-wu composed these words or merely recorded lyrics he had heard, but his general interest in song forms leads me to believe these poems are probably from Wei Ying-wu's own hand.

We encounter less ambiguity in a set of poems attributed to Chang Chih-ho (730–810), who likewise moved south from the capital. Chang Chih-ho was a member of the imperial Han-lin Academy under Emperor Su-tsung (r. 756–762), but he later retired to the southeast where he became known as the "Old Fisherman of the Lakes" (Yen-po tiao-sou). The nine poems attributed to him are all songs expressing a relaxation in subject matter which parallels the less formal lifestyle Chang Chih-ho chose in withdrawing from the imperial court. Chang Chih-ho left five poems to the tune "Fisherman's Song" ("Yü-fu," 7-7-3-3-7), of which the first two are translated below:

I.

In front of the Western Pass mountains, white egrets fly,
In the waters flowing through peach blossoms, the mandarin fish are fat.
A grey bamboo hat
A green straw cape,
In the slanting wind and light rain, it is not necessary to return.

II.

On the fishing platform the fisherman uses coarse hemp for clothing,
Two by two and three by three, small boats pass by.
Knowing the use of the oars,
Experienced at riding the current,
On the Long River's white waves he is never anxious.[4]

It is quite clear that these poems are Chang Chih-ho's own compositions. First, they self-consciously exploit the standard imagery of eremitic Taoist poetry. The peach blossoms in the first poem suggest the famous utopian retreat of T'ao Ch'ien (365–427), the Peach Blossom Spring (T'ao-hua yüan), and the references to simple attire and not needing to return are also conventional motifs of the voluntary recluse. The poetic speaker emphasizes his persona as the rustic sage by insisting on the Taoist spontaneity or "non-action" (*wu-wei*) of his activity, in tune with the flux of the current.

Chang Chih-ho's poems are given further authenticity by a poem written in response by his elder brother, Chang Sung-ling:

Tune: "Yü-fu"
Responding to My Younger Brother Chih-ho

Joy is the wind and waves, fishing is leisure.
By the grass hut pines and cypress have already reached their peak.
The waters of Lake T'ai,
The hills of Tung-t'ing,
Wildly the wind and waves rise and he must return.[5]

Just as Chang Chih-ho refers to the Yangtze (the "Long River," Ch'ang-chiang) in his second poem, similarly Chang Sung-ling localizes the leisurely pleasures of the lifestyle of the hermit fisherman and identifies the figure with his specific surroundings with references to Lake T'ai (T'ai-hu) and its Tung-t'ing Island (Tung-t'ing shan). This is an early example of literati filling in words to the same *tz'u* form for social exchange between themselves.[6]

There also survive a number of poems in *tz'u* forms by Wang

Chien (768-833), who distinguished himself primarily by writing a sequence of about one hundred *chüeh-chü shih* poems describing the life of women in the imperial harem.[7] Among his poems to *tz'u* patterns is a set of verses to the tune "Chiang-nan san-t'ai." Wang Chien apparently never went to the Chiang-nan region himself; his poem uses stereotyped local references which indicate that by the first quarter of the ninth century the conventions of southern *tz'u* poetry were well known in the northern capital:

> Tune: "Chiang-nan san-t'ai"
>
> In Yangchou by the edge of the pond, a young woman;
> In Ch'ang-kan at the market, a merchant.
> For three years they have not received any news:
> Each one bows before the spirits, seeking divine intervention.[8]

Though this poem is in a regular quatrain form (6-6-6-6), its bourgeois content and straightforward presentation reflect its origins in the song style. It is interesting to compare a song on a similar theme attributed to a T'ang courtesan from the Chiang-nan region named Liu Pien-ch'un:

> Do not become a merchant's wife:
> Golden hairpins are pawned for petty cash.
> Morning after morning gazing at the mouth of the river:
> By mistake I seem to recognize so many other men's boats.[9]

In the singing girl's poem, the neglected wife's bitter frustration is concretely expressed in her actions. Reduced to poverty, she must sell her jewelry; with nothing to do but wait for her traveling husband to sail home, she is repeatedly disappointed that when she thinks she might recognize his boat it always turns out to belong to someone else. Her intense subjectivity contrasts strikingly with the detached point of view in the Wang Chien poem, in which an omniscient speaker describes both of the separated lovers relatively dispassionately. While the impact of the courtesan's poem comes from her palpable longing and resentment, Wang Chien's poem appeals to the audience's pity for the helpless situation of the lovers who feel that only a miracle could effect their reunion.

The fluidity of the conventional song motifs in circulation in the Mid-T'ang period is also apparent in the following two verses from a set of *tz'u* by Wang Chien to the tune "T'iao-hsiao" but more fully entitled "T'iao-hsiao within the Palace" ("Kung-chung t'iao-hsiao"). Some of the poems in this group depict palace women, like those in the one hundred poems on the imperial harem, while others describe local Chiang-nan merchants' lovers, as in the "Chiang-nan san-t'ai" poem above:

Tune: "Kung-chung t'iao-hsiao"

I.

Round fan
Round fan,
When illness comes to the beautiful woman you cover her face.
Her jade face has been haggard and sad for three years:
Who will again tune up her pipes and strings?
Pipes and strings
Pipes and strings,
Amidst spring grass the road to Chao-yang is cut off.

II.

Willow
Willow,
At dusk standing by the White Sand Ford.
Ahead of the boat, the river waters are so vast:
The merchant and young woman are heartbroken.
Heartbroken
Heartbroken,
Partridges flying at night miss their mates.[10]

Wang Chien's *tz'u* have a charming, direct appeal which must have been enhanced by their musical settings, but they do not add considerable literary refinement to the popular material. It is not until poets like Liu Yü-hsi and Po Chü-yi make a more serious and self-conscious effort in their literati imitations of popular songs that we see a significant stylistic difference in the results.

Liu Yü-hsi had a checkered official career in Ch'ang-an, for he was successively exiled and then recalled. He was never sent to the Chiang-nan region, but rather was once banished to Szechwan. There he encountered and became intrigued by the melancholy popular tradition of the "Bamboo Branch Songs" ("Chu-chih ch'ü").

In the introduction to his nine imitations of the "Bamboo Branch Songs" Liu Yü-hsi describes how the local youth play flutes, beat drums, and dance as they sing sets of songs to this tune. Then he reveals his ambivalent judgment of the quality of such songs:

> Although they are vulgar [*ts'ang-ning*] and undifferentiated, they contain deep feeling and subtlety, and they have the same voluptuous tone as the poem "Little bay of the Ch'i" ["Ch'i ao," a love song from the *Shih ching*]. In the past, when Ch'ü Yüan [343?-278 B.C.] lived near the Yüan and Hsiang Rivers, where the common people summoned the spirits, many of the local songs were coarse and crude [*pi-lou*]. Yet he composed the "Nine Songs" ["Chiu-ko"], which are still sung and danced in the Ching and Ch'u regions even today. Therefore I have also written nine pieces to the "Bamboo Branch" tune, to enable those who are skilled at music to disseminate them. They are recent additions to the tradition, so that those who come later and hear the music of the Pa region will know the origins of these altered styles.[11]

It is significant that Liu Yü-hsi compares himself with Ch'ü Yüan, another Confucian literatus exiled to a remote region of local shamanistic cults and ritual music. It is unclear whether or not the "Nine Songs" were in fact composed, recorded, or transmitted by Ch'ü Yüan, but they are traditionally attributed to this prototype of the individual Chinese poet, who thus provides a convenient model for Liu Yü-hsi to point to in justifying his own imitations of local popular songs. Liu Yü-hsi self-consciously places himself in an ongoing poetic tradition. His sensitivity to the need to record the current repertoire probably indicates his awareness of living in a period of literary transition, when the local popular styles were about to be superseded and overshadowed by literati adaptations.

Indeed Liu Yü-hsi's polished versions of the "Bamboo Branch Songs" are said to have been used by local Szechwan singers for a long time after he composed them.[12] This is quite plausible, for his style retains the simplicity and repetition of the popular song. For example, Liu Yü-hsi's second poem to this tune reads:

The mountain peach trees' red blossoms fill the hilltops;
The Shu rivers' spring waters beat against the mountains as they flow.
Flowers' hue easily fades like my lover's feelings;
Waters flow on without end like my grief.[13]

The celebration of the local color of the Szechwan region is made explicit in the reference to the rivers of Shu, the older term for the Szechwan area. The impact of this poem comes from the speaker's association of his inner emotions (*ch'ing*) with the external scene (*ching*).

Liu Yü-hsi was strongly attracted to the various contemporary song forms, and we have records of many of his experimentations with them. In some of these the poetic speaker assumes the voice of a courtesan:

Tune: "Lang t'ao sha"

On the shores of Parrot Island, waves beat on the sand.
From the blue mansion, I gaze out at spring in the setting sun.
Carrying mud in their beaks the swallows hurry to return to nest for the
    night;
Only my crazy lover does not long for home.[14]

The conventional contrast between birds who fly and nest in pairs and lovers who are separated unifies the quatrain form of this neglected woman's lament. Her direct complaint is only mildly subdued in the last line.

Elsewhere, Liu Yü-hsi distinguishes himself as one of the earliest literati poets to use the *tz'u* form to express his personal feelings in a context which was not an exchange of poems between lovers. Liu Yü-hsi had traveled with Po Chü-yi in the Chiang-nan region, including two weeks of sightseeing in Yangchou. Later, Po Chü-yi expressed his nostalgia for the south in a series of poems to the tune "Yi Chiang-nan" (3-5-7-7-5). Liu Yü-hsi responded in

the same tune pattern, but from his own perspective in the northern city of Lo-yang:

> *Harmonizing with Lo-t'ien [Po Chü-yi]'s Spring Tz'u,*
> *Following the Rhythm and Form of the "Yi Chiang-nan" Song*

Spring has gone.
Many times it honored this man from Lo-yang:
The delicate willows bending in the wind as if they are waving their sleeves,
The clusters of orchids dripping with dew seem to be wetting their hand-
      kerchiefs.
Alone I sit, suppressing a frown.[15]

Here the lament for the south is only implicitly expressed, in the
gestures of farewell projected onto the willows and the orchids, and
in the poetic speaker's attitude.

It is interesting that Liu Yü-hsi responded in a more contemplative, personal tone, because Po Chü-yi's "Yi Chiang-nan" poems,
though artful, present a relatively conventional celebration of the
delights of the Chiang-nan area:

I.

Chiang-nan is wonderful!
Once I knew its scenery so well.
The sun rises, river flowers are redder than fire;
Spring comes, river waters are as blue as indigo.
How could I not long for Chiang-nan?

II

When I remember Chiang-nan,
What I remember most is Hangchou.
From mountain temples I would search for the cassia tree in the moon,
From the pavilion, I would watch the crests of waves from my pillow.
When can I again repeat that trip?

III

When I remember Chiang-nan,
What I next remember is Wu palaces.
A cup of Wu wine, leaves of spring bamboo,
A pair of dancing Wu beauties, wine-flushed hibiscus faces.
When can I meet them again? [16]

The alluring charm of these poems gracefully balances colorful evocations of the local Chiang-nan scenery and sensual pleasures with unqualified direct expressions of enthusiasm. The point of view is clearly not that of a local resident. Rather, the temporary visitor—the official from the north— expresses his appreciation for the regional delights, in a style quite similar to that employed in the "P'u sa man" poems attributed to Li Po (translated above, chapter 3), but perhaps using a tune pattern derived from a local song or musical style.

With Po Chü-yi we reach the culmination of our survey of literati imitations of popular *tz'u* songs, not only because soon after the death of Po Chü-yi in 846 a new style evolved, but also because Po Chü-yi's fame was so widespread that any poems attributed to him were probably performed and transmitted with considerable alacrity, especially among the singing girls of his acquaintance in Chiang-nan. Po Chü-yi's work was said to be popular even among the common people. He himself reported finding his poems inscribed on walls of inns and monasteries he visited, and it was claimed that courtesans who knew his poetry could ask a higher price. Thus, Po Chü-yi represents the peak in the prestige of mutual poetic exchange between courtesans and literati.

In spite of his avowed intention to emphasize serious didactic poetry, Po Chü-yi significantly advanced song forms and poetic musicality with his verses in simple diction, vivid imagery, and plain style. He and his close friend Yüan Chen initiated a movement to promote "new folk songs" (*hsin yüeh-fu*), which were poetic ballads of social significance not set to music; the separation of the words from the music was intended to stress the verbal message.

In the High T'ang period *chüeh-chü* or *yüeh-fu shih* poetry set to music had been loosely referred to as *ch'ü* or song, as in the case of the three poets—Wang Chih-huan, Wang Ch'ang-ling, and Kao Shih—who secretly listened to singing girls performing their *chüeh-chü* compositions. The Mid-T'ang attempt to distinguish the *shih* form from song forms indicates a growing awareness of the important role played by song forms, for songs were gradually coming to be associated more specifically with the *tz'u* genre. However, Po Chü-yi is also recognized for the success of his compositions in the *tz'u* form.

Having served in Chiang-nan for many years, first as prefect of Hangchou and then as prefect of Suchou, Po Chü-yi was intimately familiar with the southern courtesan culture. He often referred to a *tz'u* identified by its reference to the drizzling rain which he had heard performed in the south by a Chiang-nan singing girl named Wu Erh-niang.[17] The poem to the tune "Ch'ang hsiang-ssu" (3-3-7-5-3-3-7-5) attributed to Po Chü-yi is perhaps a record of Miss Wu's song, or, more likely, Po Chü-yi's somewhat refined version of it:

Darkly painted eyebrows
Lightly painted eyebrows,
Her cicada hair hanging loose, clouds fill her gown.
At Yang-t'ai streams of rain return.
High on Wu-shan,
Low on Wu-shan,
At dusk in drizzling rain, he does not return.
In the empty room alone she bides her time.[18]

This poem is replete with standard images from the "Kao-t'ang fu," a prose-poem attributed to Sung Yü (third century B.C.), in which a king from the state of Ch'u experiences a sexual initiation in the Kao-t'ang pavilion on Mount Wu (Wu-shan), near Tung-t'ing Lake (Tung-t'ing hu). A goddess comes to him in a dream in the form of clouds and rain, then leaves as suddenly as she arrived.[19] But though Miss Wu's song uses the language of the "Kao-t'ang fu," it reverses the roles, so that the woman rather than the

man receives the sexual favors of a lover whose comings and goings
she is powerless to control.

If the courtesan Wu Erh-niang's song indicates that the classical *fu* motifs had been incorporated into the popular culture, Po
Chü-yi's own poetry shows the influence of such motifs in literati
imitations of popular songs. Thus, the process has come full cycle
in Po Chü-yi's poems such as the following, in which he compares
a real woman to a dream goddess of mist and clouds:

Tune: "Hua fei hua" (3-3-3-3-7-7)

Flowers are not [real] flowers,
Mist is not [real] mist.
At midnight she came,
At dawn she left.
She came like a spring dream, how long did she stay?
She went like morning clouds, and could not be found anywhere.[20]

Though the style is plain and simple, the theme of this poem fore-
shadows the new style of *tz'u* poetry which developed in the Late
T'ang period. The contrast between appearance and reality, and
the dreamlike quality of experience, are hallmarks of Wen T'ing-
yün's poetry. Though his treatment is quite original, his material
is derived from sources like some of the fine *tz'u* poems by Mid-
T'ang literati such as Po Chü-yi.

In general, literati *tz'u* poetry during the century from 755 to
850 tends to be closely tied to its social and musical context. Poems
written in the *tz'u* form were generally intended for public musical
performance, so they have a universal rather than a particular or
occasional appeal. Though they tend to use conventional images
and emphasize the grief of separated lovers in straightforward
popular style, the *tz'u* form may also be used for personal communication and lyrical self-expression. Poets attracted to the *tz'u*
form before 850 had almost all lived in the Chiang-nan region where
the courtesan culture flourished. The development of the *tz'u* genre
in this period was largely based on the social and literary interaction between the literati and local singing girls. The alternative form
to the *shih* allowed for more relaxation, experimentation, and emo-

tionality. This literary freedom was closely associated with the social and sensual freedom of the Chiang-nan region.

Changes in *Tz'u* Form and Content after 850

Liu Yü-hsi died in 842 and Po Chü-yi died in 846. After approximately 850 a new style of *tz'u* composition developed. There
are various reasons for this change, though none so dramatic as
the An Lu-shan Rebellion which had led to marked changes in poetic style a century earlier. Nevertheless, with the mounting instability of the T'ang centralized government, the degree of disaf-
fection was increasing among literati—potential scholar-officials, who
often did not find suitable positions. Their exclusion from official
circles may be related to their desire for an alternative literary form.
At the same time, the *tz'u* genre was gradually gaining acceptance
among the educated elite, who felt progressively freer to make fuller
use of its unique inherent characteristics. Finally, and perhaps most
importantly, in the Late T'ang period two major literary figures,
Wen T'ing-yün and Wei Chuang, devoted significant effort to the
writing of *tz'u* poetry. As a result, in place of the casual, experimental or secondary *tz'u* compositions of Mid-T'ang poets before
850, the Late T'ang period produced serious, complex, and elegant *tz'u* poems, which set the stage for the full flowering of the
genre in the Five Dynasties and Sung periods.

Kang-i Sun Chang makes a sharp distinction between the *tz'u*
written before and after circa 850, primarily on formal metrical
grounds. Following Glen Baxter, Suzuki Torao, Hu Shih, and
others, she stresses that most of the early *hsiao-ling* or short *tz'u*
written by literati before 850 more or less adhered to the regular
chüeh-chü quatrain form, with a few interpolations. She argues
persuasively, by counting the number of characters in a poem, that
the literati in the earlier period preferred to use the tune patterns
with twenty to twenty-eight characters, just like the *chüeh-chü*
(twenty characters in a quatrain with five characters per line, or
twenty-eight characters in a quatrain with seven characters per line),
in four distinct "line-units," while the contemporary popular songs

recorded in the Tun-huang manuscripts characteristically use longer, less regular forms with more variations.[21] After circa 850, she continues, the *hsiao-ling* tune patterns generally used by literati who wrote *tz'u* show greater length and more structural flexibility.[22]

In my view, the formal similarity between the *chüeh-chü* and the early *tz'u* has been overemphasized and reflects a misunderstanding of the origins of the *tz'u,* by looking for prototypes in the elite *shih* tradition rather than in the music of the popular culture. While it is true that literati before 850 generally tended to favor the more regular *tz'u* forms, the examples quoted in the previous pages demonstrate that from the Early and High T'ang periods on there are numerous examples of poems written in lines of clearly unequal length. The interpolations which scholars such as Baxter and Suzuki perform on the long and short lines to make them fall into a pattern of four line-units seem to me highly dubious, especially without evidence of the musical rhythms to which these songs were sung. In any case, it is clear that the *ch'ang-tuan tz'u* with lines of unequal length did not suddenly spring to life after 850, but rather, this development was the culmination of a long, gradual process.

However, in the Late T'ang period there were significant changes. Perhaps the most clear-cut contrast, as Kang-i Sun Chang point out, is between the single stanza or *tan-tiao* form in the Mid-T'ang and the double stanza or *shuang-tiao* form which replaced it after circa 850.[23] Two-stanza forms are common in the Tun-huang manuscripts and they became increasingly prevalent in literati *tz'u* at the end of the ninth and into the tenth centuries. But coupled with these structural changes are significant Late T'ang developments in poetic tone, imagery, and techniques which are more central to this study.

Wen T'ing-yün was a pioneer in developing aspects of the new style, though his poetry also shows the influence of the popular tradition with which he was intimately familiar because he spent much of his time in the entertainment quarters. Wen T'ing-yün began his attempts to pass the *chin-shih* examination early in the *t'ai-chung* period (847–859) but, according to the *Old T'ang History,* when he first arrived in the capital, the other scholars unanimously admired him, but his own scholarly behavior was self-indulgent and improper, and he did not pay attention to external appearances. He was capable in playing string and wind instruments and in composing *tz'u* poetry which tended toward the voluptuous. He went out gambling and drinking with the untrustworthy sons of dukes and ministers such as P'ei Ch'eng and Ling Hu-kao; they would be drunk for the whole day. Thus year after year he did not earn the *chin-shih* degree.

After a brief period of service in Hsiang-yang, Wen T'ing-yün went south to the lower Yangtze region. "When he arrived, he extravagantly patronized brothels with newly appointed young officials. . . . He also asked for money from the Yang-tzu Yüan. He became so drunk he violated the night curfew, and was beaten by a supervisory officer who injured his face and broke his teeth." Wen T'ing-yün filed a complaint in Yangchou, and though no charges were pressed,"ever since then his foul conduct was known in the capital. When he returned to Ch'ang-an, he wrote letters to the dukes and ministers to clear himself of false charges."[24] But though Wen T'ing-yün received a few minor positions, he remained best known for his fine poetry and his disreputable lifestyle. He was alleged to have carried on a relationship with the famous courtesan Yü Hsüan-chi after she had become a Taoist nun (see chapter 3). He died about 870, a decade before the Huang Ch'ao Rebellion.

Wen T'ing-yün belonged to the large class of highly educated men who frequented the entertainment quarters during the period described in Sun Ch'i's *Pei-li chih*. From his close contact with the singing girls and musicians there, Wen T'ing-yün had an excellent command of current popular music. At this time the growing entertainment establishments needed new songs to expand their repertoire, and it is likely that Wen T'ing-yün, unsatisfied with his mediocre official appointments, supported himself in part by writing song words for the courtesans to perform at establishments like the Yang-tzu Yüan, where it is said he "asked for money." Another tenth-century source, the *T'ang Chih-yen*, confirms this interpretation in its record that Wen T'ing-yün's "reputation for literary talent was widespread, but he did not care about trivial details of behavior. He considered literary works as commercial goods, and therefore discerning men scorned him."[25]

Perhaps as a result of this commercial motivation, Wen T'ing-yün's oeuvre was very large, but the two T'ang collections of his *tz'u* poetry, *Wo-lan chi* (3 *chüan*) and *Chin-ch'üan chi* (10 *chüan*), have both been lost. The most complete selection of his extant *tz'u* poems is the sixty-six pieces included in the *Hua-chien chi*.

Wen T'ing-yün's single-stanza (*tan-tiao*) *tz'u* directly reflect the influence of the popular tradition with which he was so closely involved. Many of these songs even assume the persona or point of view of the courtesan—who would perform them— as in the following example:

Tune: "Meng Chiang-nan"

My combing and washing are finished.
Alone I lean against the tower for watching the river.
A thousand sails have passed out of sight: all were not his.
The setting sun ardent, the waters distant;
Heartbroken: the white duckweed islet.[26]

The tune "Meng Chiang-nan" is a variant on "Yi Chiang-nan," but here we do not find the personal nostalgia for the south of a literatus who has returned to the north. On the contrary, the poem is a generalized complaint of a lonely woman watching for her lover's boat to return, thus similar to the song of the courtesan Liu Pien-ch'un cited above. The feeling in this poem is projected onto the landscape, but the straightforward language of emotions is also borrowed from the popular tradition.

In another single-stanza poem, Wen T'ing-yün combines the conventional motifs of the frontier lament with those of the courtesan:

Tune: "Fan nü yüan"

On the sand south of the shoal startled geese rise;
Flying snow for one thousand li.
Equipage with jade rings,
Arrows with golden tips;

Year after year on a military campaign.
In the painted tower, the pain of separation in the brocade screen's emp-
    tiness.
Apricot flowers turn red.[27]

Again, the circumstances and emotions of the poem are explicitly
stated, as in popular songs ("year after year on a military campaign"; "the pain of separation"). Wen T'ing-yün's poem is tightly
unified, with the imagery of the first four lines representing the
soldier's situation while the last two lines indicate the woman's point
of view. Yet the combination of straightforward exposition of the
setting and imagistic evocation of a mood is basic to the popular
style, as in the following anonymous single-stanza poem from the
Tun-huang manuscripts:

#138 (P. 3271, S. 6537)
Tune: "Yüeh shih tz'u"

The chrysanthemums turn yellow, reeds are turning white; geese fly south.
A tribal flute and a foreign lute: tears dampen my clothing.
This long separation from you: waters of the autumn river.
Once it sets off on its eastward flow, when will it return?

The images in the anonymous song are utterly conventional and
less varied than those in Wen T'ing-yün's poem, but the technique of beginning with imagery suggestive of the frontier and
separation and then specifying the human situation just before the
end is clearly shared by both works. However, the popular song
uses a one-to-one correspondence between imagery and exposition, so that the natural phenomena of autumn are linked directly
to human sadness and military service is the direct cause for tears,
whereas in the Wen T'ing-yün poem the imagistic associations are
more open-ended and ambiguous.[28]

Though anonymous poems often juxtapose images without
syntactic connectives, and in certain poems Wen T'ing-yün may
be imitating the fragmentary and abrupt qualities of popular songs,
the extreme parataxis of these two one-stanza poems by Wen T'ing-

yün is a literary innovation which is also characteristic of his style in longer *tz'u* of two stanzas. The last two lines of the "Meng Chiang-nan" poem have no logical or sequential connectives, so the reader or listener must supply the associations—for example, between the flaming sunset and passionate love, between the distant flow of water and endless grief, or more ambiguously between the island's isolation and the neglected woman's despair. The "Fan nü yüan" poem, which at first appears concrete and explicit, likewise requires that the audience "fill in the gaps,"[29] linking the long flight of the anxious geese with the separated lovers' desire for reunion, understanding that even the finest military equipment, jade-studded or gold-embossed, cannot bring solace to a frontier soldier, or explaining the emptiness within the brocade screen by the soldier's absence and knowing that just as spring flowers blossom and then fall, so also the neglected woman will reach and pass her prime. The entertainment hall audience, familiar with the conventions of frontier and boudoir laments like the one to the tune "Yüeh shih tz'u," would not only have no difficulty supplying these associations, but would also derive pleasure and satisfaction from doing so. The fact that Wen T'ing-yün was composing song words for actual performance before a live audience of his own colleagues and acquaintances may have made him particularly aware of the audience's active engagement in listening and interpreting. Consequently, the performance context may offer at least a partial explanation for Wen T'ing-yün's daring to take the poetic risk of relying on the audience to supply the ultimate coherence to the poem.

Though Wen T'ing-yün takes only slight risks in his single-stanza poems, he is more bold in his longer *tz'u*. In many cases he briefly explains the human situation, in terms borrowed from the popular tradition: "She has not received news from him for a long time" or "They met among the flowers but now they are separated." However, even this sort of minimal narrative setting is not necessary, and frequently Wen T'ing-yün allows the imagery to carry the full burden of the poem, a significant departure from the folk song style:

Tune: "Keng lou tzu" II

Behind my back, the river tower;
Arched over the sea, the moon.
On the city wall the sound of the dawn horn weeping,
Willows on the bank move;
Mist over the island darkens,
Two columns of traveling wild geese separate.

The road leads to the capital,
Returning sails passing by;
Just now fragrant grasses are about to fade.
The candle in a silver holder is consumed,
The constellation Jade Cord hangs down:
A single crow from the village cock.[30]

Here the social circumstances are only implied by the imagery, but the associations are perfectly clear to anyone familiar with the genre. The tower, moon, road, and sails all suggest separation and longing for reunion. Distance is associated with the relentless passage of time: though the moon and constellation Draco ("Jade Cord") are still visible, the city wall watchman's horn and the village cock's crow have already announced the new day, indicating that time cannot be escaped. The mist obscuring the island suggests the frustration of desire, and the parted geese stand for the separated lovers. The tone is one of despair: the sleepless woman's candle has now burned down, and the grasses will soon wither. Wen T'ing-yün's poetic imagery not only exhibits lovely patterns of stillness and motion, silence and sound, nature and artifice; it also entirely contains the human situation and emotions with no explicit expository statement.

Wen T'ing-yün's tendency to juxtapose images without articulating their interrelationships has often been noticed by critics. Kange-i Sun Chang calls it the "rhetoric of implicit meaning."[31] Lois Fusek emphasizes that "Wen T'ing-yün leaves much to his reader, and the very nature of his art is to conceal itself."[32] Yü P'ing-po writes, "The *tz'u* of Fei-ch'ing [Wen T'ing-yün] often select various compatible images and place them together randomly, letting them blend spontaneously."[33] Though of course the ar-

rangement of images is not random, it may appear that way because of the lack of logical or causal sequence. Many of Wen T'ing-
yün's images are repeated over and over again, so that each one is
crammed with multiple associations. Jonathan Chaves points out
that "this consistency allowed Wen to experiment endlessly with
the limited elements at hand"; the result is a richly textured poetry in which explicit narrative explanation is unnecessary, for "the
imagery tells us by itself."[34] In other words, the function of Wen
T'ing-yün's imagery is strengthened because it is not secondary
ornamentation for more direct exposition; rather, it is the essence
of the poem.

The process of interpreting the implicit associations of Wen
T'ing-yün's imagery encourages the audience to participate in the
emotional or psychological state being evoked by the poem. The
focus of most Wen T'ing-yün poems is on the solitary woman, whose
isolation is often emphasized by the walls, screens, and curtains
which surround her. Wen T'ing-yün moves his subject indoors and
into her own mind, then he raises questions for the audience about
the relationships between life and dreams, nature and artifice, reality
and appearance. In the following poem, the static position of the
helpless neglected woman behind the curtains contrasts with the
lively imaginative process suggested by the imagery:

Tune: "Keng lou tzu" III

Willow silks are long,
Spring rain is light.
Beyond the flowers, the sound of the waterclock far away
Startles frontier geese,
Arouses city wall crows;
On the painted screen, golden partridges.

Fragrant mist is thin,
Penetrates the curtains.
Sadness: the ponds of the house of Hsieh.
Behind the red candle,
Brocade curtains hang down.
The dream is long, you do not know.[35]

The poem contains no explicit emotional rhetoric except the vague association of sadness with the Hsieh House (Hsieh *chia*), which may refer both to the decline of the formerly great Southern Dynasties Hsieh family and to a specific brothel by that name. However, willow "silks" *(ssu)* suggests its homophone "love thoughts" *(ssu);* the frontier geese and city wall crow suggest a man away on a military campaign; and line three evokes both the distance and the duration of the lovers' separation. The structure contrasts the external and the internal in the shift between the two stanzas, yet unifies the two frames of reference by the repetition of "long" in the first and last lines, creating a sense of continuing cycles of this endless longing. Moreover, the layers of curtains which surround the woman and cut her off from the real outside world suggest that her experience may be imaginary, or perhaps the final line indicates that all of the foregoing was a dream. Certainly the apparent nonsequitors in the imagery resemble dream-thoughts, open to various interpretations. Are the distant birds really alarmed by the sound of the waterclock? Are the geese and crows real and the partridges artificial? Or are the partridges part of the sequence of birds apparently frightened by the sound? Does the mist permeating the curtain awaken the dreamer? The purpose of raising these questions is not to seek fixed answers, but to show the kind of mental process a reader or listener might experience.

This is the kind of ambiguity which characterizes Wen T'ing-yün's style of suppressed emotion, which is projected onto objects, sublimated into tedious chores such as dressing and putting on cosmetics, rechanneled into dreams, fantasies, and doubts. Wen T'ing-yün's mastery of the two-stanza *shuang-tiao* form adds a two-dimensionality to the *tz'u* rarely found earlier: the two stanzas may contrast external and internal, past and present, real and artificial, and other such pairs of opposites, but the distinctions are never clear-cut; rather, overlaps, circularity and shifting points of view are suggested. Similarly, in poems by Wen T'ing-yün which use dialogue, it is often unclear when speakers change, and the reader is again forced to keep shifting his own perspective. Such complexity in the *tz'u* was deliberate on Wen T'ing-yün's part; Kang-i Sun Chang points out that Wen T'ing-yün did not use this ambiguous style in his more formal *lü-shih* poetry: "Nowhere could one find better proof of the poet's conscious choice between the two literary genres."[36]

Wen T'ing-yün's layering of associations, evocative overtones, and interiority are innovations which became associated with the *Hua-chien chi* style because during the next century many poets tried to imitate his techniques. To find the source of Wen's paratactic imagistic style, however, one need not look to the two middle parallel couplets of a *lü-shih*.[37] Chaves rightly argues that "the themes and the imagery which Wen employed in his *tz'u* was utterly traditional," but he points only to the *shih* tradition of neglected wife poetry.[38] Instead, we can more clearly trace the origins of Wen T'ing-yün's influential imagistic richness to the popular song tradition. The intense subjectivity and ambiguous open-endedness which Wen T'ing-yün added are significant, but the purpose of this study is to emphasize the continuities in the ongoing developing process of the *tz'u* from its seventh- and eighth-century beginnings until its tenth-century maturity.

The other great and innovative poet of the Late T'ang period, Wei Chuang, was also strongly influenced by the popular song style, and though he lived several decades later than Wen T'ing-yün, his poetic debts to the courtesans' lyrics of the entertainment quarters are often even more apparent.

Wei Chuang was a more diligent student than Wen T'ing-yün, but just before he attempted to pass the *chin-shih* examination, the rebel Huang Ch'ao sacked the city of Ch'ang-an in 881. With the capital in chaos, Wei Chuang wandered around southern cities for the next ten years, finding refuge from the country's political turmoil in the cultural life of the entertainment quarters. He returned to Ch'ang-an in 893, where he finally attained the *chin-shih* degree, and served as a minor official. In 897 he went to Ch'eng-tu, Szechwan. There he became a close advisor to Wang Chien, the ruler of Szechwan, who after the collapse of the T'ang dynasty declared himself Emperor of the (Former) Shu dynasty in 907. Because of his high offices under Wang Chien, Wei Chuang is often associated with the Former Shu dynasty, even though he died in 910, only three years after its founding.[39]

Scholars frequently contrast Wei Chuang and Wen T'ing-yün, not only in their official careers but also in their poetic styles. Wei Chuang's style is traditionally described as "clear and vigorous" (*ch'ing-chün*), while Wen T'ing-yün's style is said to have "deep beauty" (*shen-mei*). On the other hand, Wang Kuo-wei, who generally disparaged Late T'ang *tz'u* poetry, preferred Wei Chuang's "depth of emotion" (*ch'ing-shen*) and "artistry in diction" (*yü-hsiu*) to what he considered Wen T'ing-yün's more shallow style.[40] Compared to Wen T'ing-yün's tone of dreamlike detachment, Wei Chuang's straightforward presence is striking. In his poems to the tune "P'u sa man," for example, he openly describes amorous encounters with the "red sleeved" courtesans at the "green windows" of the entertainment halls. As in the following illustration, the point of view of the literatus spending his time "among the flowers" of Chiang-nan courtesans may be maintained throughout the poem:

Tune: "P'u sa man" I

Now I still remember the pleasures of Chiang-nan;
Then I was young, and my spring clothing was light.
Riding on my horse, I leaned on the arched bridge,
The towers were filled with red sleeves beckoning me.

Gold hinges on kingfisher folding screens:
Drunk I entered the clusters of flowers to spend the night.
Now when I again see flower branches—
Until my hair turns white, I swear I will not return home.[41]

The directness of the exposition, the flower euphemisms for the courtesans, and the formulaic phrases of admiration (especially in the first and last lines) recall the popular style. Wei Chuang's poetry is distinguished by its unadorned diction and economy of expression.

Not only does Wei Chuang not hide behind the female persona, he even dares to be explicitly autobiographical. There remain two poems in which he refers to the official celebrations with courtesans in honor of the successful candidates for the *chin-shih* degree, specifically indicated as such by the tune title, "Hsi ch'ien ying" ("Joy in the Flight of the Orioles," a conventional metaphor for passing a high exam or being promoted to high office).[42] Another pair of poems is said to have been a personal lament over the loss of his concubine:

> Wei Chuang had a beautiful concubine who was fond of literature and excelled in literary pursuits. The founder [of the Former Shu dynasty, Wang Chien] used the excuse of having her instruct his palace women as a pretext for forcibly taking her away from Chuang. Chuang wrote the words to "Yeh chin men" in longing for her. When the concubine heard it, she could not eat and so she died.[43]

Though the situation in the poem could be generalized, the initial motivation for this composition, as presumably with folk songs, may well have been a particular personal experience. The urgency of the simple, direct language certainly supports the autobiographical reading:

Tune: "Yeh chin men"

In vain he longs for her:
There is no way to send news to her,
The Heavenly Ch'ang O, beyond human contact;
To send a letter, where would he search for her?

Newly awakened from sleep, she is languorous,
She cannot bear to pick up the remnants of her lover's letters.
The garden full of fallen flowers: the loneliness of spring.
Heartbroken: the fragrant grass turns green.[44]

The first stanza is apparently from the man's point of view, though the speaker is ambiguous because in this case he is reduced to the helpless passivity which usually befalls the abandoned woman. The concubine who has been taken away he likens to Ch'ang O, the goddess who stole the elixir of immortality and fled to the moon, where she had to remain, forever unattainable. However, the two separated lovers, and the speakers of the two stanzas, are poetically united by their slight contact through letters, even though he

is afraid they will not get through and she is reluctant to read them.
Six of the eight lines of this poem are about broken human contact; where Wen T'ing-yün would use a series of interrelated images, Wei Chuang focuses on the letters and the difficulty of communication. Though this Wei Chuang poem is dominated by
exposition, it concludes with standard images of the passage of time,
in a conventional form which recalls the closure of Wen T'ing-yün's
"Fan nü yüan" and popular songs such as the one to the tune "Yüeh
shih tz'u" (see above). Wei Chuang has selected current popular
materials and placed them in a setting which has particular impact
because of the very simplicity and directness of its presentation.

The candor of Wei Chuang's poetry is evident even when he
writes from the point of view of the courtesans who performed his
songs in the entertainment halls. Wei Chuang does not strictly adhere to the conventional tone of melancholy lament, and indeed
many of his poems are invitations to enjoy the available pleasures
of Chiang-nan, as in the following lyrics to a tune which is called
"The City by the River":

Tune: "Chiang-ch'eng tzu"

Her favors generous, her charms many; feelings are easily hurt.
The waterclock drips slowly,
She loosens her mandarin duck garments.
When her red lips have not yet moved,
He already senses her mouth's rouged fragrance.
Gently she raises the embroidered quilt and extends her white hand;
Moving aside the phoenix pillow,
She pillows her handsome lover.[45]

Just as Wen T'ing-yün at times composed imagistic poems with no
exposition, Wei Chuang occasionally wrote this sort of direct expository poem with minimal imagery, demonstrating what Kang-i
Sun Chang calls the "rhetoric of explicit meaning."[46] In place of
Wen T'ing-yün's nominal images and parataxis, Wei Chuang uses
many verbs, hypotactic continuity, and temporal sequence. The
listener or reader responds to the palpably vivid situation rather
than to evocative or ambiguous imagistic overtones.

Wei Chuang's straightforward presentation is sometimes influenced by the use of colloquial expressions and direct dialogue
of the popular tradition. Moreover, the conventional images of songs
like the following, from the Tun-huang manuscripts' *Yün-yao chi*,
reverberate in his work:

#013 (S. 1441, P. 2838)
Tune: "P'o chen tzu"

The sun is warm, the wind is gentle, there is lovely scenery.
Flying orioles seem to ask me:
"Now is the time that flowers offer their beauty at Yüeh Stream:
Only you are separated from your lover by a thousand hills and ten thou-
          sand crossings.
He alone must be lost and captured in the dust."

Plum blossoms' snow falls and settles on the sad ground;
In vain is fragrant sandalwood balm applied to the singer's lips.
The path is covered with thick growth, fragrant grass turns green.
On my red cheeks constantly can be seen pearly tears.
Letters are not easy to send.

Here the series of images seems almost randomly arranged, whereas
Wei Chuang's works are masterfully condensed and pointed. Instead of a static scene of passive melancholy, he often presents immediate activity or dramatic confrontations. Many of Wei Chuang's
tz'u depict the actual moment of parting, or recreate it in a vivid
memory. In the following example the lonely woman is described
with traditional diction, but rather than listlessly waiting she actively climbs the tower. Though the imagery approaches the banal,
the originality of the poem is found in the poignancy of her tearful
response. Her final disappointment is emphasized by its contrast
to the initial hopeful gesture she makes of looking actively for her
lover:

Tune: "Mu-lan hua"

Alone she ascends the small tower, spring is almost over.
Sadly she gazes toward the Jade Pass, along the fragrant grass road.

News is cut off,
She does not meet anyone.
Knitting her fine brows she returns through the embroidered door.

She sits and watches falling flowers, in vain she sighs.
Her silk sleeves are spotted with dampness, from red tears dripping.
A thousand hills, ten thousand rivers, never crossed before:
Her soul in dreams would like to learn, but where would she search for
    him?[47]

The images here are all familiar, and recall the popular song style.
The lush fragrant grass of summer and the falling flowers indicate
late spring, which is associated with passing youth and loss of hope.
The long road and countless hills and rivers emphasize the distance of the separation. The embroidered door and rouge-stained
tears on silk sleeves indicate the woman's unappreciated beauty.
News is conventionally cut off, and one would not know where to
look for the lover even if it were possible, as in the "Yeh chin men"
song above. But Wei Chuang's poem, however derivative in imagery, is tightly unified in structure, with the action of climbing
the tower in the first stanza, and the disappointed response in the
second, joined by a logical causal relationship between the two. The
anonymous *Yün-yao chi* poem attempts a meaningful sequence:
aroused by the orioles' chiding, the separated woman responds to
the evidence of late spring with the same tearful despair, but the
transitions between images and between sections of the poem, as
is characteristic of oral literature, are more abrupt and aesthetically unsatisfying.

    Wei Chuang's more active style, acquired from the popular
tradition but enhanced by his personal voice and focused presentation, makes an interesting contrast with Wen T'ing-yün's more free-
ranging and remote impersonality. In a characteristic poem, Wen
T'ing-yün presents the internal emotional experience of a woman
who dwells on a memory until it gains the elusive quality of a dream:

    Tune: "P'u sa man" I

In the jade tower, a bright moon and a long remembrance:
The willow silks were soft and slender, the spring was languorous.

Outside the gate the grass grew thick;
When I parted from you, I heard the horse neigh.

A painted silk with golden kingfishers,
A fragrant candle melts into tears.
Flowers fall, the cuckoo cries out;
By the green window, remnants of a dream gone astray.[48]

A poem by Wei Chuang to the same tune presents a similar situation: by moonlight a lover leaves the tower and goes out the gate, not to return to the sad woman who is left by the green window:

Tune: "P'u sa man" II

In the red tower, the night we parted, to bear such sorrow!
The fragrant lamp, the tasseled curtain half rolled up.
The waning moon when I went out the gate;
And the beautiful woman said good-bye with tears.

The lute with golden kingfisher feathers,
On its strings the voice of an oriole,
Urging me soon to return.
By the green window, she was like a flower.[49]

Wei Chuang uses a few images identical to Wen T'ing-yün's (the tower, the gate, tears, flowers, and the "green window") and many slight variations ("red tower" for "jade tower," "fragrant lamp" for "fragrant candle," "waning moon" for "bright moon," "tasseled curtain" for "willow silks," "oriole voice" for "cuckoo cry," and golden kingfishers on the lute rather than on the curtain), but in spite of the remarkable overlaps in imagery, the poems are strikingly different in tone. The action in Wei Chuang's poem is present; in Wen T'ing-yün's poem it is only a fragmentary memory. Wen T'ing-yün's poem has a circular structure: it begins and ends with "remembrance" and "dream," and could continue to follow that repeated cycle endlessly. Wei Chuang's poem, on the other hand, progresses from the parting to the request to return, and implies the possibility of future developments extending beyond the scope of the poem. The point of view in Wei Chuang's poem is that of the man who is actively though reluctantly departing; the perspective in Wen T'ing-yün's poem is that of the passive woman. Thus, the emotions and sensations are immediate and intense in the Wei Chuang poem, while they are muted by passing time in the Wen T'ing-yün poem. The scene is more remote in the Wen T'ing-yün poem as well—the willows, the spring, and the grass beyond the gate are all distant—but in the Wei Chuang poem there is no landscape outside the boudoir. Wen T'ing-yün also creates a sense of distance by projecting emotional attributes onto objects: the horse cries out and the candle sheds tears; the falling flowers are at most impersonal metaphors for the woman, and the cuckoo is an emblem of tragic loss. But in Wei Chuang's poem the people express the emotions directly ("to bear such sorrow!" and "said good-bye with tears"); and in her lute song the woman—who herself has the voice of an oriole and is "like a flower"—urges her lover to return in her own voice.

Wen T'ing-yün's poem characteristically establishes a powerful mood of melancholy distraction, where dreams and memories overshadow the present, and all objects in the environment carry metaphoric associations with the emotional state of the subject. Wei Chuang's poem is representative of his ability to create the impact of a dramatic presentation, where the actors bear the burden of self-expression, only supplemented and underscored by the implications of elements of the scene.[50] Both poets use the conventional diction which developed in the popular song style, but the changes in the way that material is used demonstrates the degree of refining and recasting possible by literati. Wen T'ing-yün's imaginative recreation of a psychological state, with all its layering of multiple associations and aesthetic distance, is probably the more original and distinctive. Wei Chuang is perhaps closer to the intimate, unself-conscious directness of the popular tradition, but his artful reshaping of the folk elements into an intensely condensed, cohesive whole, characterized by sharp contrasts and explicit expressions of strong emotions, often in a personal lyric voice, probably had more influence on the *tz'u* styles which developed in the eleventh and twelfth centuries.[51]

The Late T'ang Imperial Style and
Its Popular Audience

If the *tz'u* poems by Wen T'ing-yün and Wei Chuang demonstrate the extent to which popular poetic styles had "trickled up"
to the elite literati by the end of the tenth century, it is also possible to show that at the same time *tz'u* poetry composed by members of the elite was well known and influential among the semiliterate. A set of poems from the Tun-huang manuscripts presents
an unusual, and perhaps rather extreme, case of musical interaction among different social classes, moving from high to low culture. These songs cluster around those attributed to the penulti-
mate T'ang ruler, Emperor Chao-tsung (Li Chieh, r. 888–904), and
others written in response by members of the lower classes to whom
the Emperor's songs had "trickled down."

We know that the young Chao-tsung was a patron of the arts,
and of popular music in particular. For example, early in 894, when
Li Mao-chen, the military governor of Feng-hsiang, who in fact
controlled more than fifteen western prefectures, came to court,
he was presented with a heavily guarded banquet performance by
thirty singing girls in the inner palace.[52] Certainly the Emperor's
own compositions in the *tz'u* form were influenced by this kind of
popular music currently in fashion in his own court; at the same
time, there is evidence in the Tun-huang manuscripts that poems
of unattributed authorship were composed in response to songs
thought to have been written by Chao-tsung himself.

First we have two poems conventionally attributed to Emperor Chao-tsung in various anthologies.[53] Of course the attribu
tion to the Emperor may still be spurious, but a least it is supported by a widespread legend. Historical records show that after
Li Mao-chen and his allies attacked Ch'ang-an in 895, Chao-tsung
fled for his life. En route he was intercepted by Han Chien, the
prefect of Hua-chou, who kept him under forced "protection" in
Hua-chou from the seventh month of 896 until the Emperor returned to Ch'ang-an in the eighth month of 898.[54] The *Old T'ang
History* records that in the seventh month of 897, after a year of

virtual captivity, "the Emperor, accompanied by his scholars and members of the royal family, climbed Ch'i-yün lou and gazed toward Ch'ang-an in the West. The Emperor ordered his musicians to sing *tz'u* songs he had composed himself to the tune of 'P'u sa man.' When the performance was over, everyone's tears fell, wetting their lapels."[55] These are the two poems which evidently were composed by the Emperor on this occasion, both to the tune "P'u sa man":

#046 (S. 2607)

I climb the tower and gaze afar toward the Ch'in palace:
All I see are pairs of swallows darting about.
The Wei River flows in a line,
A thousand mountains join with ten thousand hills.

Wilderness mist covers the distant trees;
On the paths, travelers are gone.
Where are the heroes
To welcome my return to the Imperial Palace?

#047 (S. 2607)

Blowing and whirling beneath the Three Peaks,
In the autumn wind it is often damp and wet.
My heart breaks when I recall the immortal palace,
Dark and dim in mist and fog.

Lost in thoughts and reveries, I often go to sleep,
Speechless for so long, as if I am drunk.
When will I ever return?
Does heaven understand, or not?

Following these two well-known lyrics, the Tun-huang manuscripts also contain three other poems to the same tune which were apparently likewise written at or near the same time.[56] The first poem of response reinforces the Emperor's lament from the point of view of a loyal subject:

#048 (S. 2607, P. 3128)

For a thousand years they struggled for power over the Phoenix Gates;
When will someone present a strategy for restoring peace to the country?
The imperial chariot is at Three Peaks:
Heaven is the same, but affairs on earth are changed.

The universe detests partiality;
Now the Emperor is a traveler covered with dust.
Beyond the inner chambers are loyal and steadfast ones
Longing to help the righteous sovereign.

The Emperor's poem opens with a veiled reference to his own palace in Ch'ang-an, now occupied by mean "swallows" rather than loyal servants; the response poem also begins with a reference to the palace—for "Phoenix Gates" by synecdoche indicates the imperial city—and the displaced subjects who should be in control. The Emperor's poem then places the contemporary political events in a broader temporal and spatial context, and the response poem follows in this vein by skillfully contrasting human mutability with the constancy of nature. In the second stanza, the Emperor's poem emphasizes desolation in nature as in the human realm; the response poem is first more abstract (l. 5), then more concrete (l. 6); "loyal and steadfast ones" echoes "heroes" in line 7 and the final line is a flattering version of the Emperor's closing sentiment. The response poem finally makes sense only in the context of the model, another indication of the intertextuality of the Tun-huang corpus.

The second poem of response harmonizes with the model not thematically, but by repeating the final word of nearly every line of Chao-tsung's second poem. The repetition is often clumsy, however, and is not evident in the translation; the poem itself seems quite insignificant if not considered as a response to the model. This response was apparently composed by an artisan, appointed to supervise reconstruction of the palace, which may account for its literary shortcomings;[57] the manuscript is also damaged, which does not improve the final product as we have it:

#050 (S. 2607)

I have always been ashamed of my ambition to serve in office;
Now the enlightened sovereign, making his tour, generously favored me:
I am appointed Master Builder to see to repairing the palace;
I offer . . .* without end.

Serving the country, how could anyone ever go to sleep?
Restoring order, no one can be drunk.
Set a time for return,
Hoping, at the edge of heaven, always . . .*

This response is a technical rather than a thematic echo; the speaker is so self-absorbed that he regards the imperial palace only as the object of his own work. If the last line also used the final word of the model, *chih* ("to know"), it would probably read, "Hoping, even at the edge of heaven, that the Emperor will always remember (know) me."

The third poem of response is more highly poeticized, substituting repeated imagery for imitation of narrative content:

#051 (S. 2607)

In the imperial gardens, drop by drop, red threads hanging;
In the wind, they fall down, dampening the trellis.
The willows' color is just now lingering,
The dark palace is reflected in the clear pond.

Whenever I think of the imperial Phoenix Gates,
I only regret the many long years of separation.
Counting the days until the return:
As sure as South Mountain which cannot be budged.

The first four lines of this response are notable for their originality. Nostalgia is evoked by the delicate picture of the palace garden, and intensified by the conceit in which the tendrils of blossoms are said to hang down as if they are dripping, and their falling on the trellis below is likewise depicted as the effect of drops of water: the whole extended metaphor obliquely suggests human tears.

*Ellipses indicate a lacuna in the original manuscript.

Not only are the loyalist sentiments and imperial images in all five poems similar, but the wording even echoes the Emperor's model. #050 in particular adheres closely to the diction and rhymes of Chao-tsung's #047, but common knowledge of the original poem also seems indicated by the repetition in line seven of both #050 and #051 of the "return" trope.[58] Moreover, the manuscripts contain yet another poem to the same tune, apparently written the following year (898) when the Emperor did return to the capital, which strongly harks back to the tone and language of the original, including a variation on the "return" figure in line seven:

#049 (S. 2607)

Ever since the imperial chariot stayed at Three Peaks,
With all our hearts day and night we longed for our enlightened ruler.
He should properly be within the Forbidden City;
Reed organ songs have been quiet for a long time.

Government officials are dispersed to the South and the North,
Who is concerned about the nation?
This night the imperial carriage returns:
We must establish the stability of the country.[59]

These examples illustrate how difficult it is to make fine distinctions in levels of literature. It would appear that the poems Emperor Chao-tsung composed for the occasion were not oral in any strict (Parry/Lord) sense: the poet and audience were not illiterate, the composition was probably not spontaneous and may have even anticipated the actual visit to Ch'i-yün lou, and the style was not conspicuously formulaic. However, as Ruth Finnegan has demonstrated, a poem does not necessarily have to fulfill these requirements in order to be part of an oral tradition. Chao-tsung's lyrics were introduced to the audience through a live performance, and though they may have been written down by a court scribe they were simultaneously transmitted through oral/aural means. Although we do not possess the original written record of Chao-tsung's songs, we may imagine that it existed quite early, if not even before the first performance. Nevertheless, it seems most likely that the written text was not the only—and probably not even the primary—means by which the poems became well known, and there may have been extensive oral distribution, during this time of social and political upheaval similar to the period of the An Lu-shan Rebellion, by musicians dispersed from the court and among the bewildered, insecure populace. As in the case of early sixteenth-century English "broadside" ballads, often concerning political topics or current events, which were sung by itinerant street singers at fairs and markets as samples to induce the audience to buy the printed sheets on which the songs were published for cheap sale, the distribution of popular songs often involves considerable interaction between written and oral modes.[60]

The origins of the three poems responding to Chao-tsung's—#048, #050, and #051—are likewise probably mixed and may even represent joint or collective authorship, and/or composers from a broad social spectrum. The literary refinement of the anonymous poem #048 suggests the hand of a sophisticated poet, perhaps a member of the original party which visited the Ch'i-yün lou; whereas the precious conventionality of #051 may imply an author of less talent but nevertheless well versed in poetic craft. And the virtually formulaic quality of #050 clearly indicates that it was modeled on Chao-tsung's #047. Although we may speculate that the anonymous authors of these songs were all loyal subjects somehow connected with the imperial court in exile, the collective voice in all three poems of response suggests that they speak for a wider social group. One is reminded of popular accounts of another Emperor in exile, Li Yü, or Li Hou-chu (937–978), the Last Ruler of the Southern T'ang dynasty, whose *tz'u* songs of patriotic nostalgia were said to have had such a potent subversive effect among the conquered populace that the deposed sovereign was finally put to death by his Sung captors to eliminate his eloquent loyalist poetic threats to the new regime.[61] It is readily conceivable that the poems of the exiled Emperor Chao-tsung gained widespread circulation because of their political and emotional, as well as poetic, appeal. We know Chao-tsung's poems were transmitted in various written versions; I propose there was a rather large and varied corpus of lyrics written on the same theme to the same tune, using similar language, images, and/or attitudes, which likewise circulated among the people—including both more "literary" and more "folk" versions. The Tun-huang manuscripts may happen to preserve only a few of this group of lyrics, a sample representing a series of variations ranging from orally transmitted loyalist popular songs to highly sophisticated courtly poems written by literati in response to the Emperor's model, and probably including many intermediate mixtures of these two extremes.

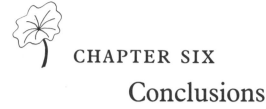

CHAPTER SIX

Conclusions

THE publication of the *Hua-chien chi* anthology in 940 marks the culmination of the first stage in the development of *tz'u* poetry. The purpose of the anthology, as stated in Ou-yang Chiung's Preface, was to demonstrate that the poetry in the *tz'u* form had been artistically refined and socially accepted to the point where it could be used by members of the elite class publicly and without apology. By 940 the climactic claim was that the literati *tz'u* style, although derived from the popular style, had developed sufficiently that it might finally displace the courtesans' repertoire, and "Southern singing girls will stop singing songs of the lotus boat."

We have traced the gradual process of the development of *tz'u* poetry through the T'ang dynasty, emphasizing the continued significance of the popular culture, especially the art of the entertainment quarters, represented by Ou-yang Chiung as "songs of the lotus boat." From Emperor Hsüan-tsung's court to the Mid-T'ang and Late T'ang scholar officials who served or traveled in Chiangnan, the influence of current popular songs was reflected in literati *tz'u* tune patterns, themes, and imagery. However, after the stylistic innovations of Wen T'ing-yün and Wei Chuang, many literati began writing *tz'u* poems based on those highly educated poets' style rather than on the popular culture. On the other hand, tenth-century poets whose artistic talents were inferior to those of Wen T'ing-yün, although they tried to imitate his elegant refinement, often had to fall back on the conventional motifs and well-known straightforward situations of the popular tradition which were easier to emulate.

Wang Chien established in 907 the Former Shu dynasty, which lasted until 925; it was soon followed by the Later Shu dynasty (934–965) under Meng Ch'ang (919–965), whose splendid court cultivated the arts, including the sponsorship of the *Hua-chien chi* anthology. Isolated geographically and culturally from the military, political, and social chaos of most of the rest of China, the Shu court tried to restore in their Szechwan retreat some of the former prosperity and cultural glory of the T'ang dynasty. This remote little world was strikingly similar to the decadent Liang court society of the sixth century which produced the *Yü-t'ai hsin-yung*. Yet as only one of the southern "Ten Kingdoms" *(shih-kuo)* competing for control of China during the tenth century, the Shu state felt a particular need to demonstrate its own achievements, and a feeling of local pride informs the compilation of the *Hua-chien chi* by the minor Shu official Chao Ch'ung-tso. The works of eighteen poets are represented in this anthology, and most of the authors had strong Szechwan connections. Among those who did not, Wen T'ing-yün and Huang-fu Sung (ninth century) died before the end of the T'ang dynasty. Wei Chuang served in the Former Shu administration, but Chang Pi (middle tenth century) and Ho Ning (898–955) apparently had positions elsewhere. The remaining thirteen of the *Hua-chien chi* poets were all either born in Szechwan and/or served under the Shu government.

The attitude reflected in the *tz'u* of the Szechwan poets is retrospective. In their nostalgia for the T'ang, they were attracted by the tone of Wen T'ing-yün's poetry, and they shared his interest in looking back upon memories or dreams of a past happiness. The Shu poets in the *Hua-chien chi* also emulated Wen T'ing-yün's ornate imagistic style and detached impersonal tone. While emperor-poets such as Li Ching (916–961) and Li Yü (937–978) of the Southern T'ang dynasty (937–976), located in the lower Yangtze region, were making major innovative contributions to the *tz'u* genre developing out of Wei Chuang's more straightforward presentation and personal lyric voice, the Western Shu poets in the upper Yangtze area of the far west were attempting to perpetuate a style which for them epitomized the melancholy elegance of the Late T'ang period. The only two T'ang poets whom Ou-yang Chiung mentions as literary precursors in his Preface to the *Hua-chien chi* are Li Po and Wen T'ing-yün.

But although Ou-yang Chiung claims that the five hundred literati *tz'u* collected in the *Hua-chien chi* are vastly superior to common folk songs, in fact it is difficult to support such a sharp distinction between two types of poetry. This study has shown that historically there was constant interaction, socially and literarily, between the popular and the elite cultures, and that the influence traveled in both directions between the higher and lower classes. Various anecdotes and other historical records indicate that performances of *tz'u* songs were probably joint enterprises, in which the literati participated alongside the musicians. Certainly, the audience was socially mixed, and the performers must have tailored their performances to please the various elements in the audience.

Moreover, *tz'u* poetry cannot be categorized according to the old controversy about oral versus written literature. As Ruth Finnegan has shown, the only clear criterion for oral poetry is the performance context. Whether or not a poem was composed or transmitted with the aid of writing, the distinctive qualities of orality appear when the performance is direct and unmediated by the written word.[1] Thus it could well be argued that even poems originally composed with brush and ink by literati such as Wang Chih-huan or Wen T'ing-yün entered the corpus of oral literature when they were performed by singing girls in entertainment halls. However, this argument is problematic, because since the song words were still simultaneously familiar to at least some members of the audience in their written form, even the criterion of performance becomes blurred with other forms of transmission. Like the T'ang writers who made no precise distinctions between the performed song (*ch'ü*) and the written song words (*ch'ü-tzu tz'u*), we must also accept the overlapping commonalities of the two modes of presentation.

Furthermore, in thematic and stylistic characteristics we also find similarities between popular and elite *tz'u*. We have already considered the broad diversity of the poems found in the Tun-huang manuscripts, even including poems by literati such as Wen T'ing-yün, Ou-yang Chiung, and Emperor Chao-tsung. The *Hua-chien chi* collection is also hardly homogeneous. Not only do Wen T'ing-yün and Wei Chuang use markedly different styles, but the work of their contemporary Huang-fu Sung, for example, does not resemble either of their styles. Huang-fu Sung's twelve poems, on the contrary, closely resemble folk songs. Generally in one stanza, they use plain and colloquial language, stock images and simple narrative exposition. Huang-fu Sung's deliberate imitation of the folk song style is most apparent in his *carpe diem* poems and his exuberant verses which must at least approximate the kind of piece Ou-yang Chiung called "songs of the lotus boat," set to the tune named "Gathering Lotus."

Tune: "Ts'ai lien tzu"

Water lilies and fragrant lotus across the vast stretch of water,
Raise oars!
A young girl exuberant and playful, picks lotus until late;
Youth!
Evening comes, the splashing water dampens her in the boat,
Raise oars!
Making her remove her red skirt and wrap up the ducks.
Youth!

The boat glides, the lake shines, overflowing with autumn,
Raise oars!
With desire she watches a young boy letting his boat drift,
Youth!
Impetuously across the water she throws lotus seeds,
Raise oars!
As the news spreads and people hear of it, she is bashful for half a day.
Youth![2]

This poem announces the popular mode in its refrains and subject matter. In addition to the general associations of lotus with love, the lotus seeds were regarded explicitly as love tokens, and drifting boats were associated with spontaneous moods.

In general, poems concerning drifting boats tend to exhibit

the least refined styles, perhaps because the subject matter is the pleasure and satisfaction of the spontaneous, informal lifestyle. There are several carefree boating poems in the Tun-huang manuscripts. One of these, #058, expresses childlike wonder that as the boat glides along the mountains appear to be moving, but on careful inspection one realizes that only the boat is actually moving. Another, #061, describes an old fisherman in the rain who has not moored his boat but leaves it to drift in any direction while he enjoys his jug of wine in this peaceful natural setting. Some such poems praising the joys of the simple life of ease seem to be reacting against a more formal lifestyle, as did Chang Chih-ho in his "Fisherman's Songs" (see chapter 5). This attitude is explicit in another Tun-huang text:

#063 (P. 3128, S. 2607)
Tune: "Huan hsi sha"

Putting aside my classics of *Poetry* and *History*, I board the fishing boat.
Wearing a straw coat and a bamboo hat, I carry a fishing rod.
Rowing into the depths of the blue waves:
A succession of several beaches.

Formerly I was not a fisherman,
But the passing of time conceals virtue and wisdom.
Therefore I hide my body under cliffs and swamps,
And do not attend court.

The imagery of a comparable song in the *Hua-chien chi* by Ku Hsiung (middle tenth century) is more lush, but the rejection of worldly concerns, self-consciously confessed, is similarly explicit:

Tune: "Yü ko-tzu"

At dawn the wind is clear,
The quiet lake is green.
Leaning against the balustrade, I concentrate on watching the rare birds.
The painted curtain hangs down,
The kingfisher screen is folded,
My sleeves are full of perfume of lotus fragrance.

Wonderful to express my feelings,
To eagerly gaze around.
My body relaxed and heart tranquil, the ordinary life is sufficient.
My wine cup is full,
Light and darkness rush on.
For fame and profit I have no desire to compete and strive.[3]

Whereas the lotus picking songs probably represent a folk motif adopted by the literati, the fisherman's songs—which imply the ancient Confucian and Taoist attitudes toward the simple fisherman as the exemplary sage who merely follows the flow—are more likely to have developed from self-conscious literati origins to merge with the popular tradition.

Nevertheless, in spite of reciprocal influence coupled with formal, thematic, and imagistic similarities, there are clearly generalizable differences between the popular and elite styles. In the oral tradition we often find the predictable characteristics, such as more narrative and dramatic situations, more dialogue and shifting points of view, more direct expression of emotions and colloquial diction. The rejection of many of these features by the literati reveals the kind of aesthetic values which informed their poetic style: Wen T'ing-yün, for example, substituted static scenes for action, a unified detached perspective for encounters, oblique expression of feelings, and objectification in an elegant style. The following pair of poems contrasts an anonymous Tun-huang song with a Wen T'ing-yün poem and indicates which aspects of the popular style Wen T'ing-yün chose to adopt and which to avoid:

#119 (P. 3137)
Tune: "Nan ko-tzu"

I regret having married this playboy husband,
A playboy who cannot be relied on.
Plucking flowers, breaking willows, he is loathed by others.
Night after night he comes home sunk in drunkenness:
After a thousand calls, he still does not respond.

I turn and watch the moon beyond the curtain;
Inside the canopy decorated with mandarin ducks is a lamp

Which clearly reveals this heartless man.
I ask him, "What little affairs . . . ?"
He shakes his head and says, "Never."

Wen T'ing-yün
Tune: "P'u-sa man" II

Night comes with the shining moon; it is just now midnight.
Inside the rolled up curtains all is silent, there is no one to talk to.
From deep within, musk incense lingers;
At bedtime she leaves on her thin makeup.

"I still regret the years gone by;
How can I bear to recall the past?"
Flowers fall and the moonlight fades,
The embroidered quilt knows the chill of dawn.[4]

Both poems are spoken in the voice of a lonely, disappointed woman; in both, she is in her bedroom on a moonlit night, behind curtains and surrounded by embroidered fabrics suitable for a scene of love-making, which is of course not achieved. But in the Tunhuang poem the social situation is emphasized: we know that the husband is a philanderer, often drunk and unresponsive to his wife. The folk song is structured by the narrative events, whereas the Wen T'ing-yün poem is devoid of explicit narration. The solitary desolation of the woman in the second poem is indicated by the imagistic description of her physical surroundings and her ambiguous inner thoughts of the past which only implicitly suggest her lover's absence. The extreme depersonalization of the Wen T'ing-yün poem is emphasized by the conceit in the last line: the lonely woman's awareness of the coldness of sleeping alone is transferred to the quilt.

The popular song employs devices often noted above, such as dialogue and direct question-and-answer confrontation. Images such as "plucking flowers, breaking willows" are also formulaic in this style. These techniques, with their flavor of the popular tradition, were avoided by the literati, who substituted static, impersonal scenes filled with suggestive objects surrounding a solitary female figure; indeed, Wen T'ing-yün emphasizes she has "no one to talk to." But not only do literati use the general situation of the neglected wife in their *Hua-chien chi* style *tz'u;* they also pick up and give fuller play to the imagery, which is secondary to the narrative in the popular song (lines 6–7). This emphasis and elaboration of the imagery indicates an important step in the literary evolution of elite *tz'u* poetry, which may be traced back to Liang dynasty Palace Style poems and even earlier to *shih* poems on the theme of the neglected wife.

Another striking difference between popular and elite styles is the treatment of figurative language. Overt descriptions of parts of the woman's body are common in the Tun-huang poems, but rare in the *Hua-chien chi* style. Instead, a woman's beauty is described obliquely, by association with her surroundings, or ornaments. These evocative objects often carry the weight of the whole poem; the poem would collapse without them. In contrast, similes and metaphors are frequently mere ornaments to embellish the narrative or emotive substance of popular poetry. The figures of speech in a Tun-huang poem often stand out as distinct from the fabric of the poem.

In a Wen T'ing-yün poem there is often a delicate balance between a woman's boudoir furnishings and her emotional situation: the screens and curtains which surround her harmonize with her psychological withdrawal, the cold bedcovers express her sense of desolation, a finely embroidered gown complements her tender sensitivity. This integration is rarely achieved in a Tun-huang poem, where the imagery sometimes seems an obligatory gesture or a contrivance. In extreme cases, the fictionality of the similes is emphasized, as in the following relatively self-conscious example from the *Yün-yao chi:*

#005 (S. 1441, P. 2835)
Tune: "T'ien hsien tzu"

Swallows chatter and orioles call in the middle of the third month.
Mist drenched willow tendrils: a profusion of golden threads.
On the Wu-ling Terrace there is an immortal goddess,
She carries a singer's fan,

Her incense spreads freely;
A layer of clouds lingers over the Chiu-hua Mountains.

Ornaments of jade cover her head, flowers cover her face.
But this rejected concubine: one, then two, secret tears fall.
The tears' pearls are like getting pearls that seem real:
She holds them, they do not scatter,
Who knows what is their limit?
Strung together on red silk they should be worth a million.

Just as the willow silks are conventionally compared to golden threads, tears are likened to pearls. But in this poem the metaphor takes on a life of its own in a clever conceit: the tears are so pearl-like it seems they could be held in the hand or strung into a necklace. This technique calls attention to the artificiality of the style, and the wit of the poet. In place of the *hua-chien* style of poised, harmonious integration, the popular style exhibits a refreshing liveliness and immediacy, which may be jolting but has its own vitality and punch.

The variations and stylistic range of the Tun-huang corpus may be demonstrated in the following poem, also from the *Yün-yao chi*. Here within a single poem the style is mixed. The delicate interplay between the human subject and the external world which the *hua-chien* poets strove to achieve is shown in the first four-and-a-half lines, but then the tone abruptly shifts and the detached, impersonal static scene is interrupted by a direct emotional outburst. This immediate speaking voice is one of the characteristics of the popular style which poets like Wen T'ing-yün generally suppressed. Again, though it disrupts the smooth blending of elements, it achieves a direct impact lacking in Wen T'ing-yün's more guarded and distanced style:

#012 (S. 1441, P. 2838)
Tune: "P'o chen tzu"

Lotus face, willow eyebrows, bashful manners;
Black silk hair, she finishes gathering it into clouds.
Warm sun, soft breeze, flowers carry charm;

Painted pavilions, carved beams, swallows chatter again.
Rolling up the curtains, I resent the man who's gone.

Pearl tears of loneliness forever falling.
I burn incense and pray to every spirit.
It must be that beautiful women from the Hsiao and Hsiang Rivers are
    replacing me;
He doesn't remember the beginning of our affair, love inside the silk cur-
    tains.
The abandoned one, in vain I am passing my spring.

In spite of the abrupt shift, this poem is in fact successfully unified. The narrative details of the woman's suffering are perhaps
more extensive than would be necessary in the more subtle literati
style, but they do present a balanced contrast with the images of
returning spring and female beauty, youth, and potential for love
in the first stanza. All of the optimism of spring and youth are denied by the second stanza, culminating with the final line, in which
the abandoned woman's youth and the season of spring are merged
into a perfect identification between subject and scene.

The majority of the isolated independent lyrics from the Tun-
huang manuscripts are love poems, and many of them may have
originated, as did the Chao-tsung and other topical poems, as occasional pieces composed in response to a particular situation, or
as variations on such model poems. The occasion may have been
an actual life experience, as in the case of Wei Chuang's loss of his
concubine (see chapter 5), or it may have been a literary theme, as
in the revival of the Meng Chiang-nü legend. The songs seem to
have been understood in a broader context than that specified in
the poem itself because of accumulated associations—for example,
a lonely woman generally implies a husband away at the frontier,
she is often occupied in making winter clothes for him, and so on.
By presenting a single moment the Meng Chiang-nü poem can imply the entire story. Moreover, there is a fluidity to the perspective
even within a single poem, and a sense of composition by combination of different motifs, voices, and points of view. Rather than
the static scenes of Palace Style and *Hua-chien chi* poetry, the Tun-
huang poems tend to emerge—often *in medias res*—out of a vigor-

ous narrative background. Thus, poetic images and attitudes evoke situations as well as moods. Given the particular circumstances of performance of the extant Tun-huang *tz'u* poems, which of course represent only a small fraction of the contemporary cultural knowledge and assumptions, it is especially challenging for us to try to approximate the information and expectations of the T'ang dynasty audience. However, reading the poems with no sense of their rich social context is unacceptably limited, and we must try as much as possible to recreate the audience background and performance context.

The audience was not necessarily the same for every *tz'u* in the Tun-huang manuscripts. Some of these songs were local products; others were probably carried to Tun-huang from Ch'ang-an and perhaps even Suchou or Hangchou. Just as the composers of the poems ranged from emperors and literati to artisans and semi-literate courtesans, those for whom the songs were performed also represented a broad social spectrum. Thus the nature and degree of audience understanding was not fixed. The thematic content of particular lyrics—such as traveling merchants' songs, students' songs, and patriotic songs—suggests somewhat specialized audiences and occasions. Perhaps performances were held in the marketplace, or particular meeting halls. Similarly, many of the love songs were performed in erotic settings or urban entertainment quarters, usually by courtesans. It was there that the ninth-century literati in the audience learned the tunes and themes which they eventually adopted and modified to create the *hua-chien* style. Thus, the popular *tz'u* audience became the creators of the literary *tz'u*, indicating a complex interaction among social and literary levels.

In 1907, exactly a millennium after the fall of the T'ang dynasty, when Sir Aurel Stein manipulated Wang Tao-shih to allow him to remove a large quantity of manuscripts from cave #17 in Tun-huang, he did not know the contents or implications of the materials he procured. However, in comparing himself to the Buddhist pilgrim Hsüan-tsang, Stein revealed that he intuitively grasped the cultural significance of these texts and relics. In spite of the ethical questions surrounding Stein's and Pelliot's acquisitions, their value in helping us understand the nonelite cultural circumstances of T'ang China cannot be overestimated. They show us that even the simplest popular love song is part of a vast common repertoire which defines a range of thematic conventions, stylistic norms, and possible narrative contexts which are necessary for our appreciation of the texts. And since the elite *tz'u* genre grew out of this network of texts, we cannot evaluate the contributions of the literati without understanding the social and literary contexts which influenced them. Attention to the circumstances of performance sheds new light on the characteristics of literati *tz'u* poetry, and also enables us to appreciate the charm and appeal of the popular *tz'u* songs in their own right.

NOTES

ABBREVIATIONS USED IN NOTES AND BIBLIOGRAPHY

HJAS   *Harvard Journal of Asiatic Studies*
JAOS   *Journal of the American Oriental Society*
SPPY   *Ssu-pu pei yao*
TSCC   *Ts'ung-shu chi-ch'eng*

PREFACE

1. Chao Ch'ung-tso, ed., *Hua-chien chi, SPPY*, vol. 332, "Hsü," 2a.
2. All citations of popular poems from the Tun-huang manuscripts follow the numbering system in the definitive edition by Jen Erh-pei, *Tun-huang ch'ü chiao-lu* (Shanghai: Wen-i lien-ho ch'u-pan she, 1955), with reference also to the Stein (S.) or Pelliot (P.) manuscript number in which the poem occurs. All translations of poems are mine.
3. *Hua-chien chi*, 10.7a–7b.

CHAPTER ONE: INTRODUCTION

1. An extended description of the process of composing different *tz'u* lyrics to a particular tune pattern is found in Lois Fusek, tr., *Among the Flowers: The "Hua-chien chi"* (New York: Columbia University Press, 1982), pp. 1–3.
2. Wan Shu, comp., *Tz'u-lü*, (1687; rpt. with supplements by Hsü Pen-li and Tu Wen-lan), *SPPY*, vols. 483–84.
3. Wang I-ch'ing, et al., comp., *[Ch'in-ting] tz'u-p'u* (1715; rpt. Taipei: privately printed, 1964). See also Glen W. Baxter, *Index to the Imperial Register of*

Tz'u Prosody (Ch'in-ting tz'u-p'u) (Cambridge, Mass.: Harvard University Press, 1956).

4. A handful of materials on Sung dynasty music survive: for example, see L. E. R. Picken's reconstruction of a few *tz'u* songs in "Secular Chinese Songs of the Twelfth Century," *Studia Musicologica Academiae Scientiarum Hungaricae*, 8 (1966):125–72. But comparable evidence from the T'ang is severely limited. L. E. R. Picken has transcribed the musical notation for a dozen *Shih ching* poems in "Twelve Ritual Melodies of the T'ang Dynasty," *Studia Memoriae Bela Bartok Sacra* (Budapest, 1956):147–73. Yet popular music remains inaccessible; although some Tun-huang manuscripts (e.g., P. 3808 and S. 5443) contain what appears to be musical transcription, the system used is not understood. Rulan Chao Pien explains that the notation for the set of twenty-five melodies for the *p'i-p'a* found in one Tun-huang manuscript is so unusual that it cannot be reliably deciphered (see *Sonq Dynasty Musical Sources and their Interpretation* [Cambridge, Mass.: Harvard University Press, 1967], p. vii).

5. The best recent study of the origins of *tz'u* poetry is Kang-i Sun Chang's *The Evolution of Chinese "Tz'u" Poetry* (Princeton: Princeton University Press, 1980), especially chapter 1, pp. 1–32. See also James J. Y. Liu, *Major Lyricists of the Northern Sung* (Princeton: Princeton University Press, 1974), pp. 3–4; and Liu Ta-chieh, *Chung-kuo wen-hsüeh fa-chan shih* (Shanghai: Chung-hua shu-chü, 1949), vol. 2, pp. 1–13.

6. Hu Shih, "Tz'u ti ch'i-yüan," in Appendix to his *Tz'u hsüan* (1927; rpt. Shanghai: Shang-wu yin-shu kuan, 1930), pp. 1–22. Hu Shih's scholarship actually confirms the position of older critics such as Chu Hsi (1130–1200), whose explanation he quotes concerning the addition of *fan-sheng* ("floating words") to the regular *shih* meter to fill out the more varied song rhythms (p. 9).

7. Quoted near the end of Hu Shih's article, p. 18.

8. Baxter, "Metrical Origins of the *Tz'u*," *HJAS*, 16 (1953):108–45; rpt. in *Studies in Chinese Literature*, ed. John L. Bishop (Cambridge, Mass.: Harvard University Press, 1965), pp. 203–6.

9. Ibid., pp. 217–20, p. 223.

10. Suzuki Torao, "Shigen," in his *Shina bungaku kenkyū* (Kyotō, 1922), 459–78; Baxter, "Metrical Origins," pp. 191–96.

11. Baxter, "Metrical Origins," pp. 194–97.

12. All of these works emphasize selections from the thirty poems in the earliest collection of *tz'u* known as the *Yün-yao chi*. Chu Tsu-mou (Hsiao-tsang) begins his vast collection, *Ch'iang-ts'un ts'ung-shu* (Preface 1917; Shanghai: n.p., 1922), with eighteen poems from the *Yün-yao chi*. Lo Chen-yü includes eighteen poems from the *Yün-yao chi* and six other short songs in his *Tun-huang ling-shih* (1924; rpt. in *Lo Hsüeh-t'ang hsien-sheng ch'üan-chi*, series 3, vol. 7 [Taipei: Wen-hua ch'u-pan kung-ssu, 1968]). Liu Fu transcribes fourteen of the *Yün-yao chi* poems (pp. 127–31) and seven other short songs in his *Tun-huang to-so* (Preface 1925; n.p.: Kuo-li chung-yang yen-chiu li-shih yü-yen yen-chiu-suo chuan-k'an, no. 2, 1931), vol. 2, pp. 127–31 and 133–34.

13. Wang Chung-min, *Tun-huang ch'ü-tzu-tz'u chi* (Shanghai: Shang-wu yin-shu kuan, 1950).

14. Wang Chung-min, *Tun-huang ch'ü-tzu-tz'u chi* (1950; rev. ed. Shanghai: Shang-wu yin-shu kuan, 1956).

15. Jen Erh-pei, *Tun-huang ch'ü ch'u-t'an* (Shanghai: Wen-i lien-ho ch'u-pan she, 1954); and *Tun-huang ch'ü chiao-lu*.

16. Jen Erh-pei, *Tun-huang ch'ü ch'u-t'an*, pp. 201–5, 220–46, et passim.

17. Shih-chuan Chen, "Dates of Some of the Tunhuang Lyrics," *JAOS*, 88, no. 2 (April–June 1968):261–70.

18. Jao Tsung-yi, "Tun-huang ch'ü chih t'an-chiu," in Jao Tsung-yi and Paul Demiéville, *Airs de Touen-houang (Touen-houang k'iu)* (Paris: Editions du Centre National de la Recherche Scientifique, 1971). See, for example, Jao Tsung-yi's interpretation of the year "Jen-wu" on the manuscript catalogued as S. 4332, which he claims should actually be 802 rather than 742 as Chen argued (pp. 188–90; adapted into French, pp. 19–20).

19. Shih-chuan Chen, "The Rise of the Tz'u, Reconsidered," *JAOS*, 90, no. 2 (April–June 1970):240.

20. *Chiao-fang chi*, ed. Ts'ui Ling-ch'in, in *Ku-chin i-shih*, ed. Wu Kuan (Shanghai: Shang-wu yin-shu kuan, 1937), vol. 29, pp. 1a–10a. A convenient modern edition is the *Chiao-fang chi chien-ting*, ed. Jen Pan-t'ang [Erh-pei] (Shanghai: Chung-hua shu-chü, 1962); on p. 4 Jen states that 65 percent of the Tun-huang tune titles appear in the *Chiao-fang chi*.

21. Jao Tsung-yi, "Yin-lun," in *Airs de Touen-houang*, pp. 185–86; adapted into French, pp. 13–14.

22. Albert B. Lord, *A Singer of Tales* (Cambridge, Mass.: Harvard University Press, 1960), p. 54 et passim. The legacy of the rigid Parry-Lord distinctions is still being perpetuated by a few staunch disciples such as David E. Bynum who recently attacked Wang Ching-hsien's oral-formulaic analysis of the *Shih ching* in *The Bell and the Drum: Shih Ching as Formulaic Poetry in an Oral Tradition* (Berkeley: University of California Press, 1974)—which actually generally adheres rather closely to the Parry-Lord theory—as too loose because it suggests the possibility of a transitional stage between oral and written literature ("The Bell, the Drum, Milman Parry and the Time Machine," *Chinese Literature: Essays, Articles, Reviews*, 1, no. 2 (July 1979):241–53.

23. Gregory Nagy, *The Best of the Achaeans: Concepts of the Hero in Archaic Greek Poetry* (Baltimore: Johns Hopkins University Press, 1979), p. 3.

24. Albert Lord, "Homer as Oral Poet," *Harvard Studies in Classical Philology*, 72 (1968):46.

25. Leonard Charles Muellner, *The Meaning of Homeric EYXOMAI Through Its Formulas* (Innsbruck: Inst. f Sprachwissenschaft d. Univ. Innsbruck, 1976), p. 15. An excellent example of uncovering this traditional depth is Richard Sacks' forthcoming *The Traditional Phrase in Homer: Two Studies*.

26. Nagy, p. 3.

27. See R. F. Leslie, ed., *Three Old English Elegies: The Wife's Lament, The*

Husband's Message, The Ruin (Manchester: Manchester University Press, 1961), especially the Introduction. See also Larry D. Benson, "The Literary Character of Anglo-Saxon Formulaic Poetry," *Publications of the Modern Language Association*, 81 (1966):334–41.

28. Ruth Finnegan, *Oral Poetry: Its Nature, Significance, and Social Context* (New York: Cambridge University Press, 1977), p. 29 et passim.

29. Ibid., p. 24.

30. Maurice Freedman, "On the Sociological Study of Chinese Religion," in *Religion and Ritual in Chinese Society*, ed. Arthur P. Wolf (Stanford: Stanford University Press, 1974), p. 23.

31. David Johnson, "Chinese Popular Literature and Its Contexts," *Chinese Literature: Essays, Articles, Reviews*, 3, no. 2 (July 1981):225.

32. Ibid., p. 226.

33. Patrick Hanan, "The Early Chinese Short Story: A Critical Theory in Outline," in *Studies in Chinese Literary Genres*, ed. Cyril Birch (Berkeley: University of California Press, 1974), pp. 299–338.

34. Wang Ching-hsien, *The Bell and the Drum: Shih Ching as Formulaic Poetry in an Oral Tradition*, p. 27.

35. Finnegan, p. 80.

36. *Hua-chien chi*, 1.9b.

CHAPTER TWO: THE TUN-HUANG MANUSCRIPTS

1. This legend is probably at least partly spurious. Chang Hsi-hou points to evidence that men began carving out these caves as early as the end of the third century or the beginning of the fourth century ("Tun-huang ho Mo-kao k'u te li-shih yen-ke," in his *Tun-huang wen-hsüeh* [Shanghai: Ku-chi ch'u-pan she, 1980], p. 4).

2. This explanation of the caves' history is described in Peter Hopkirk, *Foreign Devils on the Silk Road* (London: John Murray, 1980), pp. 156–57.

3. See Chang Hsi-hou, pp. 8–9.

4. Aurel Stein, *Ruins of Desert Cathay* (London: MacMillan, 1912), vol. 2, p. 169. Stein also described his expeditions and their finds in a more scholarly form in *Serindia, Detailed Report of Explorations in Central Asia and Westernmost China* (Oxford: Clarendon Press, 1921), especially pp. 791–830.

5. Stein, *Ruins of Desert Cathay*, p. 169.

6. Ibid., p. 171.

7. Ibid., p. 172.

8. Ibid., p. 178.

9. Ibid., p. 190.

10. Ibid., p. 179.

11. Ibid., p. 180.

12. Ibid., p. 180.

13. See Jeannette Mirsky, *Sir Aurel Stein: Archaeological Explorer* (Chicago: University of Chicago Press, 1977), pp. 278–79. Stein boasted to a friend that "all which the 'Thousand Buddhas' has yielded has cost the Govt. only some £130" (quoted in Mirsky, p. 280). The Stein collection is described in Lionel Giles, *Descriptive Catalogue of the Chinese Manuscripts from Tunhuang in the British Museum* (London: British Museum, 1957).

14. See, for example, Arthur Waley, "Afterword," *Ballads and Stories from Tun-huang* (London: Allen and Unwin, 1960), pp. 237–38.

15. Hopkirk, p. 6.

16. Ibid., especially pp. 111ff., 145–55.

17. Mirsky, p. 254.

18. Stein, *Ruins of Desert Cathay*, p. 190.

19. See Mission Pelliot, *Les Grottes de Touen-Houang* (Paris, 1920–1924), 6 vols. The Pelliot collection is at present being meticulously catalogued, but only the first volume listing five hundred manuscripts (P. 2001–P. 2500) has so far been published by the Bibliothèque Nationale Département des Manuscrits, *Catalogue des Manuscrits chinois de Touen-Houang: Fonds Pelliot Chinois* (Paris· Bibliothèque Nationale, 1970).

A provisional catalogue of the Pelliot collection, "Po Hsi-ho chieh-ching lu," is found in Wang Chung-min's general *Tun-huang i-shu tsung-mu so-yin* (Peking: Shang-wu yin-shu kuan, 1962), pp. 253–313. Many of the non-Buddhist manuscripts from the Pelliot collection are also described in Wang Chung-min's *Tun-huang ku-chi hsü-lu* (Peking: Shang-wu yin-shu kuan, 1958).

20. See Hopkirk, chapter 13, "Pelliot—The Gentle Art of Making Enemies," pp. 177–89; also pp. 4–6.

21. Hopkirk, pp. 190–207. For a catalogue of the Ōtani collection see Kantōchō hakubutsukan, "Ōtani ke shuppin mokuroku," in *Shin Saiiki ki*, vol. 2 (Kyoto, 1937). The Oldenburg collection at the U.S.S.R. Academy of Sciences is catalogued by M. Vorob'eva-Desiatovskaia et al., *Opisanie kitaiskikh rukopisei Dun'khuanskogo fonda Instituta naradov Azii*, 2 vols. (Moscow: Izd-vo vostochnoy lut-ry, 1963 and 1966). See also Paul Demiéville, "Manuscrits de Touen-houang à Leningrad," *T'oung Pao*, 51, no. 4 (1964):355–76.

22. Hopkirk, pp. 209–22.

23. The manuscripts in the Peking collection were catalogued in 1931 by Ch'en Yüan, *Tun-huang chien-yü lu* (Peking, 1931). Wang Chung-min's *Tun-huang i-shu tsung-mu so-yin* is a worldwide catalogue which includes the Tokushi collection and the Yamanouchi collection at Ryūkoku University in Kyoto, as well as the small private collections of Hashikawa Tokio, Li Cheng-to, Lo Chen-yü, and others. For a general survey, see Kanda Kiichirō, *Tonkō gaku gojūnen* (Tokyo: Nigen-sha, 1960).

24. Lionel Giles estimates that of the seven thousand complete manuscripts and six thousand fragments in the Stein collection alone, about eighty-five percent concern Buddhist subjects (*Six Centuries at Tunhuang* [London: The China Society, 1944], p. 7).

25. The earliest dated manuscript is S. 797 in the British Museum, dated 406 A.D.; the latest document is M. 1696 (Φ. 32A) in the Leningrad collection, dated 1002 A.D. See Fujieda Akira, "The Tunhuang Manuscripts, A General Description," Part II, *Zinbun*, no. 10, 1969, pp. 17–39, for an analysis of dating methods for Tun-huang manuscripts based on calligraphic changes, and a description of scribes and "copying offices," primarily for Buddhist texts. A chronological survey of the manuscripts dated from 406 to 995 in the British Museum collection is presented in a series of six articles by Lionel Giles, all titled "Dated Chinese Mss. in the Stein Collection," in the *Bulletin of the School of Oriental and African Studies*, 7 (1935):809–35; 8 (1936):1–26; 9 (1937):1–25; 10 (1940):317–34; and 11 (1943):149–73.

26. For a detailed description, see Ma Shih-ch'ang, "Kuan-yü Tun-huang ts'ang-ching tung te chi-ko wen-t'i," *Wen-wu*, 1978, no. 12, pp. 22–28.

27. See, for example, Chang Hsi-hou, p. 8.

28. Ma Shih-ch'ang, pp. 28–30.

29. Stein, *Ruins of Desert Cathay*, p. 188.

30. Fujieda Akira, "The Tun-huang Manuscripts," in Donald D. Leslie, Colin Mackerras, and Wang Gungwu, eds., *Essays on the Sources for Chinese History* (Columbia, South Carolina: University of South Carolina Press, 1975), p. 128.

31. Studies in English include Waley, *Ballads and Stories from Tun-huang;* Eugene Eoyang, "Word of Mouth: Oral Story Telling in the Pien-wen" (Ph.D. dissertation, Indiana University, 1971); Richard E. Strassberg, "Buddhist Storytelling Texts from Tun-huang," *Chinoperl Papers*, 8 (1978):39–99; David Johnson, "The Wu Tzu-hsü *Pien-wen* and Its Sources," *HJAS*, 40, no. 1 (June 1980):93–156; and 40, no. 2 (December 1980):465–505; and Victor H. Mair, "Lay Students and the Making of Written Vernacular Narrative: an Inventory of Tun-huang Manuscripts," *Chinoperl Papers*, 10(1981):5–96. Also consult the notes and bibliographies of these studies for additional references.

32. See Victor H. Mair, *Tun-huang Popular Narratives* (Cambridge: Cambridge University Press, 1983).

33. Denis Twitchett, review of Arthur Waley's *Ballads and Stories from Tun-huang*, in *Bulletin of the School of Oriental Studies*, 214, no. 2 (1961):376.

34. See Dante Alighieri, *La Commedia secondo l'antica vulgata*, ed. Giorgio Petrocchi, 4 vols., vol. 1, *Introduzione* (Milano: Arnoldo Mondadori Editore, 1966), p. 60.

35. Giles, *Six Centuries at Tunhuang*, p. 12.

36. Ibid., p. 44; see also pp. 10–11. Examples of such colophons are found in S. 4366, S. 3935, and P. 2.

37. See Fujieda Akira, "The Tun-huang Manuscripts," who concurs that many of the non-Buddhist manuscripts discovered in the cave library were used at these monastic schools as schoolboys' exercises in calligraphy and composition (pp. 126–27).

38. Waley, *Ballads and Stories from Tun-huang*, p. 239.

39. Ibid., p. 239.

40. Most of these features are discussed in detail in Jen Erh-pei's *Tun-huang ch'ü ch'u-t'an*. For an illustrated but perhaps too generalized overview of elements of the popular style in Tun-huang songs, see Kang-i Sun Chang, pp. 19–25.

41. *Tun-huang ch'ü ch'u-t'an*, pp. 265–67ff. The "broad field of vision" of the Tun-huang poems is also emphasized by Wang Chung-min, *Tun-huang ch'ü-tzu-tz'u chi* (1950; rpt. 1954), "Hsü-lu," p. 8.

42. See Lin Mei-i, "Lun Tun-huang ch'ü ti she-hui hsing," *Wen-hsüeh p'ing-lun*, 2 (1976):107–44, who stresses that the frequency of military campaigns, the growth of urban centers, popular customs, holidays, traditional stories, political competitiveness and instability, and popular religion account for the range of subject matter in the Tun-huang poems. See also Jen Erh-pei, *Tun-huang ch'ü ch'u-t'an*, p. 268.

43. *Tun-huang ch'ü ch'u-t'an*, p. 285.

44. The views of various Chinese critics are outlined in Jen Erh-pei, *Tun-huang ch'ü ch'u-t'an*, pp. 283–97.

45. Kang-i Sun Chang, p. 1 and p. 12.

46. Jen Erh-pei, *Tun-huang ch'ü ch'u-t'an*, p. 258.

47. See Chen, "Dates of Some of the Tunhuang Lyrics," pp. 267–70.

48. Nine of the "song sequences in fixed forms" have been translated into French by Demiéville, in Jao Tsung-yi and Demiéville, *Airs de Touen-Houang*, pp. 100–7, 116–18, 120, 122–25.

49. Chen, "Dates of Some of the Tunhuang Lyrics," pp. 264–65.

50. Fujieda Akira, "The Tun-huang Manuscripts, A General Description," Part I, *Zinbun*, no. 9 (1966):25–26.

51. This text is reproduced in facsimile in Jao Tsung-yi and Demiéville, Plate VI. Demiéville identifies the Avenue of Heaven (*T'ien chieh*) as the main north-south thoroughfare of T'ang dynasty Lo-yang (p. 112).

CHAPTER THREE: THE RISE OF *Tz'u* POETRY BEFORE 755

1. The *Shih ching*, a collection of 305 songs of oral origin, was compiled in the sixth century B.C. For a complete English translation see Arthur Waley, *The Book of Songs* (1937; rpt. New York: Grove Press, 1960). For a study of the oral tradition of the *Book of Songs* see Wang Ching-hsien, *The Bell and the Drum*.

2. Liu Ta-chieh, *Chung-kuo wen-hsüeh fa-chan shih*, 3 vols. (1949; rpt. Shanghai: Chung-hua shu-chü, 1962), vol. 2, p. 539.

3. Jen Erh-pei, *Tun-huang ch'ü ch'u-t'an*, p. 268.

4. Chang Hsi-hou, p. 21.

5. P'eng Ting-ch'iu et al., eds., *Ch'üan T'ang shih* (Peking: Chung-hua shu-chü, 1960), ch. 889, p. 10041.

6. *Hua-chien chi*, 1.4b–5a.

7. *Tsun-ch'ien chi*, in *Ch'iang-ts'un ts'ung-shu*, ed. Chu Tsu-mou, vol. 1, p. 30b and p. 29b. These attributions were first identified by Wang Chung-min,

Tun-huang ch'ü-tzu-tz'u chi (1950; rpt. 1954), "Fan-li," remarks on P. 3994, p. 6.

8. The Tun-huang manuscripts provide the most complete extant source for the *Yün-yao chi* anthology, though some or all of its thirty poems have been reprinted in other collections (see chapter 1, note 12). A useful modern annotated edition is P'an Chung-kuei's *Tun-huang Yün-yao chi hsin-shu* (Taipei: Shih-men t'u-shu kung-ssu, 1977).

9. *Hua-chien chi*, "Hsü," 1b. My translation. For a complete annotated translation of the Preface see Fusek, *Among the Flowers*, pp. 33–36.

10. *Hua-chien chi*, "Hsü," 2a. My translation.

11. Kang-i Sun Chang, pp. 17–25.

12. Ibid., p. 18.

13. *Hua-chien chi*, "Hsü," 1a–1b. Translated by Fusek, *Among the Flowers*, pp. 34–35.

14. *Hua-chien chi*, "Hsü," 1b. My translation.

15. Hans H. Frankel, *The Flowering Plum and the Palace Lady* (New Haven: Yale University Press, 1976), p. 50.

16. Marilyn Jane Coutant Evans, "Popular Songs of the Southern Dynasties" (Ph.D. dissertation, Yale University, 1966), p. 18. For a more general discussion, see Hans H. Frankel, *"Yüeh-fu* Poetry," in *Studies in Chinese Literary Genres*, ed. Cyril Birch, especially pp. 94–96.

17. For a more complete list of such puns see Wang Yün-hsi, *Liu-ch'ao yüeh-fu yü min-ko* (Shanghai: Wen-i lien-ho ch'u-pan she, 1955), pp. 127–28.

18. Kuo Mao-ch'ien, ed., *Yüeh-fu shih-chi*, SPPY ed., vol. 457, 44.6b.

19. See ibid., 44.8a–45.3a.

20. Ibid., 44.5b.

21. See David T. Roy, "The Theme of the Neglected Wife in the Poetry of Ts'ao Chih," *Journal of Asian Studies*, 19, no. 1 (November 1959):25–31; and Jonathan Chaves, "The 'Neglected Lover' and 'Beautiful Woman' Imagery in Early Chinese Poetry," Part I of "The Tz'u Poetry of Wen T'ing-yün" (M.A. essay, Columbia University, 1966), pp. 4–34.

22. Sui Shu-sen, ed. *Ku-shih shih-chiu shou chi shih* (Peking: Chung-hua shu-chü, 1955), p. 27.

23. *Yüeh-fu shih-chi*, 44.7b.

24. See Anne Birrell's complete translation, *New Songs from a Jade Terrace* (London: Allen and Unwin, 1982). Birrell calculates that 502 of the 656 poems date from the beginning of the fifth to the middle of the sixth century (p. 3).

25. Hsü Ling, ed., *Yü-t'ai hsin-yung*, *SPPY*, vol. 459, "Hsü," p. 2a. For an annotated translation of the Preface, see James Robert Hightower, "Some Characteristics of Parallel Prose," in *Studia Serica: Bernhard Karlgren Dedicata* (Copenhagen: Ejnar Munksgaard, 1959), pp. 77–91; rpt. in *Studies in Chinese Literature*, ed. John L. Bishop (Cambridge, Mass.: Harvard University Press, 1965), pp. 125–35. On the interpretation of the confluent rivers, see p. 133, n. 5; and Stephen Owen, *The Poetry of the Early T'ang* (New Haven: Yale University Press, 1977), p. 16. The Preface is also translated in Birrell, *New Songs from a Jade Terrace*, pp. 339–43.

26. On the Liang court context, see John Marney, *Liang Chien-wen ti* (Boston: G. K. Hall, 1976), and Anne Birrell, *The Cult of Imperfection: Courtly Love Poetry in Early Medieval China* (forthcoming).

27. Ronald Miao gives an excellent presentation of the history and conventions of the genre in "Palace-Style Poetry: The Courtly Treatment of Glamour and Love," in *Studies in Chinese Poetry and Poetics*, vol. 1, ed. Ronald C. Miao (San Francisco: Chinese Materials Center, 1978), pp. 1–42.

28. *Yü-t'ai hsin-yung*, 10.13b.

29. Ibid., 10.15a.

30. Ibid., 7.7b.

31. Ibid., 8.10a–10b. This is one of three poems in response to Hsiao I, the Prince of Hsiang-tung.

32. Fusek, *Among the Flowers*, pp. 23–27. See also Miao, pp. 2–5, 33–34, and 39–42. The metaphor has ancient roots, of course, in the story of the banished official Ch'ü Yüan and his yearning to be reunited with his king.

33. For an overview of literary adaptations of the popular elements of the mulberry girl tradition in early Chinese poetry, see Jean-Pierre Diény, *Pastourelles et Magnanarelles* (Geneva and Paris: Librairie Droz, 1977).

34. "Letter of Admonition to the Duke of Tang-yang Ta-hsin" (*Chieh Tang-yang kung Ta-hsin shu*), in *Ch'üan Liang wen*, 11.1a, in Yen K'o-ch'ün, ed., *Ch'üan Shang-ku San-tai Ch'in Han San-kuo Liu-ch'ao wen* (Shanghai: Chung-hua shu-chü, 1958), vol. 3, p. 3010.

35. See L. Carrington Goodrich and Ch'ü T'ung-tsu, "Foreign Music at the Court of Sui Wen-ti," *JAOS*, 69, no. 3 (1949):148–49, for the seven types, the last of which they interpret as referring to the imported music of Japan.

36. An overview of the musical categories in the Sui and T'ang from the perspective of the Sung scholar Kuo Mao-ch'ien (1132-1198?) is given in *Yüeh-fu shih-chi*, 79.1a-1b.

37. This neat three-part division of types of music is articulated by another Sung scholar, Shen Kua (1030-1094), in *Meng ch'i pi-t'an* (*Ssu-pu ts'ung-k'an hsü-pien*, 2d ed., 1934, vol. 79, 5.9a). Unfortunately, the terms are not always distinguished so precisely, and there was probably considerable ambiguity and overlapping of categories in the High T'ang, while the new music was continually being introduced.

38. Tu Yu (735–812), *T'ung-tien* (facsimile of the 1538 Canton ed.; rpt. Taipei: I-wen yin-shu kuan, 1963), 146.1a-3a.

39. Baxter, "Metrical Origins of the Tz'u," p. 196; see also chapter 1.

40. Shen Kua, 5.9a.

41. Chen, "The Rise of the Tz'u, Reconsidered," p. 234.

42. "Yin-yüeh chih," part three, *Chiu T'ang shu*, ed. Liu Hsü, et al., *chüan* 30 (Peking: Chung-hua shu-chü, 1975), vol. 4, p. 1089.

43. Jen Erh-pei, *Tun-huang ch'ü ch'u-t'an*, pp. 197–200.

44. The most thorough study of the social and institutional history of T'ang music is Kishibe Shigeo, *Tōdai ongaku no rekishiteki kenkyū* (Tokyo: Tokyo University Press, 1960). He discusses Hsüan-tsung's music offices in vol. 1, espe-

cially pp. 21–28, and suggests 714 as the most likely date of the founding of the *chiao-fang* on p. 64 et passim. See also Kang-i Sun Chang, pp. 8–9.

45. See chapter 1, note 20.

46. Wang P'u, ed., *T'ang hui-yao* (Peking: Chung-hua shu-chü, 1955), vol. 2, ch. 33, especially pp. 609–10, 614–19. Shih-chuan Chen counts 242 tune titles, though Jen Erh-pei mentions the figure 253 (*Tun-huang ch'ü ch'u-t'an*, p. 222); Shih-chuan Chen calculates that only fifteen tune titles in the *Chiao-fang chi* and the *T'ang hui-yao* overlap, giving a total of 570 tunes known in the High T'ang period ("The Rise of the Tz'u, Reconsidered," p. 234).

47. Baxter gives a partial list of poems in irregular meters by the Sung poet Pao Chao (d. 466), as well as the transitional figure Shen Yüeh, and Liang dynasty poets Hsü Mien, T'ao Hung-ching, Wang Yün, Chang Shuai, Hsü Ling, Hsiao Yen and Hsiao Kang; he also discusses controversial attributions of *t'u* poems to Emperor Yang of the Sui dynasty ("Metrical Origins of the Tz'u," pp. 191–92).

48. *Yüeh-fu shih-chi*, 69.4a–4b.

49. Stephen Owen, *The Poetry of the Early T'ang* (New Haven: Yale University Press, 1977), p. 7. Owen's study is unusual in its acknowledgement of the debt of Early T'ang court poetry to the earlier traditions. It clearly demonstrates that the conventions of Early T'ang poetry "all had their origins in the court poetry of the Southern Dynasties" (ibid.).

50. Meng Ch'i, ed., *Pen-shih shih*, in *Ts'ung-shu chi-ch'eng*, vol. 2546, p. 15. For the text of the poem, see also Lin Ta-ch'un, ed., *T'ang Wu-tai tz'u* (Hong Kong: Shang-wu yin-shu kuan, 1963; rpt. 1976), p. 1. The "Hui-po yüeh" form is four six-character lines.

51. *T'ang Wu-tai tz'u*, p. 1. Four six-character lines.

52. Ibid., p. 2. Four six-character lines. See also Baxter, "Metrical Origins of the Tz'u," pp. 199–200; and Paul W. Kroll, "The Dancing Horses of T'ang," *T'oung Pao*, 67, nos. 3–5 (1981):240–68.

53. *T'ang Wu-tai tz'u*, p. 4. Four seven-character lines.

54. The *Tsun-ch'ien chi* is generally assumed to have been compiled about 900 (see Jen Erh-pei, *Tun-huang ch'ü ch'u-t'an*, p. 338 et passim), though this is doubted by others who place it as late as the Ming. A plausible compromise is suggested by Shizukuishi Kōichi, who believes the *Tsun-ch'ien chi* was compiled during the Sung ("Sonzenshū zakkō," in *Kangakkai zasshi*, 9, no. 1 [June, 1941]:97–106).

55. *Tsun-ch'ien chi*, in *Ch'iang-ts'un ts'ung shu*, vol. 1, p. 1a. The poem is also recorded in *Ch'üan T'ang shih*, vol. 12, ch. 889, p. 10040.

56. *Tsun-ch'ien chi*, vol. 1, pp. 3b–5b; *Ch'üan T'ang shih*, vol. 12, ch. 890, pp. 10050–52. Sixteen *tz'u* poems attributed to Li Po are translated by Elling O. Eide in his *Poems by Li Po* (Lexington, Kentucky: Anvil Press, 1983), pp. 29–38.

57. Kang-i Sun Chang, pp. 29–30.

58. Yang Hsien-yi, "Li Po yü 'P'u sa man,' " in *Ling-mo hsin-chien* (Shang-

hai: Chung-hua shu-chü, 1947), pp. 1–8. Jen Erh-pei concurs, and adds the date of 745 for Li Po's "Ch'ing-p'ing yüeh" (*Tun-huang ch'ü ch'u-t'an*, p. 222).

59. Chang Wan, " 'P'u sa man' chi ch'i hsiang-kuan chih chu wen-t'i," *Ta-lu tsa-chih*, 20, no. 1 (1960):19–24; 20, no. 2 (1960):15–17; 20, no. 3 (1960):27–32. A very similar "P'u sa man" poem, with six lines out of eight nearly identical to this version, though somewhat rearranged, is attributed to Wei Chuang, and the remaining two lines are similar to a couplet another "P'u sa man" by Wei Chuang, in *Hua-chien chi*, 2.7b.

60. *T'ang Wu-tai tz'u*, pp. 5–6 (7-7-5-5 5-5-5-5).

61. Not only were *yüeh-fu* and songs "the most widely anthologized of [Li Po's] works, they also occurred in anecdotes and comments about his poetry far in excess of their proportions [about one-fifth] in his present collection" (Stephen Owen, *The Great Age of Chinese Poetry: The High T'ang* [New Haven: Yale University Press, 1981], p. 119; see also p. 130).

62. Owen, *The Great Age of Chinese Poetry*, p. 128.

63. For the date of 922, see Jen Erh-pei, *Tun-huang ch'ü ch'u-t'an*, p. 204.

64. See ibid., p. 222.

65. Kuo P'u, ed., *Mu T'ien-tzu chuan*, SPPY, vol. 77, 3.1a. The "White Cloud Song" is the first of the legendary songs from antiquity mentioned at the beginning of the Preface to the *Hua-chien chi* to show the noble lineage of the popular song tradition (*Hua-chien chi*, "Hsü," 1a).

66. Kang-i Sun Chang, pp. 108–9. Chang compares the *man-tz'u* and *hsiao-ling* forms on pp. 110–12.

67. See, for example, Chang Hsi-hou, pp. 23–24; and Cheng Tu [Cheng Chen-to], *Chung-kuo su-wen hsüeh shih* (1954; rpt. Taipei: Shang-wu yin-shu kuan, n.d.), vol. 1, p. 129.

68. Kang-i Sun Chang gives examples of the common use of the term *yün-yao* to refer to casual *tz'u* compositions by literati (p. 16), and also argues convincingly that in the ninth through eleventh centuries literati were actively writing *man-tz'u* derived from the *Yün-yao chi* (p. 123).

69. *Ch'üan T'ang shih*, vol. 10, ch. 641, p. 7348.

70. A similar social situation is presented in the other *Yün-yao chi* poem to the same tune, #020, translated by Kang-i Sun Chang, "Appendix II," p. 214. Kang-i Sung Chang translates one other *Yün-yao chi* poem, #002 (p. 213). The latter is also translated by Demiéville, along with the first poem of the *Yün-yao chi*, #001 (Jao Tsung-yi and Demiéville, *Airs de Touen-houang*, pp. 115–16).

CHAPTER FOUR: POPULAR *Tz'u* POETRY IN THE ENTERTAINMENT
QUARTERS AFTER 755

1. See my *Wang Wei* (Boston: G. K. Hall, 1981), especially chapter two; and Stephen Owen, *The Great Age of Chinese Poetry*.

2. For a discussion in formal terms of the emergence of the *tz'u* as a "countergenre" to the *shih*, see Kang-i Sun Chang, pp. 4–5.

3. Baxter basically follows this tradition, as articulated by Hu Shih. See also, for example, Liang Ch'i-hsün, *Tz'u-hsüeh* (1932; rpt. Hong Kong: Hui-wen ko shu-tien, n.d.), pp. 9b–10a; and Hu Yün-i, *Chung-kuo tz'u shih* (Hong Kong: I-wen ch'u-pan she [1970?]), especially pp. 6–20.

4. See Kishibe Shigeo, pp. 82–106.

5. Robert H. Van Gulik, *Sexual Life in Ancient China* (Leiden: E. J. Brill, 1974), pp. 27–28. For a clear and concise overview, see Sue Gronewold, *Beautiful Merchandise: Prostitution in China 1860–1936*, in *Women and History*, no. 1 (New York: Haworth Press, 1982), pp. 4–5.

6. See Yao Hsin-nung, "When Sing-song Girls Were Muses," *T'ien Hsia Monthly*, 4 (April 1935):476.

7. This list of four groups is derived from Robert des Rotours, *Courtisanes Chinoises à la fin des T'ang* (Paris: Presses Universitaires de France, 1968), "Introduction," pp. 11–14.

8. *Pen-shih shih*, p. 11.

9. For a discussion of the question of authorship, see Des Rotours, "Introduction," pp. 16–21.

10. On the dating of the composition of the *Pei-li chih*, see ibid., pp. 15–16.

11. Ibid., pp. 21–24.

12. Sun Ch'i, *Sun Nei-Han Pei-li chih*, TSCC, vol. 2733, "Hsü," p. 1.

13. Van Gulik, p. 178.

14. Ibid., p. 181.

15. See Yao Hsin-nung, p. 474.

16. Sun Ch'i, "Hsü," p. 1.

17. Ibid.

18. The text is identical in the two versions, P. 2809 and P. 3911; for facsimile reproductions, see Jao Tsung-yi and Demiéville, Plates XX and XXII–XXIII.

19. About fifty of Yü Hsüan-chi's poems are included in *Ch'üan T'ang shih*, ch. 803, pp. 9047–56.

20. See Arthur Waley, *The Life and Times of Po Chü-i (772–846 A.D.)* (London: Allen and Unwin, 1949), pp. 196–97.

21. See *Ch'üan T'ang shih*, ch. 803, pp. 9035–46.

22. Ibid., ch. 356, pp. 3996–97.

23. Po Hsing-chien, "Li Wa chuan," in *T'ang-jen ch'uan-ch'i hsiao-shuo*, Ssu-pu ts'ung-k'an (rpt. Taipei: Shih-chieh shu-chü, 1972), pp. 100–7.

24. Tuan An-chieh, ed., *Yüeh-fu tsa-lu*, in Wu Kuan, ed., *Ku-chin i-shih*, vol. 29, p. 6b. Also cited in Kishibe Shigeo, vol. 1, pp. 357–58. The date of the *Yüeh-fu tsa-lu* is uncertain, and various points during the ninth century have been suggested. Kishibe Shigeo proposes that it was compiled during the *t'ai-chung* era (849-859) (vol. 2, p. 426), although most Chinese editions claim a date two or

three decades later. See Martin Gimm, *Das Yüeh-fu tsa-lu des Tuan An-chieh: Studien zur Geschichte von Musik, Schauspiel und Tanz in der T'ang-Dynastie* (Wiesbaden: Otto Harrassowitz, 1966), p. 58.

25. *Yüeh-fu tsa-lu*, p. 7a.

26. Ibid., pp. 6b–7a.

27. See *Yüeh-fu shih-chi*, ch. 28; and Joseph R. Allen, III, "Early Chinese Narrative Poetry: The Definition of a Tradition," (Ph.D. dissertation, University of Washington, 1982), especially chapter 3.

28. Julia Kristeva, *Semiotikè: Recherches pour une sémanalyse* (Paris: Editions du Seuil, 1969), p. 146.

29. The short fragment, P. 3319, is reproduced in Jao Tsung-yi and Demiéville, Plate XXVII. For P. 3911 see Plate XXII, and for P. 2809 see Plate XIX. Demiéville also translates the four stanzas as a single poem, or a single sequence of four poems (pp. 114–15). Wang Chung-min, on the other hand, separates the two pairs as in the original manuscripts (*Tun-huang ch'ü-tzu-tz'u chi*, p. 29).

30. Jao Tsung-yi and Demiéville, p. 59.

31. See Waley, *Stories and Ballads from Tun-huang*, pp. 145–49.

32. For a more thorough analysis, see Ch'iu-kuei Wang, "The Formation of the Early Versions of the Meng Chiang-nü Story," *Tamkang Review*, 9, no. 2 (Winter 1978), 111–40.

33. Jen Erh-pei, *Tun-huang ch'ü ch'u-t'an*, p. 304.

34.. Ibid., pp. 302–3.

35. See Finnegan, pp. 116–18; and Frankel, "*Yüeh-fu* Poetry," pp. 77, 82, 91–93.

36. Jen Erh-pei, *Tun-huang ch'ü ch'u-t'an*, p. 462.

37. "My neighbor to the east had a daughter . . ." is familiar from ballads such as the anonymous *K'ung-ch'üeh tung-nan fei* ("Southeast Fly the Peacock"), and the *Ch'in-fu yin* ("The Lament of the Lady of Ch'in") by Wei Chuang, preserved in the Tun-huang manuscripts. The trope of the nobleman so startled by the sight of a beautiful woman that he drops his whip also occurs ubiquitously; in the Tun-huang *tz'u*, see, for example, #037.

38. Jen Erh-pei, *Tun-huang ch'ü ch'u-t'an*, p. 462; see also p. 348. Jen dates this pair of songs in the early eighth century due to an apparent reference to it in a poem by Ts'en Shen (715-770) (p. 462).

39. *T'ang Wu-tai tz'u*, pp. 20–21.

40. See Chang Chung-chiang, *Li-tai chi-nü yü shih-ko* (T'ao-yüan, Taiwan: Chih-ch'üan ch'u-pan she, 1966), p. 21.

CHAPTER FIVE: T'ANG *Tz'u* POETRY BY LITERATI AFTER 755

1. Hsüeh Yung-jo, ed. *Chi-i chi*, TSCC, vol. 2698, ch. 2, pp. 8–9.

2. Owen, *The Great Age of Chinese Poetry*, p. 166.

3. *T'ang Wu-tai tz'u*, p. 9.

4. Ibid., p. 12; see also *Ch'üan T'ang shih*, ch. 308, p. 3491 and ch. 890, p. 10053.

5. *T'ang Wu-tai tz'u*, pp. 13–14; this is the only poem by Chang Sung-ling included in the *Ch'üan T'ang shih* (ch. 308, p. 3492 and ch. 809, p. 10053).

6. Baxter claims that Liu Yü-hsi's response to Po Chü-yi's *tz'u* to the tune "Yi Chiang-nan," in the early ninth century, is "the first avowed instance of the practice of *t'ien tz'u*" (filling in words to a given tune pattern, "Metrical Origins of the *Tz'u*," p. 219), but as we have seen other evidence shows that the practice did not begin in the ninth century but must date back at least to the High T'ang (see chapter 3).

7. See William H. Nienhauser, Jr., "The Imperial Presence in the Palace Poems of Wang Chien (c. A.D. 768-833)," *Tamkang Review*, 8, no. 1 (April 1977):111–22.

8. *T'ang Wu-tai tz'u*, p. 18.

9. Chang Chung-chiang, p. 23.

10. *T'ang Wu-tai tz'u*, pp. 19–20.

11. Ibid., pp. 25–26; and *Ch'üan T'ang shih*, ch. 365, p. 4112.

12. Arthur Waley, *The Life and Times of Po Chü-i*, p. 167.

13. *T'ang Wu-tai tz'u*, p. 26; *Ch'üan T'ang shih*, ch. 365, p. 4112.

14. *T'ang Wu-tai tz'u*, p. 29.

15. Ibid., p. 22.

16. Ibid., pp. 31–32.

17. Po Chü-yi's references to Wu Erh-niang's song in various places in his works are listed by Baxter, "The Metrical Origins of the Tz'u," p. 216, n. 77.

18. *T'ang Wu-tai tz'u*, p. 37.

19. See Lois Fusek, "The 'Kao-T'ang Fu,' " *Monumenta Serica*, 30 (1972–73):392–425.

20. *T'ang Wu-tai tz'u*, p. 31.

21. Kang-i Sun Chang, pp. 26–28.

22. Ibid., pp. 30–32.

23. See Kang-i Sun Chang, pp. 27–32, who perceptively shows how a poet's way of handling the transition from the first to the second stanza "reflects not only his stylistic predilections but also . . . his personal relationship to the world in general" (pp. 31–32).

24. Liu Hsü, et al., ed., *Chiu T'ang shu, chüan* 190 *hsia, lieh-chüan* 140 *hsia* (Peking: Chung-hua shu-chü, 1975), vol. 15, pp. 5078–79.

25. Wang Ting-pao, ed., *T'ang Chih-yen* (Shanghai: Ku-tien wen-hsüeh ch'u-pan she, 1957), p. 121.

26. *Hua-chien chi*, 2.3a.

27. Ibid., 2.4a.

28. For another example of a single-stanza *tz'u* by Wen T'ing-yün compared with a Tun-huang song, see Kang-i Sun Chang, pp. 60–61.

29. This aspect of reader (or audience) response is discussed in relation to narrative prose by Wolfgang Iser, in "Indeterminacy and the Reader's Response

in Prose Fiction," in *Aspects of Narrative,* ed. J. Hillis Miller (New York: Columbia University Press, 1971), pp. 1–45.

30. *Hua-chien chi,* 1.4b.

31. Kang-i Sun Chang, pp. 37–39.

32. Fusek, *Among the Flowers,* "Introduction," p. 16.

33. Yü P'ing-po, *Tu tz'u ou-te* (Taipei: K'ai-ming shu-tien, 1957), p. 15.

34. Chaves, pp. 44 and 46.

35. *Hua-chien chi,* 1.3b.

36. Kang-i Sun Chang, p. 54.

37. As does Kang-i Sun Chang, pp. 54–55.

38. Chaves, p. 38.

39. The most complete study of Wei Chuang in English is John Timothy Wixted's *The Song-Poetry of Wei Chuang (836–910 A.D.)* (Tempe, Arizona: Center for Asian Studies, Arizona State University, Occasional Paper No. 12, 1979), which includes a biographical introduction.

40. Wang Kuo-wei, *Jen-chien tz'u-hua,* ed. Hsü T'iao-fu (Peking: Jen-min wen-hsüch ch'u-pan she, 1960), p. 247. For an annotated translation, see Adele Austin Rickett, *Wang Kuo-wei's Jen-chien Tz'u-hua: A Study in Chinese Literary Criticism* (Hong Kong: Hong Kong University Press, 1977), p. 88.

41. *Hua-chien chi,* 2.7b.

42. Ibid., 3.4a–4b.

43. Wu Jen-ch'en, ed., *Shih-kuo ch'un-ch'iu* (facsimile reproduction; Taipei: Kuo-kuang shu-tien, 1962), 40.5b.

44. *Hua-chien chi,* 3.2a.

45. Ibid., 3.2a.

46. Kang-i Sun Chang, p. 49 and passim.

47. *Hua-chien chi,* 3.6b–7a.

48. Ibid., 1.2a.

49. Ibid., 2.7b.

50. Kang-i Sun Chang not only emphasizes the general tendency toward narrative presentation in Wei Chuang's style, but also analyzes his series of five poems to the "P'u sa man" tune—of which this is one—as an extended narrative sequence (pp. 45–49).

51. On Five Dynasties and Northern Sung *tz'u* poetry see Kang-i Sun Chang, pp. 63–209; and James J. Y. Liu, *Major Lyricists of the Northern Sung.*

52. "Chao-tsung pen-chi," *Chiu T'ang shu, chüan* 20, vol. 3, p. 751 (also cited in Kishibe Shigeo, vol. 1, p. 359).

53. Jen Erh-pei cites slight variations from the Tun-huang manuscript version of one of these poems in eight other collections, including the *Hsin Wu-tai shih,* the *Meng-ch'i pi-t'an,* and the *T'ang-shih chi-shih,* as well as the *Ch'üan T'ang shih (Tun-huang ch'ü ch'u-t'an,* p. 405).

54. See Robert M. Somers, "The End of the T'ang," in *The Cambridge History of China,* vol. 3, *Sui and T'ang China, 589–906,* Part I, ed. Denis Twitchett (New York: Cambridge University Press, 1979), pp. 776–79.

55. "Chao-tsung pen-chi," *Chiu T'ang shu, chüan* 20, vol. 3, p. 762.

56. Jen Erh-pei believes the five poems date from 897 (*Tun-huang ch'ü ch'u-t'an*, p. 256).

57. Jen Erh-pei indicates the literary shortcomings of #050 and identifies its author as a workman assigned to the construction of the Emperor's temporary palace in Hua-chou in *Tun-huang ch'ü chiao-lu*, p. 38.

58. Ibid., p. 38.

59. Jen Erh-pei argues that this poem was written by people in the palace on the night of the Emperor's return in 898 (*Tun-huang ch'ü ch'u-t'an*, p. 256). The second poem using similar diction which Jen identifies as also having been written in 898 is #045 (ibid.).

60. See Finnegan, pp. 162–63.

61. A version of this perhaps sentimentalized story is recounted in Alan Ayling and Duncan Mackintosh, trs., *A Collection of Chinese Lyrics* (New York: Chelsea House, 1965), p. 29.

CHAPTER SIX: CONCLUSIONS

1. See Finnegan, especially pp. 17–28.
2. *Hua-chien chi*, 2.6a–6b.
3. Ibid., 7.6b.
4. Ibid., 1.3a.

BIBLIOGRAPHY

Note: See abbreviations list on p. 155.

Allen, Joseph R., III. "Early Chinese Narrative Poetry: The Definition of a Tradition." Ph.D. dissertation, University of Washington, 1982.

Aoki Masaru 青木正兒. "Shikaku no chōtanku no hattatsu no gen'in ni tsuite" 詞格の長短句の發達の原因に就て. In his *Shina bungei ronsō* 支那文芸論薮. Tokyo, 1923. Pp. 67–85.

Ayling, Alan, and Duncan Mackintosh. *A Collection of Chinese Lyrics*. New York: Chelsea House, 1965.

Baxter, Glen W. *Index to the Imperial Register of Tz'u Prosody (Ch'ing-ting tz'u-p'u)*. Cambridge, Mass.: Harvard University Press, 1956.

—— 'Metrical Origins of the *Tz'u*." *HJAS*, 16 (1953): 108–45. Rpt. in *Studies in Chinese Literature*, ed. John L. Bishop. Cambridge, Mass.: Harvard University Press, 1965. Pp. 186–225.

Benson, Larry D. "The Literary Character of Anglo-Saxon Formulaic Poetry." *Publications of the Modern Language Association*, 81 (1966): 334–41.

Bibliothèque Nationale Département des Manuscrits. *Catalogue des Manuscrits Chinois de Touen-Houang: Fonds Pelliot Chinois*. Paris: Bibliothèque Nationale, 1970.

Birrell, Anne. *The Cult of Imperfection: Courtly Love Poetry in Early Medieval China*. Forthcoming.

—— *New Songs from a Jade Terrace: An Anthology of Early Chinese Love Poetry, Translated with Annotations and an Introduction.* London: Allen and Unwin, 1982.

Bynum, David E. "The Bell, the Drum, Milman Parry and the Time Machine." *Chinese Literature: Essays, Articles, Reviews*, 1, no. 2 (July 1979): 241–53.

Chang Chung-chiang 張忠江. *Li-tai chi-nü yü shih-ko* 歷代妓女與詩歌. T'ao-yüan, Taiwan: Chih-ch'üan ch'u-pan she, 1966.

Chang Hsi-hou 張錫厚. *Tun-huang wen-hsüeh* 敦煌文學. Shanghai: Ku-chi ch'u-pan she, 1980.

Chang, Kang-i Sun. *The Evolution of Chinese "Tz'u" Poetry: From Late T'ang to Northern Sung.* Princeton: Princeton University Press, 1982.

Chang Wan 張琬 (pseud.). "P'u sa man chi ch'i hsiang-kuan chih chu wen-t'i" 菩薩蠻及其相關之諸問題. *Ta-lu tsa-chih*, 20, no. 1 (1960): 19–24; 20, no. 2 (1960): 15–17; 20, no. 3 (1960): 27–32.

Chao Ch'ung-tso 趙崇祚, ed. *Hua-chien chi* 花間集. *SPPY*, vol. 465.

Chaves, Jonathan. 'The Tz'u Poetry of Wen T'ing-yün." M.A. Essay, Columbia University, 1966.

Chen Shih-chuan. "Dates of Some of the Tunhuang Lyrics." *JAOS*, 88, no. 2 (April-June 1968): 261–70.

—— "The Rise of the Tz'u, Reconsidered." *JAOS*, 90, no. 2 (April-June 1970): 232–42.

Ch'en Yüan 陳垣. *Tun-huang chieh-yü lu* 敦煌劫餘錄. Peking, 1931.

Cheng Tu 鄭篤. *Chung-kuo su-wen-hsüeh shih.* 中國俗文學史. 1954; rpt. Taipei: Shang-wu yin-shu kuan, n.d. 3 vols.

Chu Tsu-mou 朱祖謀 [Hsiao-tsang 孝藏], ed. *Ch'iang-ts'un ts'ung-shu* 彊村叢書. Preface 1917; Shanghai: n.p., 1922.

Dante Alighieri. *La Commedia secondo l'antica vulgata.* Ed. by Giorgio Petrocchi. 4 vols. Milano: Arnoldo Mondadori Editore, 1966.

Demiéville, Paul. "Manuscrits de Touen-houang à Leningrad." *T'oung Pao*, 51, no. 4 (1964): 355–76.

Des Rotours, Robert. *Courtisanes Chinoises à la fin des T'ang, entre circa 789 et le 8 janvier 881.* Translation of *Pei-li Tche (Anecdotes du quartier du Nor) par Souen K'i.* Paris: Presses Universitaires de France, 1968.

Diény, Jean-Pierre. *Pastourelles et Magnanarelles: Essai sur un thème littéraire chinois.* Geneva and Paris: Librairie Droz, 1977.

Eide, Elling O. *Poems by Li Po*. Lexington, Kentucky: Anvil Press, 1983.

Eoyang, Eugene. "Word of Mouth: Oral Story Telling in the Pien-wen." Ph.D. dissertation, Indiana University, 1971.

Evans, Marilyn Jane Coutant. "Popular Songs of the Southern Dynasties: A Study in Chinese Poetic Style." Ph.D. dissertation, Yale University, 1966.

Finnegan, Ruth. *Oral Poetry: Its Nature, Significance, and Social Context*. New York: Cambridge University Press, 1977.

Frankel, Hans H. *The Flowering Plum and the Palace Lady: Interpretations of Chinese Poetry*. New Haven: Yale University Press, 1976.

—— "*Yüeh-fu* Poetry." In *Studies in Chinese Literary Genres*, ed. Cyril Birch. Berkeley: University of California Press, 1974. Pp. 69–107.

Freedman, Maurice. "On the Sociological Study of Chinese Religion." In *Religion and Ritual in Chinese Society*, ed. Arthur P. Wolf. Stanford: Stanford University Press, 1974. Pp. 19–41.

Fujieda Akira. "The Tun-huang Manuscripts." In *Essays on the Sources for Chinese History*, ed. Donald D. Leslie, Colin Mackerras, and Wang Gungwu. Columbia, South Carolina: University of South Carolina Press, 1975. Pp. 120–28.

—— "The Tunhuang Manuscripts, A General Description." Part I, *Zinbun*, no. 9 (1966): 1–32; Part II, *Zinbun*, no. 10 (1969): 17–39.

Fusek, Lois. *Among the Flowers: The "Hua-chien chi."* New York: Columbia University Press, 1982.

—— "The 'Kao-T'ang Fu.'" *Monumenta Serica*, 30 (1972–73): 392–425.

Giles, Lionel. "Dated Chinese Mss. in the Stein Collection." *Bulletin of the School of African and Oriental Studies*, 7 (1935): 809–35; 8 (1936): 1–26; 9 (1937): 1–25; 10 (1940): 317–34; and 11 (1943): 149–73.

—— *Descriptive Catalogue of the Chinese Manuscripts from Tunhuang in the British Museum*. London: British Museum, 1957.

—— *Six Centuries at Tunhuang: A Short Account of the Stein Collection of Chinese Mss. in the British Museum*. London: The China Society, 1944.

Gimm, Martin. *Das Yüeh-fu tsa-lu des Tuan An-chieh: Studien zur Geshichte von Musik, Schauspiel und Tanz in der T'ang-Dynastie*. Wiesbaden: Otto Harrassowitz, 1966.

Goodrich, L. Carrington, and Ch'ü T'ung-tsu. "Foreign Music at the Court of Sui Wen-ti." *JAOS*, 69, no. 3 (1949): 148–49.

Gronewold, Sue. *Beautiful Merchandise: Prostitution in China 1860–1936*. In *Women and History*, no. 1. New York: Haworth Press, 1982.

Hanan, Patrick. "The Early Chinese Short Story: A Critical Theory in Outline." In *Studies in Chinese Literary Genres*, ed. Cyril Birch. Berkeley: University of California Press, 1974. Pp. 299–338.

Hightower, James Robert. "Some Characteristics of Parallel Prose." In *Studia Serica: Bernhard Karlgren Dedicata*. Copenhagen: Ejnar Munksgaard, 1959. Pp. 77–91. Rpt. in *Studies in Chinese Literature*, ed. John L. Bishop. Cambridge, Mass.: Harvard University Press, 1965. Pp. 107–39.

Hopkirk, Peter. *Foreign Devils on the Silk Road: The Search for the Lost Cities and Treasures of Chinese Central Asia*. London: John Murray, 1980.

Hsiao Kang 蕭綱. "Letter of Admonition to the Duke of Tang-yang Ta-hsin" (*Chieh Tang-yang kung Ta-hsin shu* 誡當陽公大心書). In *Ch'üan Liang wen* 全梁文, 11.1a. In *Ch'üan Shang-ku San-tai Ch'in Han San-kuo Liu-ch'ao wen* 全上古三代秦漢三國六朝文, ed. Yen K'o-ch'ün 嚴可均. Shanghai: Chung-hua shu-chü, 1958. 4 vols. Vol. 3, p. 3010.

Hsiao Kuo-chün 蕭國鈞. *T'ang Wu-tai tz'u chih ti-yü fa-chan* 唐五代詞之地域發展. Hong Kong: Tz'u ch'ü hsüeh-hui, 1970.

Hsü Ling 徐陵, ed. *Yü-t'ai hsin-yung* 玉臺新詠. *SPPY*, vol. 459.

Hsüeh Yung-jo 薛用弱, ed. *Chi-i chi* 集異記. *TSCC*, vol. 2698.

Hu Shih 胡適. "Tz'u ti ch'i-yüan" 詞的起源. In Appendix to his *Tz'u hsüan* 詞選. Shanghai: 1927; rpt. Shang-wu yin-shu kuan, 1930.

Hu Yün-i 胡雲翼. *Chung-kuo tz'u-shih* 中國詞史. Hong Kong: I-wen ch'u-pan she [1970?].

Iser, Wolfgang. "Indeterminacy and the Reader's Response in Prose Fiction." In *Aspects of Narrative*, ed. J. Hillis Miller. New York: Columbia University Press, 1971. Pp. 1–45.

Jao Tsung-yi 饒宗頤 and Paul Demiéville. *Airs de Touen-houang (Touen-houang k'iu* 敦煌曲). Paris: Editions du Centre National de la Recherche Scientifique, 1971.

Jen Erh-pei 任二北 [Pan-t'ang 半塘, pseudonyms of Jen Na 訥], ed. *Chiao-fang chi chien-ting* 教坊記箋訂. Shanghai: Chung-hua shu-chü, 1962.

—— *Tun-huang ch'ü chiao-lu* 敦煌曲校錄. Shanghai: Wen-i lien-ho ch'u-pan she, 1955.

—— *Tun-huang ch'ü ch'u-t'an* 敦煌曲初探. Shanghai: Wen-i lien-ho ch'u-pan she, 1954.

Johnson, David. "Chinese Popular Literature and Its Contexts." *Chinese Literature: Essays, Articles, Reviews*, 3, no. 2 (July 1981):225–33.

—— "The Wu Tzu-hsü *Pien-wen* and Its Sources." *HJAS*, 40, no. 1 (June 1980):93–156; and 40, no. 2 (December 1980):465–505.

Kanda Kiichirō 神田喜一郎. *Tonkō gaku gojūnen* 敦煌學五十年. Tokyo: Nigen-sha, 1960.

Kantōchō hakubutsukan 關東廳博物館. "Ōtani ke shuppin mokuroku" 大谷家出品目錄. In *Shin Saiiki ki*, vol. 2. Kyoto, 1937.

Kishibe Shigeo 岸辺成雄. *Tōdai ongaku no rekishiteki kenkyū* 唐代音楽の歴史的研究. Tokyo: Tokyo University Press, 1960. 2 vols.

Kristeva, Julia, *Semiotikè: Recherches pour une sémanalyse* Paris: Editions du Seuil, 1969.

Kroll, Paul W. "The Dancing Horses of T'ang." *T'oung Pao*, 67, nos. 3–5 (1981), pp. 240–68.

Kuo Mao-ch'ien 郭茂倩, ed. *Yüeh-fu shih chi* 樂府詩集. *SPPY*, vols. 456–458.

Kuo P'u 郭璞 ed. *Mu T'ien-tzu chuan* 穆天子傳. *SPPY*, vol. 77.

Leslie, R. F., ed. *Three Old English Elegies: The Wife's Lament, The Husband's Message, The Ruin*. Manchester: Manchester University Press, 1961.

Liang Ch'i-hsün 梁啓勳. *Tz'u hsüeh* 詞學. 1932; rpt. Hong Kong: Hui-wen ko shu tien, n.d.

Lin Mei-i 林玫儀. "Lun Tun-huang ch'ü ti she-hui hsing" 論敦煌曲的社會性. *Wen-hsüeh p'ing-lun*, 2 (1976):107–44.

Lin Ta-ch'un 林大椿, ed. *T'ang Wu-tai tz'u* 唐五代詞. Hong Kong: Shang-wu yin-shu kuan, 1963, rpt. 1976.

Liu Fu 劉復. *Tun-huang to-so* 敦煌掇瑣. Preface 1925. N.p.: Kuo-li chung-yang yen-chiu li-shih yü-yen yen-chiu-suo chuan-k'an, no. 2, 1931.

Liu Hsü 劉昫, et al., ed. *Chiu T'ang shu* 舊唐書. Peking: Chung-hua shu-chü, 1975.

Liu, James J. Y. *Major Lyricists of the Northern Sung, A.D. 960–1126*. Princeton: Princeton University Press, 1974.

Liu Ta-chieh 劉大杰. Chung-kuo wen-hsüeh fa-chan shih 中國文學發展史. Shanghai: Chung-hua shu-chü, 1949. 2 vols.

Lo Chen-yü 羅振玉. *Tun-huang ling-shih* 敦煌零拾. 1924; rpt. in *Lo Hsüeh-t'ang hsien-sheng ch'üan-chi* 羅雪堂先生全集, series 3, vol. 7. Taipei: Wen-hua ch'u-pan kung-ssu, 1968.

Lord, Albert B. "Homer as Oral Poet." *Harvard Studies in Classical Philology*, 72 (1968): 1–46.

—— *A Singer of Tales*. Cambridge, Mass.: Harvard University Press, 1960.

Ma Shih-ch'ang 馬世長. "Kuan-yü Tun-huang ts'ang-ching tung te chi-ko wen-t'i" 關于敦煌藏經洞的幾個問題. *Wen-wu*, 1978, no. 12, pp. 21–33.

Mair, Victor H. "Lay Students and the Making of Written Vernacular Narrative: an Inventory of Tun-huang Manuscripts." *Chinoperl Papers*, 10 (1981): 5–96.

—— *Tun-huang Popular Narratives*. Cambridge, England: Cambridge University Press, 1983.

Marney, John. *Liang Chien-wen ti*. Boston: G. K. Hall, 1976.

Meng Ch'i 孟啓, ed. *Pen-shih shih* 本事詩. *TSCC*, vol. 2546. Pp. 1–16.

Miao, Ronald C. "Palace-Style Poetry: The Courtly Treatment of Glamour and Love." In *Studies in Chinese Poetry and Poetics*, vol. 1. Ed. by Ronald C. Miao. San Francisco: Chinese Materials Center, 1978. Pp. 1–42.

Mirsky, Jeannette, *Sir Aurel Stein: Archaeological Explorer*. Chicago: University of Chicago Press, 1977.

Mission Pelliot. *Les Grottes de Touen-Houang*. Paris, 1920–1924. 6 vols.

Muellner, Leonard Charles. *The Meaning of Homeric EYXOMAI Through Its Formulas*. Innsbruck: Inst. f. Sprachwissenschaft d. Univ. Innsbruck, 1976.

Nagy, Gregory. *The Best of the Achaeans: Concepts of the Hero in Archaic Greek Poetry*. Baltimore: Johns Hopkins University Press, 1979.

Nienhauser, William H., Jr. "The Imperial Presence in the Palace Poems of Wang Chien (c. A.D. 768–833)." *Tamkang Review*, 8, no. 1 (April 1977): 111–22.

Owen, Stephen. *The Great Age of Chinese Poetry: The High T'ang*. New Haven: Yale University Press, 1981.

—— *The Poetry of the Early T'ang.* New Haven: Yale University Press, 1977.

P'an Chung-kuei 潘重規. *Tun-huang Yün-yao chi hsin-shu* 敦煌雲謠集新書. Taipei: Shih-men t'u-shu kung-ssu, 1977.

P'eng Ting-ch'iu 彭定求, et al., eds. *Ch'üan T'ang shih* 全唐詩. Peking: Chung-hua shu-chü, 1960. 12 vols.

Picken, L. E. R. "Secular Chinese Songs of the Twelfth Century." *Studia Musicologica Academiae Scientiarum Hungaricae*, 8 (1966): 125–72.

—— "Twelve Ritual Melodies of the T'ang Dynasty." In *Studia Memoriae Bela Bartók Sacra.* Budapest, 1956. Pp. 147–73.

Pien, Rulan Chao. *Sonq Dynasty Musical Sources and their Interpretation.* Cambridge, Mass.: Harvard University Press, 1967.

Po Hsing-chien 白行簡. "Li Wa chuan" 李娃傳. In *T'ang-jen ch'uan-ch'i hsiao-shuo* 唐人傳奇小說. Ssu-pu ts'ung-kan ed. Rpt. Taipei: Shih-chieh shu-chü, 1972. Pp. 100–7.

Rickett, Adele Austin. *Wang Kuo-wei's Jen-chien Tz'u-hua: A Study in Chinese Literary Criticism.* Hong Kong: Hong Kong University Press, 1977.

Roy, David. "The Theme of the Neglected Wife in the Poetry of Ts'ao Chih." *Journal of Asian Studies*, 29, no. 1 (November 1959): 25–31.

Sacks, Richard. *The Traditional Phrase in Homer: Two Studies.* Forthcoming.

Shen Kua 沈括. *Meng ch'i pi-t'an* 夢溪筆談. Ed. Chang Yüan-chi 張元濟. *Ssu-pu ts'ung-k'an hsü-pien*, 2nd ed., 1934, vol. 79.

Shizukuishi Kōichi 雫石皓一. "Sonzenshū zakkō" 尊前集雜考. In *Kangakkai zasshi* 漢學會雜誌, 9, no. 1 (June 1941): 97–106.

Somers, Robert M. "The End of the T'ang." In *The Cambridge History of China*, vol. 3, *Sui and T'ang China, 589–906*, Part I. Ed. Denis Twitchett. New York: Cambridge University Press, 1979.

Stein, M. Aurel. *Ruins of Desert Cathay: Personal Narrative of Explorations in Central Asia and Westernmost China.* London: MacMillan, 1912. 2 vols.

—— *Serindia, Detailed Report of Explorations in Central Asia and Westernmost China.* Oxford: Clarendon Press, 1921.

Strassberg, Richard E. "Buddhist Storytelling Texts from Tunhuang." *Chinoperl Papers*, 8 (1978): 39–99.

Sui Shu-sen 隋樹森, ed. *Ku-shih shih-chiu shou chi-shih* 古詩十九首集釋. Peking: Chung-hua shu-chü, 1955.

Sun Ch'i 孫棨. *Sun Nei-Han Pei-li chih* 孫內翰北里誌. *TSCC*, vol. 2733.

Suzuki Torao 鈴木虎雄. "Shigen" 詞源. In his *Shina bungaku kenkyū* 支那文學研究. Kyoto, 1922. Pp. 259–78.

Ts'ui Ling-ch'in 崔令欽, ed. *Chiao-fang chi* 教坊記. In *Ku-chin i-shih* 古今逸史, ed. Wu Kuan 吳琯. Shanghai: Shang-wu yin-shu kuan, 1937, vol. 29, pp. 1a–10a.

Tu Yu 杜佑. *T'ung-tien* 通典. Facsimile of 1538 Canton ed.; rpt. Taipei: I-wen yin-shu kuan, 1963.

Tuan An-chieh 段安節, ed. *Yüeh-fu tsa-lu* 樂府雜錄. In *Ku-chin i-shih*, ed. by Wu Kuan. Shanghai: Shang-wu yin-shu kuan, 1937. Vol. 29.

Twitchett, Denis. Review of Arthur Waley's *Ballads and Stories from Tun-huang*. *Bulletin of the School of Oriental Studies*, 214, no. 2 (1961): 375–76.

Van Gulik, Robert H. *Sexual Life in Ancient China: A Preliminary Survey of Chinese Sex and Society from ca. 1500 B.C. till 1644 A.D.* Leiden: E. J. Brill, 1974.

Vorob'eva-Desiatovskaia, M., et al. *Opisanie Kitaiskikh rukopisei Dun'khuanskogo fonda Instituta naradov Azii.* Moscow: Izd-vo vostoch-noy lut-ry, 1963, 1966, 2 vols.

Wagner, Marsha L. *Wang Wei.* Boston: G. K. Hall, 1981.

Waley, Arthur. *Ballads and Stories from Tun-huang.* London: Allen and Unwin, 1960.

—— *The Book of Songs.* 1937; rpt. New York: Grove Press, 1960.

—— *The Life and Times of Po Chü-i (772–846 A.D.).* London: Allen and Unwin, 1949.

Wan Shu 萬樹, comp. *Tz'u-lü* 詞律. Preface dated 1687; rpt. with supplements by Hsü Pen-li 徐本立 and Tu Wen-lan 杜文瀾. *SPPY*, vols. 483–84.

Wang, Ching-hsien. *The Bell and the Drum: Shih Ching as Formulaic Poetry in an Oral Tradition.* Berkeley: University of California Press, 1974.

Wang Ch'iu-kuei. "The Formation of the Early Versions of the Meng Chiang-nü Story." *Tamkang Review*, 9, no. 2 (Winter 1978): 111–40.

Wang Chung-min 王重民. *Tun-huang ch'ü-tzu-tz'u chi* 敦煌曲子詞集.

Shanghai: Shang-wu yin-shu kuan, 1950. Rev. ed. 1956.

—— *Tun-huang i-shu tsung-mu so-yin* 敦煌遺書總目索引. Peking: Shang-wu yin-shu kuan, 1962.

—— *Tun-huang ku-chi hsü-lu* 敦煌古籍叙錄. Peking: Shang-wu yin-shu kuan, 1958.

Wang I-ch'ing 王奕清, et al., comp. *Ch'in-ting tz'u-p'u* 欽定詞譜. Preface dated 1715; rpt. Taipei: privately printed, 1964.

Wang Kuo-wei 王國維. *Jen-chien tz'u-hua* 人間詞話. Ed. Hsü T'iao-fu 徐調孚. 1939; rpt. Peking: Jen-min wen-hsüeh ch'u-pan she, 1960.

Wang P'u 王溥. *T'ang hui-yao* 唐會要. Peking: Chung-hua shu-chü, 1955. 3 vols.

Wang Ting-pao 王定保, ed. *T'ang Chih-yen* 唐摭言. Shanghai: Ku-tien wen-hsüeh ch'u-pan she, 1957.

Wang Yün-hsi 王運熙. *Liu-ch'ao yüeh-fu yü min-ko* 六朝樂府與民歌. Shanghai: Wen-i lien-ho ch'u-pan she, 1955.

Wixted, John Timothy. *The Song-Poetry of Wei Chuang (836–910 A.D.)*. Tempe, Arizona: Center for Asian Studies, Arizona State University, Occasional Paper No. 12, 1979.

Workman, Michael E. "The Bedchamber *Topos* in the *Tz'u* Songs of Three Medieval Chinese Poets: Wen T'ing-yün, Wei Chuang, and Li Yü." In *Critical Essays on Chinese Literature*, ed. by William H. Nienhauser, Jr. Hong Kong: The Chinese University of Hong Kong, 1976. Pp. 167–86.

Wu Jen-ch'en 吳任臣, ed. *Shih-kuo ch'un-ch'iu* 十國春秋. Facsimile reproduction; Taipei: Kuo-kuang shu-tien, 1962.

Yang Hsien-yi 楊憲益. "Li Po yü P'u sa man" 李白與菩薩蠻. In *Ling-mo hsin-chien* 零墨新箋. Shanghai: Chung-hua shu-chü, 1947. Pp. 1–8.

Yao Hsin-nung. "When Sing-song Girls Were Muses." *T'ien Hsia Monthly*, 4 (April 1935): 474–83.

Yü P'ing-po 俞平伯. *Tu tz'u ou-te* 讀詞偶得. Taipei: K'ai-ming shu-tien, 1957.

GLOSSARY OF CHINESE NAMES
AND TERMS

Note: This Glossary excludes Chinese items already given in the Bibliography.

A ts'ao p'o 阿曹婆
An Lu-shan 安祿山
Ch'an-men shih-erh shih
　禪門十二時
Chang Ch'ang 張敞
Chang Chih-ho 張志和
Chang Hung-hung 張紅紅
Chang Pi 張泌
Chang Shuai 張率
Chang Sun 張愻
Chang Sung-ling 張松齡
Chang-t'ai 章臺
Chang Yüeh 張說
Ch'ang-an 長安
ch'ang-chia 倡家 or 娼家

Ch'ang-chiang 長江
Ch'ang hsiang-ssu 長相思
ch'ang-lou 倡樓
Ch'ang O 嫦娥
Ch'ang-ming Hsi-ho nü
　長命西河女
ch'ang-tuan chü 長短句
Chao Ch'ung-tso 趙崇祚
chao-i 昭儀
Chao-kuo 昭國
Chao-tsung (T'ang Emperor)
　昭宗
Ch'en (dynasty) 陳
Ch'en Shu-pao 陳叔寶
cheng 箏

cheng-jen yüan 征人怨
cheng-tiao 正調
Ch'eng-tu 成都
chi-kuan 妓館
chi-nü 妓女
Ch'i (dynasty) 齊
Ch'i ao 淇澳
Ch'i-chou 蘄州
Ch'i Liang 杞梁
Ch'i-t'ing 旗亭
Ch'i-yün lou 齊雲樓
chia-chi 家妓
Chiang-ch'eng tzu 江城子
chiang ching-wen 講經文
Chiang-ling 江陵
Chiang-nan 江南
Chiang-nan san-t'ai 江南三臺
Chiang Ssu-yeh (Chiang Hsiao-
   wan) 蔣孝琬
chiao-fang 教坊
Chiao-fang chi 教坊記
chiao-shu 校書
Chien-ch'i tzu 劍器子
Chien-k'ang 健康
Chien-wen (Liang Emperor)
   簡文
Ch'ien-fo tung 千佛洞
Ch'ien Shu (Former Shu)
   (dynasty) 前蜀
Ch'ien-tzu wen 千字文
chih 知
Chin-ch'üan chi 金荃集
Chin-kang ching 金剛經
chin-shih 進士

chin-t'i shih 近體詩
ch'in 琴
Ch'in-fu yin 秦婦吟
Ch'in Lo-fu 秦羅敷
Ching 荊
Ching (River) 涇
ching 景
Ching-feng Men 景風門
ch'ing 情
ch'ing-chün 清俊
ch'ing-lou 青樓
Ch'ing pei le 傾杯樂
Ch'ing-p'ing tiao 清平調
Ch'ing-p'ing yüeh 清平樂
ch'ing-shang yüeh 清商樂
ch'ing-shen 情深
Chiu-ko 九歌
Chou (dynasty) 周
chu 珠
Chu-chih ch'ü 竹枝曲
Chu Hsi 朱熹
Ch'u 楚
ch'ü 曲
Ch'ü-chiang ch'ih 曲江池
Ch'ü-chiang t'ing-tzu 曲江亭子
Ch'u Tz'u 楚辭
ch'ü-tzu tz'u 曲子詞
Ch'ü Yüan 屈原
chüan 卷
chüeh-chü 絕句
Ch'üeh t'a chih 雀踏枝
chün 郡
ch'un 春
chung-ch'ü 中曲

Chung Hung 鐘嶸

Chung-tsung (T'ang Emperor) 中宗

fa-ch'ü 法曲

Fa-t'i shih-erh shih 法體十二時

Fan nü yüan 蕃女怨

fan-sheng 泛聲

Fei-ch'ing 飛卿

Feng-hsiang 鳳翔

Feng kuei yün 鳳歸雲

Feng Yen-ssu 馮延己

fu 賦

Han (dynasty) 漢

Han Chien 韓建

Han Hung 韓翃

Han-lin 韓林

Hangchou 杭州

hao 號

Hao shih-kuang 好時光

Ho Chih-chang 賀知章

Ho man-tzu 何滿子

Ho Ning 和凝

Hou Chin (Later Chin) (dynasty) 後晉

Hou Shu (Later Shu) (dynasty) 後蜀

Hsi chiang yüeh 西江月

Hsi ch'ien ying 喜遷鶯

Hsi-ch'ü ko 西曲歌

Hsi-Hsia 西夏

Hsi-hu 西湖

Hsi Wang Mu 西王母

hsia 下

Hsia Nai 夏鼐

Hsiang (River) 湘

Hsiang-tung (Prince) 湘東王

Hsiang-yang 襄陽

Hsiao I 蕭繹

Hsiao Kang 蕭綱

hsiao-ling 小令

Hsiao Ta-hsin 蕭大心

Hsiao T'ung 蕭統

Hsiao Yen 蕭衍

Hsieh *chia* 謝家

hsien 縣

Hsin-chi hsiao-ching shih-pa chang 新集孝經十八章

Hsin Wu-tai shih 新五代史

hsin yüeh-fu 新樂府

Hsiung-nu 匈奴

Hsü Ling 徐陵

Hsü Mien 徐勉

Hsüan-tsang 玄奘

Hsüan-tsung (T'ang Emperor) 玄宗

hsüeh-shih-lang 學仕郎

Hsüeh T'ao 薛濤

Hsüeh T'ao chien 薛濤箋

Hupei 湖北

hu-pu 胡部

Hu Ying-lin 胡應麟

hu-yüeh 胡樂

hua-chien 花間

Hua-chien chi 花間集

Hua-chou 華州

Hua fei hua 花非花

Huan hsi sha 浣溪沙

Huang Ch'ao 黃巢

Huang-fu Sung 皇甫松
Hui-po yüeh 回波樂
Jen-wu 壬午
k'ai-huang 開皇
k'ai-yüan 開元
Kansu 甘肅
K'ang-hsi (Ch'ing Emperor)
　康熙
Kao Shih 高適
Kao-t'ang fu 高唐賦
Keng-lou ch'ang 更漏長
Keng lou-tzu 更漏子
ko-hsing 歌行
k'ou 口
ku-fa 古法
Ku Hsiung 顧敻
Ku-shih shih-chiu shou
　古詩十九首
ku-t'i shih 古體詩
kuan-chi 官妓
kuei-yüan 閨怨
kung 宮
kung-chi 宮妓
Kung-chung t'iao-hsiao 宮中調笑
kung-t'i shih 宮體詩
K'ung-ch'üeh tung-nan fei
　孫雀東南飛
k'ung-hou 箜篌
Lang t'ao sha 浪淘沙
Li Chieh 李傑
Li Ching 李璟
Li Ching-po 李景伯
Li Hou-chu 李後主
Li Hsün 李珣

Li Lung-chi 李隆基
Li Mao-chen 李茂貞
Li Po 李白
Li Wa 李娃
Li Yi 李億
Li Yü 李煜
Li Yüan 李原
Li yüan 梨園
Liang (dynasty) 梁
lien (lotus) 蓮
lien (love) 憐
Ling Hu-kao 令狐縞
Liu 柳
Liu chih 柳枝
Liu Hsieh 劉勰
Liu Huan 劉緩
Liu Pien-ch'un 劉采春
Liu Shih 柳氏
Liu Sung (dynasty) 劉宋
Liu Yü-hsi 劉禹錫
Liu Yung 柳永
Lo-t'ien 樂天
Lo-yang 洛陽
lü-ch'uang nü 綠窗女
Lung-hsing ssu 龍興寺
man-tz'u 慢詞
Mao Tse-tung 毛澤東
Meng Ch'ang 孟昶
Meng Chiang-nan 夢江南
Meng Chiang-nü 孟姜女
Meng Ch'ü-tzu 孟曲子
Meng Hao-jan 孟浩然
min-chi 民妓
Ming (dynasty) 明

Mo-kao k'u 莫高窟
Mo-shang sang 陌上桑
Mu-lan hua 木蘭花
Mu T'ien-tzu 穆天子
Nanching 南京
nan-ch'ü 南曲
Nan hsiang tzu 南鄉子
Nan ko-tzu 南歌子
nan-kuo ch'an chüan 南國嬋娟
Nan T'ang (Southern T'ang)
　(dynasty) 南唐
nü-yüeh 女樂
Ou-yang Chiung 歐陽烱
Pa 巴
Pai-hsüeh ch'ü 白雪曲
Pai yün-yao 白雲謠
Pao Chao 鮑昭
pei-ch'ü 北曲
Pei-li 北里
Pei-li chih 北里誌
P'ei Ch'eng 裴誠
pi-lou 鄙陋
p'i 匹
p'i-p'a 琵琶
Pieh hsien-tzu 別仙子
pien-wen 變文
p'ien-wen 駢文
P'ing-k'ang fang 平康坊
Po Chü-yi 白居易
Po Hsi-ho chieh-ching lu
　伯希和劫經錄
Po Hsing-chien 白行簡
P'o chen tzu 破陣子
pu-ya 不雅

P'u sa man 菩薩蠻
p'u-t'ung tsa-ch'ü 普通雜曲
san ch'ü 三曲
shang 商
Shen Ch'üan-ch'i 沈佺期
Shen Kua 沈括
shen-mei 深美
Shen Yüeh 沈約
shih 詩
Shih ching 詩經
Shih-erh yüeh hsiang-ssu
　十二月相思
shih-k'o 詩客
shih-kuo 十國
shou 手
Shu 蜀
shuang-tiao 雙調
ssu (love thoughts) 思
ssu (silk thread) 絲
ssu-i yüeh 四夷樂
Suchou 蘇州
Su Hsiao-hsiao 蘇小小
Su-tsung (T'ang Emperor) 肅宗
Su Wu 蘇武
su-wu 俗物
su-yüeh 俗樂
Sui (dynasty) 隋
Sun Ch'i 孫棨
Sung (dynasty) 宋
Sung Yü 宋玉
Szechwan 四川
ta-ch'ü 大曲
ta-li 大曆
ta-yeh 大業

t'ai-ch'ang-ssu 太常寺

t'ai-ch'ang ssu-pu yüeh
　太常四部樂

t'ai-chung 太中

T'ai-hu 太湖

T'ai-niang 泰娘

T'ai-tsung (T'ang Emperor)
　太宗

tan-tiao 單調

T'ang (dynasty) 唐

T'ang-shih chi-shih 唐詩紀事

T'ao Ch'ien 陶潛

T'ao-hua yüan 桃花源

T'ao Hung-ching 陶弘景

Tao lien-tzu 擣練子

t'i 體

tiao 調

tiao-ming 調名

T'iao-hsiao 調笑

T'ien chieh 天街

T'ien Ch'ih 天池

T'ien hsien tzu 天仙子

t'ien-pao 天寶

T'ien shan 天山

t'ien-tz'u 填詞

ting-ko lien-chang 定格聯章

to 多

Ts'ai lien tzu 採蓮子

ts'ang-ning 傖儜

Ts'ao T'ang 曹唐

Ts'ao Yi-chin 曹議金

Ts'en Shen 岑參

Tso-chuan 左傳

tso-yu chiao-fang 左右教坊

Tsun-ch'ien chi 尊前集

Tu Fu 杜甫

Tun-huang 敦煌

Tung Chin (Eastern Chin)
　(dynasty) 東晉

Tung-t'ing hu 洞庭湖

Tung-t'ing shan 洞庭山

t'ung-ch'ien 同前

Tzu-yeh 子夜

Tzu-yeh ko 子夜歌

tz'u 詞

tz'u-tiao 詞調

wai-kuo chih sheng 外國之聲

Wang Ch'ang-ling 王昌齡

Wang Chiang-nan 望江南

Wang Chien (poet, 768–833)
　王建

Wang Chien (ruler, 847–918)
　王建

Wang Chih-huan 王之渙

Wang Kuo-wei 王國維

Wang Tao-shih 王道士

Wang Wei 王維

Wang Yüan-lu 王圓籙

Wang Yün 王筠

Wei (dynasty) 魏

Wei (River) 渭

Wei Ch'ing 韋青

Wei Chuang 韋莊

Wei Kao 韋皋

Wei Shang-shu 韋尚書

Wei Su-chou 韋蘇州

Wei Ying-wu 韋應物

Wen (Sui Emperor) 文

Wen-hsüan 文選
wen-jen 文人
Wen T'ing-yün 溫庭筠
Wo-lan chi 握蘭集
Wu (dynasty)
Wu (Han Emperor) 武
Wu (Liang Emperor) 武
Wu Erh-niang 吳二娘
Wu-keng chuan 五更轉
Wu-ling (the "Five Tombs," frequented by aristocratic youth) 五陵
Wu-ling (place name) 武陵
Wu-ma tz'u 舞馬詞
Wu-shan 巫山
Wu-sheng ko 吳聲歌
Wu-tai (period) 五代
Wu Tseng 吳曾
wu-wei 無爲
Wu-wei tzu 無爲子
Xi'an 西安
ya-yüeh 雅樂
Yang (Sui Emperor) 煬
Yangchou 揚州
Yang-ch'un ch'ü 陽春曲
Yang-kuan 陽關
Yang-liu chih 楊柳枝
Yang-tzu yüan 陽子院
Yao Ch'ih 瑤池
yao-t'iao 窈窕

Yao Yü-ching 姚玉京
Yeh chin men 謁金門
Yen Chi-tao 晏幾道
yen ku-shih 演故事
Yen-po tiao-sou 煙波釣叟
yen-yüeh 讌樂 or 燕樂
Yi Chiang-nan 憶江南
Yin-yüeh chih 音樂志
ying-chi 營妓
yü 玉
Yü-fu 漁父
yü-hsiu 語秀
Yü Hsüan-chi 魚玄機
Yü hu-tieh
Yü ko-tzu 漁歌子
yü-kou 玉鉤
Yü mei-jen 魚美人
Yü-men 玉門
Yü-t'ai hsin-yung 玉臺新詠
Yüan (dynasty) 元
Yüan (Liang Emperor) 元
Yüan (River) 沅
Yüan Chen 元稹
yüan-ho 元和
Yüan-hsüeh 願學
yüeh-fu 樂府
yüeh-kung 樂工
Yüeh shih tz'u 樂世詞
yün-yao 雲謠
Yün-yao chi 雲謠集

FINDING LIST FOR POEMS

INDEX

NEO-CONFUCIAN STUDIES

MODERN ASIAN LITERATURE SERIES

STUDIES IN ORIENTAL CULTURE

COMPANIONS TO ASIAN STUDIES

The Classic Chinese Novel: A Critical Introduction, by C. T. Hsia. Also in paperback ed.   1968

Chinese Lyricism: Shih Poetry from the Second to the Twelfth Century, tr. Burton Watson. Also in paperback ed.   1971

A Syllabus of Indian Civilization, by Leonard A. Gordon and Barbara Stoler Miller   1971

Twentieth-Century Chinese Stories, ed. C. T. Hsia and Joseph S. M. Lau. Also in paperback ed.   1971

A Syllabus of Chinese Civilization, by J. Mason Gentzler, 2d ed.   1972

A Syllabus of Japanese Civilization, by H. Paul Varley, 2d ed.   1972

An Introduction to Chinese Civilization, ed. John Meskill, with the assistance of J. Mason Gentzlcr   1973

An Introduction to Japanese Civilization, ed. Arthur E. Tiedemann   1974

A Guide to Oriental Classics, ed. Wm. Theodore de Barry and Ainslie T. Embree, 2d ed. Also in paperback ed.   1975

Ukifune: Love in The Tale of Genji, ed. Andrew Pekarik   1982

INTRODUCTION TO ORIENTAL CIVILIZATIONS
WM. THEODORE DE BARY, EDITOR

Sources of Japanese Tradition	1958	Paperback ed., 2 vols.,	1964
Sources of Indian Tradition	1958	Paperback ed., 2 vols.,	1964
Sources of Chinese Tradition	1960	Paperback ed., 2 vols.,	1964